Invention
of the
Modern World

THE BRITISH BEE HIVE.

Invention

of the

Modern World

by

Alan Macfarlane

Odd Volumes

of the
Fortnightly Review
LES BROUZILS
2014

Odd Volumes of The Fortnightly Review

Le Ligny
2 rue Georges Clemenceau
85260 Les Brouzils
France

ODD VOLUME 3

2014

ISBN 978-0615919638

Originally published in serial form in The
Fortnightly Review's New Series online at
fortnightlyreview.co.uk in 18 instalments in 2012.

PREFACE

THE UNIQUE OPPORTUNITY and honour offered to me by being invited to give the first Wang Gouwei lectures at Tsinghua University in March 2011 has spurred me on to try to draw together many of the thoughts, both published and unpublished, which I have been gathering together over my lifetime of pursuing the riddle of the modern world.

This is a book which synthesizes a lifetime of reflection on the origins of the modern world. Through forty years of travel in Europe, Australia, India, Nepal, Japan and China I have observed the similarities and differences of cultures. I have read as widely as possible in both contemporary and classical works in history, anthropology and philosophy.

My previous attempts to understand the curious emergence of the modern world have been published in a series of books. It effectively started with *The Origins of English Individualism*, which has been published in Chinese, and is a continuation of that account. Later works dealing with this theme, particularly *The Culture of Capitalism, The Savage Wars of Peace, The Riddle of the Modern World* and *The Making of the Modern World* have as yet not been published in Chinese.

Although I speak almost exclusively of England in the following book, it was written explicitly for a Chinese audience. I wanted to explain to my Chinese friends and the audience of my lectures and readers of this book some peculiarities of the history of British civilization which might be useful for them in trying to understand the West. My assessment of what would interest a Chinese audience is based on eight visits to China since 1996 with my wife Sarah, as well as teaching a number of Chinese postgraduate students.

DURING MY VISITS over the last fifteen years I have seen the amazing transformation of China and its onward march towards equality with the west in technology and material affluence. I have also witnessed the 'clash of civilizations', not in an open and aggressive way, but at a deeper level of values and culture. In order to understand this confrontation better it seemed worthwhile exploring some of the inner dynamics of the earliest western industrializing nation.

I have long been interested in the ways in which East and West can both mutually respect each other and learn from their mutual history. I had previously studied this problem in relation to Nepal and Japan. But now China presents the most dramatic case of the need for cross-comparative understanding, both because of its size, the great depth of its history, and also the extraordinary speed of its industrial and economic growth.

The central problem for China in the future is how to retain its own distinctive culture and identity, so shaken by the events of the twentieth century, whilst also absorbing the best that Western civilization can offer. The other great problem China faces is similar to one which is facing the west in its movement into full modernity. This is the problem of social cohesion – what holds a civilization together.

This was the central philosophical and sociological problem facing those in western societies who saw that in an urban-industrial and highly mobile society, the old bonds which held people together – namely the family, status hierarchies, fixed communities, religious belief and political absolutism – were no longer strong. They could no longer hold a nation or civilization together. The 'imagined community' of the nation was a partial answer. Some countries tried intense political centralization (fascism) or utopian communitarianism (communism). Yet the experiments did not work. What alternative is there to these philosophies of the right and the left? This book tries to give an answer.

THE PROBLEMS WHICH faced thinkers like Marx, Weber and Durkheim in the late nineteenth and early twentieth centuries have become more pressing today. With greater education, faster communication, global economic markets and all the characteristics of what is now termed 'globalism', the problems are intensified.

Given that China stands at a cross-roads, its material progress fairly assured but its political and social order still to be worked out, it seems to me that it might be of benefit for the Chinese to have an account of the origins and nature of the development of modernity in the West – both its advantages but also of its costs and unintended consequences.

The case of England is particularly relevant here, for England, as I shall argue, brought 'modernity' into the world and is the oldest modern nation. Explaining its history and structure may give a Chinese audience a comparative picture of what the choices for their future are and what can be achieved.

I SHOULD EMPHASIZE that the following account may surprise or even shock those readers who have learnt at school or university something about English and European history. They are likely to have absorbed the Marx-Weber theory which dates 'modernity' either to the 'English revolution' of the English Civil War in the middle of the seventeenth century, or the 'Glorious Revolution' of 1688. Or they may have been taught that the 'watershed' when a feudal, peasant, pre-modern society turned into a capitalist and modern society occurred in the sixteenth century with the religious Reformation and the start of serious long-distance trade and Empire.

This book challenges this set of theories and argues strongly for the reinstatement of an older theory which was displaced by that of the great late-nineteenth century sociologists. It suggests that there is a great deal of continuity in England from the eleventh or twelfth century and that there is no break in the 'long arch' of modernity over the last thousand years. So some readers will have to suspend their disbelief and, hopefully, some will be persuaded by the coherence of the alternative story I tell and the evidence I present.

When I gave the lectures I likened the pursuit of an understanding of modernity to the process of filling in a jigsaw puzzle. The extraordinary change from an agrarian to an industrial world, first achieved in England, was the result of a set of interconnected features, all of which were necessary, but none of which, taken singly, were sufficient causes of modernity.

In the first case, the key to unlock modernity has to be exactly right. And it is not just a matter of getting each part right, but it must be placed in exactly the right relation to the other parts. Thus the relation of religion to politics, of the family to the economy, of games to civil society, as well as many others, needs to be exactly correct. The chances of this happening in the first case were thousands if not millions to one against. Yet it did happen and after it had been achieved it became much for others to copy the first exit from an agrarian civilization.

THE BASIC DIFFERENCE currently between England and China is that the former is fully modern. That is to say that in England the civilization is based ultimately on the individual, who alone links together the separated worlds of economy, society, religion and politics. Each individual is a microcosm of the complete society, with his or her intrinsic rights and responsibilities. China on the other hand has historically been a group-based civilization where the individual is less separated off from others, where relationships are intrinsic to a person's identity, where each person is only made complete by being joined to others. In other words, the full separation of economy, polity, society and ideology (religion) has not yet fully occurred in China.

The question this raises for the future is whether China will, can or should move further down the road of atomized, separated, individualistic civilization of the West, and how much it should retain of its relational civilization. So far it has largely individualised its market economy, but its society, polity and ideology is still quite embedded and non-individualistic.

It may be that the confrontation between two basic models of man and society cannot be resolved and ultimately a civilization has to choose one or the other. Or it may be possible to find a compromise, a hybrid, a middle way. Whatever the outcome, a clear and simple description of the competing ideology and social structure of the West may be useful for the Chinese as they work out their future.

A NUMBER OF those who attended the lectures pointed out that in practice, the separation of spheres was often ignored in the West, for example economic power and lobbying of the politicians in the United States. So it is worth stressing that this account is describing a simplified model, an attempt to keep the spheres of life separated, which in practice often fails. Very often 'corruption', as it is called, or the mixing of the spheres, occurs in practice. What is unusual, however, is that in these modern societies there is such an ideal – whereas normally in the past and still in many civilizations, it has been assumed that politics and religion, and society and economy are joined together. This is the difference – in the ideal more than in the actuality.

It is worth noting that there is an ambiguity in the use of 'English'. Until the two Crowns were merged in 1603, England and Scotland were separated. They were not formally joined until 1714 with the Act of Union. It is therefore legitimate to talk of 'England' (which for long includes Wales) until 1714. After that date it would perhaps be preferable to talk of Britain or the United Kingdom. Since much of what I am describing is in origin 'English', even when it spread to Scotland and Wales and Northern Ireland, I have tended to talk about England and the English.

Finally, as I state in the first and last chapters, although I am proud of my country and feel that it has indeed made a special contribution to world civilization, I would not wish to be thought of as what is called a 'little Englander'. England was made out of all the cultures of the world. It is a mongrel nation with such a mixture of peoples and influences that it can be said hardly to exist as a separate entity. Nor is its way morally superior to that of other civilizations. Nevertheless I find, as an anthropologist who looks back at this little island from the vantage point of the Himalayas, or Japan or China, that it is indeed a strange place which has peculiarities which have had a huge influence. My book is an attempt to analyze these features and thereby to understand better my country, the modern world and myself.

♦

ACKNOWLEDGEMENTS

THIS BOOK IS a considerably expanded version of the Wang Gouwei lectures given under the auspices of the Tsinghua Academy of Chinese Learning. I am deeply grateful for the honour of the invitation and to the Academy and also more generally Tsinghua University for giving me this opportunity to speak to their students.

In particular I would like to thank Professors Liu Dong, Li Bozhong and Liu Beicheng for their part in making the visit possible and productive. The lectures are supported by the Kaifeng Foundation and it was a special pleasure to get to know the founder and chairman of the foundation, Duan Weichong. I thank the Foundation for their generous support to me and my wife, Sarah Harrison. Finally, I would like to thank Yu Wanhui and Li Danjie who made so much effort to make our visit such a pleasure. Numerous students also contributed by their presence at the lectures and in discussions outside the classroom.

The book is a summation of a life's work and therefore I have intellectual debts to countless people, my family, my teachers, my colleagues and my students. A full acknowledgement would be very lengthy so I hope that they will all accept my general thanks and gratitude for the numerous ideas which they have shared with me.

A few people, however must be named. Among my family, my mother and father, Iris and Donald Macfarlane, gave me the love and support which helped to make me secure in my own English culture on my return from India where I had been born. Among my teachers, my school history teacher, Andrew Morgan, and my university teachers, Harry Pitt, James Campbell, Keith Thomas and Christoph von Furer-Haimendorf, gave me a grounding in history and anthropology, furthered by Jack Goody, Peter Laslett and others.

Among my friends, I am particularly indebted to Cherry and Michael Bryant, Gerry and Hilda Martin, Mark Turin and James C. Bennett. My publisher-turned-agent, John Davey, has always been encouraging. Xiaolong Guan has translated a number of my books into Chinese and added to this by translating this work. I am especially grateful to her.

Above all, however, I am indebted to my wife and intellectual companion, Sarah Harrison. She has done much of the hard work upon which this book is based, both in historical reconstruction and anthropological fieldwork. We have shared this intellectual journey now together for forty years. She has read and improved this book, as she has done almost all my others. Without her I could not have written this work and it is very much a shared creation.

– Alan Macfarlane.

CONTENTS

What question should we should ask – what is the puzzle I am trying to solve? What is modernity? What have been the favoured explanations of when and why it emerged? A brief survey of the history of attempts to set and answer this question. What is the appropriate methodology for the study of this huge topic? What evidence can we use? Was the modern world invented in the 'great divergence' of the nineteenth century, in the watershed of the rise of capitalism in the sixteenth century, or much earlier? Archives 15 May 2012.

England was a warlike, but also a trading nation. It was involved in constant warfare – but on others' soil, with others' troops,or at sea. It also built its wealth on trade. And from the seventeenth to the nineteenth centuries it created the vast Empire upon which 'the sun never set'.But how could such a tiny island do this? Archives 15 May 2012.

The nature and history of industrial and agricultural technology is one way in which England achieved and held its great Empire. By the eighteenth century England had the most technologically advanced agriculture in the world;it then used carbon energy through industrialization based on steam some fifty years before any other country. So it was powerful –but how could it escape, for the first time in history, agrarian constraints?

England had a very sophisticated capitalist economy stretching back hundreds of years. It was full of money, markets, relatively free but skilled labour, banks, limited liability, the stock exchange, mortgages and many other devices to help move capital and labour around. And it was like this for many centuries before the industrial revolution.

Chapter 5: Material life. 776

Travelers from France, Scotland and elsewhere said that England by the seventeenth or eighteenth century compared to most of Europe was by far the richest country in terms of clothes, houses, food and leisure – equaled only by the small country of Holland. This was related to late age at marriage, small families and the fact that economic advance over the centuries had not been drained by rapid population growth.

Chapter 6: Caste and Class.95

The tendency of most societies is for wealth differences to turn into legal and ritual differences, what Tocqueville calls 'caste'. England is the great exception. Its peculiar statuses of aristocrat, gentleman, yeoman, labourer were found nowhere else in the world. They were part of a hierarchical, class, society which developed from Anglo-Saxon times. Meanwhile all other Eurasian societies moved towards 'caste'. This hierarchy-with-mobility is an essential basis for modernity.

Chapter 7: Culture. 116

The English invented several of the most important competitive team games – cricket, football, and rugby – and perfected others (e.g. horse racing, shooting, tennis). These games and sports combine contract with status in an unusual way – having entered the game contractually, the arena and rules create a competitive yet uniting sentiment. The games metaphor and mentality is found through all the rest of English society in its law, politics, society and economic activity. The English also have the leisure and wealth to develop many hobbies.

Chapter 8; Kinship, friendship and population. 133

The unusually fragmented kinship system did not form the infrastructure of society. Children were sent away from home when they were young. They married for love. They placed the relationship with their married partner before that to their parents or children. In practice, most people interacted with non-kin networks in religion, politics and economy. The English family system soon became unique in Europe and later spread to America and over much of the world. Friends replaced kin as the most important contacts, but patron-client relations were weak.

Chapter 9: Civil Society. 151

The central feature of modernity is the development of associations based on 'contract', rather than communities based on birth and blood. In England, there was an enormous growth of clubs, associations and other groupings. The development of legal trusts from medieval times gave such activities the foundation on which they could develop, forming the underpinning of Anglo-American society.

Chapter 10: Power and Bureaucracy. 167

Usually power becomes more centralized and absolutist, as in the history of all of continental Europe, China and many other civilizations. England had a unique form of 'centralized feudalism' that was both directed to the centre but distributed much power to the lower levels. Without a permanent army, with the King under the Law,with a small paid bureaucracy, it developed the first real 'democracy' along unusual lines. Later it governed its huge Empire in a similar way. It employed in its schools, in its national government and in its Empire a system of indirect or delegated government which may be called the 'school prefect' system,using the local leaders to rule and hence obviating the need for a heavy political bureaucracy from the centre.

Chapter 11: Law and Violence. 191

The legal system is the key to modernity. The unique mixture of Common Law and Equity, with judge-made, precedent-based, law, with the presence of juries and the assumption of innocence until proven guilty, the absence of torture, is fundamental. There was equality before the law and the rule of law. It was a legal system with particular sophistication in its treatment of personal rights and duties and the holding of property. As Adam Smith and Max Weber realized, this was the system which underpinned modern rational capitalist economy and politics. Over the centuries it became totally different from that anywhere else in Europe.

Chapter 12: Education, Language and Art. 210

People cannot be united either in a nation or a great Empire by formal contractual ties; they need a feeling of loyalty. The unusual English educational system, especially the unique custom of sending children off very young (eight or nine)to be educated by others provided this. It is both old and central in generating the sentiments of a modern society. It also constructed the character and system of authority for later life. It was later adapted as the device for holding together the imagined empire across the globe when young children were sent home to be shaped into British identity through ten years of boarding education. At school the English learnt a particular language that both reflected and shaped their view of the world. It is flexible, practical, egalitarian, non-gendered and capable of producing great poetry and prose. The use of irony and satire was much developed and a curious playful sense of humour was widespread. It is a language that has been carried all over the world.

Chapter 13: Knowledge. 231

The unusual wealth and especially the rapid growth in the eighteenth century in both agricultural and industrial output depended considerably on the application of 'reliable knowledge'– or science – to practical matters such as wind and water power generation, steam engines and other machines, the rationalization of agriculture through fertilizers and breeding of superior animals. So the growth of knowledge and techniques, and especially the institutions of knowledge including universities and elsewhere was important, and was part of the triangle of 'knowledge: technology: mass production: back to knowledge' which lies behind modern growth.

Chapter 14: Myths of unity. 250

The cultural symbols taught in the schools expressed and created shared values through flags, parades, festivities and sports that united Britain and the Empire. They created one of the very earliest nations in the world over a thousand years ago. The cultural symbols were given legitimacy by the stories the English told about them- selves and their past, their 'myths' in the sense of stories that explain the present. In their rich literature, the great tradition they are taught in schools – Chaucer, Shake- speare, Milton, the Romantics, Austen, Dickens, the English learnt how English men and women should behave. In the many historical accounts, from Bede's Ecclesiastical History of the English People in 731 A.D., through to Winston Churchill and Simon Schama, they learnt their 'island story' and how continuous and rich it had been.

Chapter 15: Religion and ethics. 268

Formal religion has declined on the surface of much of Britain today, but all of British society is deeply soaked in the metaphysical underpinnings of Chris- tianity. This was a common European heritage, incorporating much from Greek and Roman philosophy. But in England a religion which was in a confrontation with the State from its start, and which emphasized the ethical dimensions of life, was particu- larly pronounced. Here many of the multitude of sects, Quakers, Methodists and many others, developed their own interpretations and thrived. Christianity was an essential foundation for the development of scientific thought. It also, as Weber argued, provid- ed a necessary, if not sufficient, ingredient in the development of capitalism.

Chapter 16: National character. 289

The combined effects of all that has been described before led to a strangely contradictory national character – or even, as David Hume suggested – the absence of any uniform national character at all. The

English were simultaneous individualistic and conformist, shy and extrovert, lazy and restless, childish and mature, insecure and self-confident, gentle and brutal. These are the contradictions of modernity.

Chapter 17: The English path. 309

The 'exit' from a pre-modern world was totally unexpected and not at all inevitable. The normal tendency is towards predation, absolutism, caste, over-population or other traps. The preservation of the tense balance between competing forces is difficult. The development of the modern world happened as a chance development on one small island that accidentally avoided most of the traps. If it had not happened there, it seems unlikely that it would ever have happened. Yet once it had happened, as with all great discoveries, it was not so difficult to copy. It may be useful for China, India and the other great developing countries to know a little more about the first long and difficult journey to modernity. So I have made a sketch of the developments on one small, wet, pugnacious little island which once ruled a great Empire and whose language, laws, political system, games, industrial system, science, education, family system and social structure has had such a remarkable influence on how we all live today and into the future.

Bibliography. 323

♦

INVENTION

CHAPTER 1

WHAT *IS* THE QUESTION?

THE ANSWER TO a question depends on how the question is posed. An inaccurate question gets unhelpful answers. This particularly applies to the large question of the nature, origins and future of modernity which is the theme of this book. The question is particularly difficult to pose now because it is so openly political and is constantly being changed. Certain ways of posing the question are thought of as politically incorrect, hubristic or Orientalist.

It is rather tempting, with hindsight, to believe that since the great event (the development of modern industrial, urban and scientific societies) *has* happened, it was bound to happen, and indeed, since they have now spread over much of the planet, perhaps their invention was not so difficult after all. This temptation towards inevitability and the minimizing of the magnitude of the achievement have become greater as time passes.

WHEN ENGLAND WAS the only country in the world to have made the 'escape' from agrarian constraints, and remained the only one to be able to do this for two generations, everyone agreed that it was a miracle and they all wondered how it had happened and how it could be copied. It was then 'the English', or British (because of Scotland) miracle.

In Tocqueville's day in the early nineteenth century the question seemed quite obvious. A new world was emerging; it was not just based on the technology of industrial production never before seen in the world, nor just on a self-evidently new understanding of natural laws through the growth of reliable knowledge (science), but above all by a new social, political and ideological structure, seen most dramatically in America, but starting to take the whole world in a new direction.

What Tocqueville termed the *ancien régime* countries – that is the world outside the little band of Britain, Holland and America – were faced with a different set of relations. What was this new package and how had it come about? Tocqueville never thought it was inevitable that the replacement of the *ancien régime* should have occurred, and he seriously fretted that it might collapse or be corrupted. It seemed unlikely that the two percent of the world's population in this tiny corner would convert the other ninety-eight percent.

Amazingly, many elements started to spread. Firstly this happened on parts of the Continent in the middle of the nineteenth century. Yet it still seemed so unusual that it was now termed a 'European miracle'. Even within Europe it was clearly not easy, and much of Max Weber's original inspiration came out of an attempt to understand why parts of Germany, particularly the Protestant north, were successfully industrializing, but not other parts, particularly the Catholic south. Likewise others thought it could only happen in the West. The rest of the world was stuck in what Marx called the unchanging 'Asiatic Mode of

Production', or what Sir Henry Maine thought of as the fate of 'unprogressive' societies.

A GENERATION LATER, in the 1860's at the other side of the world, Fukuzawa Yukichi saw the same thing. All of Asia was still *ancien*, but the West – and this now included parts of France, Germany and other parts of Europe – were becoming 'modern'. Unless Japan learnt the lesson and also became 'modern', then Fukuzawa knew his beloved country was doomed to become a colony of the West, just as India had long been and as China was in danger of becoming. There was no doubt in Fukuzawa's mind, just as there was no question in Max Weber's a generation later, that something extraordinary was about to happen.

So in the period 1870-1910, Japan joined the industrial world. It did so very largely by adopting many parts of the recipe which had worked in Europe. The same great change was happening in North America. So one Asiatic society and another civilization across the Atlantic achieved a break-through at about the same time. It became a Euro-American-Japanese phenomenon, and a Europe which from the third decade of the new century also included parts of the Soviet Union.

A part of the world had changed in the nineteenth century and it was now crashing into Asia. Up to the 1970's, with the work of people such as Barrington-Moore, Jones, North Thomas, Landes, Mokyr, Roberts, Diamond, Hall, Mann and Baechler, the question was focused on this puzzle.[1] There was a search for certain features in the West which made the rise of modernity occur. What had caused the European miracle, why had it happened there, then, and nowhere else?

Many elements of an answer were given, broadly spread along a continuum from the inevitabilist, 'natural tendency' arguments to those who saw it as a highly unlikely, unpredictable and chance set of events. Those who saw it as inevitable each

chose their own favourite causes – Christianity, water communications, feudalism, American minerals, coal supplies – leading inevitably to 'modernity'. Others saw it as a 'real' miracle
– in other words the result of accidental combinations, a mixture
of necessary conditions and random chance. Even so, if it was
a pure 'accident', we could at least investigate some of the contributing factors, especially those necessary if not sufficient.

Up to the 1960's it was a European miracle with two off-
shoots in Japan and the United States. Then in the next twenty
years the four 'little Tigers' were added to the 'escapees'. All
were relatively small and all either heavily influenced by Britain
and America (Singapore, Hong Kong) or Japan (Taiwan, South
Korea). So it became popular to believe that the miracle could
be exported, but only to small and heavily influenced places.

THEN, IN THE later 1980's, much of the two-thirds of the
world's population which had so far not achieved industrial and
scientific growth, namely China, India and South America, began to industrialize. This development appeared to reverse the
question. Before it had been phrased as 'How do we explain the
exceptions?' Now the question became 'Why are one or two
areas, particularly much of Africa and a good deal of central
Asia up to Pakistan and Afghanistan, still resisting the obvious
tendency?'

The 'miracle' story had found it possible to absorb 'Japanese
exceptionalism' by claiming that, as E. L. Jones put it, Japan
seems like an island which was originally off the south coast
of England – which had by chance been towed and moored off
China.[2] Yet while a paradigm can absorb a certain amount of
anomaly, as these examples of successful economic development in Asia, were joined also by parts of South East Asia and
the Pacific, and then by India in the late twentieth century, it
seemed time to revise opinions.

Gundar Frank, Blaut, Goody and others argued that the question had been wrongly posed.[3] The Orient had never really been backward so there had been no special western miracle to be investigated. Look at the current success of places which had previously been written off. All Weber's speculations about things which were inhibiting modernity in the East or encouraging it in the West – religion, a certain legal system, democracy, western logic – were irrelevant and mistaken. The East could do perfectly well without them. There was no point in even searching for analogues – such as the 'Confucian culture' theory. Basically the whole project from Montesquieu up to the 1970's had been 'Orientalist' thinking, a making of Asia into a backward area as 'the Other'. Another attack came in the work of Marshall Hodgson, who argued that suggestions that there was 'something wrong', or defective, about Islam which had slowed down its growth and finally led it to collapse in the face of the west European powers. This was nonsense. Islam was fine – it just didn't develop in the same way as the West.[4]

In some ways Ken Pomeranz and others associated with the 'California School' were the logical final instance of this revisionism.[5] In his *Great Divergence* Pomeranz argues that there was no divergence before 1800 – China and the Far East, and Eurasia across to Europe, were all roughly the same up to that date. Hence the divergence was superficial, caused by external factors such as coal and the profits of a windfall Empire in the case of Britain. In another way Goody, though critical of Pomeranz, pursues a similar line – all of Eurasia is structurally the same. He argues in a series of challenging books that there is not much structural difference except in representation between East and West. The only real deep divergence is between the post-Neolithic civilizations of Eur-Asia, and the non-Neolithic civilizations of sub-Saharan Africa.[6]

For the revisionists the problem has disappeared. The 'modern world' was never a peculiar thing. In one sense it was always everywhere, in another it was a set of surface changes in economy and technology which spread rapidly and effortlessly across the world after 1800. Modernity is a tool kit of inventions, many of them originally made in China, then stolen or borrowed and improved, and then re-exported to Asia in the nineteenth and twentieth centuries.

♦

LET ME STATE a few things about what I shall *not* be arguing in the following account. Firstly, the European miracle, as we shall start by calling it, has nothing to do with morality. Modernity, however we define it, is not necessarily morally superior to the *ancien régime*. It may be preferable to many, but it is important not to slip back into a nineteenth century evolutionary, imperial, view that if, for example, the British were the first 'modern' nation, they were thereby in some sense morally superior. God or destiny are not part of the equation.

Secondly there was absolutely nothing inevitable, necessary or pre-determined about what has happened. My argument is anti-teleological. There is no pre-destined goal of history, no set of necessary steps which we shall all climb up. Instead, there are many tendencies and traps which mean that progress is, as Gibbon and later Toynbee realized, highly unlikely, that decline and fall is the normal story.[7] In so far as there are tendencies in human history, they are towards stasis and decline. We are truly dealing with progress against the usual course of things, exceptionalism or random mutations in Darwin's terms. Even someone as wise as Adam Smith in the later eighteenth century thought there was no possible escape from the agrarian limits to growth.

This implies that it is always easy to fall off the tightrope of 'progress'. Nothing is permanently assured. Empires come and go; the Sung period in China led into 500 years of 'high level equilibrium trap'.[8] The United States, some believe, is now on the downward path, as Britain was before it.

Thirdly, I do not think that what we need to explain is a miracle created from ingredients within Europe. The origins of almost all the things that led into the invention of the modern world are from outside. Almost all the great technological inventions before 1400 were made in China, while many of the greatest scientific discoveries were in Greece, and developed within Islamic civilizations. Europe in 1300 had absorbed much of this knowledge via the great trade routes across Eurasia.

◆

THROUGHOUT THE BOOK I shall try to give some specification of what I do and do not mean by 'modernity', but here are some first clues. What I do not mean is modern technology. Nowadays and for some time, as in fascist or communist societies, it is quite possible to combine modern technologies with what I call *ancien régime* systems. On the other hand, a modern world now and in the past will indeed have a distinctively effective technology *for its period*. If that period is one where horses, windmills and watermills provide the power, it will use them particularly effectively. So we must not confuse modernity and technology. The industrial revolution is central, but it is not the defining moment of modernity. The developments in motive energy, medicine, communications and other technologies are important but do not, in themselves, distinguish the modern from the non-modern.

To be modern is not the same as to be recent, indeed to be at any particular point in time. Thus there exist today many countries which are 'modern', but also many pre- (or even perhaps post-) modern societies co-existing. The world has for many hundreds of years had societies which are 'modern' and non-modern. By my definition, Florence in the fifteenth century, Holland in the seventeenth, Britain for many centuries have all been 'modern', while France in the eighteenth century or North Korea today are *ancien régime*.

The *ancien régime* combines the separate spheres of our lives. In tribal societies people are all united within kinship as the co-ordinator; in peasant societies the social and economic are joined, as are religion and politics, and so the basic units are families and village communities – with a thin layer of literate rulers above them. Modernity makes further separations. There is no fundamental underlying principle given by kinship or religion, everything is held in check by another sphere of life.

This is Tocqueville's picture of democracy in America – a modest religion, a restrained family, a limited political power and a circumscribed economy. It is this openness, jostling of powers, which generates our modern dynamic. Once it is reduced to one infrastructure, the civilization tends to become rigid.

HOW THEN CAN we approach the problem of the origins of our modern world? If we look at modernity as a package of inter-connected features, we can separate the ingredients – and then try to reconstitute the recipe, how the ingredients should be combined, in what quantities, order, and weights.

This approach is shown in one of the most brilliant attempts to specify the conditions for the growth of wealth. Adam Smith argued that in order for there to be the development of 'wealth', all that was needed was 'peace, easy taxes, and a tolerable administration of justice'. Over time these conditions (actually incredibly difficult to establish, as Smith well know) would produce wealth 'by the natural order of things'.[9]

While Smith's three ingredients are indeed central, there are many others; a certain rationality, science, politics, religion, civil society and, above all, the liberty which comes from the separation of spheres. The task I shall set myself is to trace parts of the package back through the history of the country where Tocqueville and Weber thought modernity originated in the form which we now know – namely Britain and especially England.

This investigation is not done to promote Britain as a shining model; this country hardly brought sweetness and light to many of the peoples around the world whose countries it interfered with. It is rather that in order to understand our present world and to chart a possible course over the slippery paths of the future, we need to see where parts of the present comes from. He who understands the past will understand the present, he who understands the present may understand the future, as Orwell might have said.

I investigate this not only as a historian but also as a comparative anthropologist. I love and am proud of my country. Yet I have also spent much of my time wandering through other great civilizations, not only parts of continental Europe and America, but also on many visits to Japan, China, India, Nepal and Australia. From these distant places I have looked back on the history and culture of my own small island. I have also looked at it through the writings of a succession of external eyes, particularly those of our nearest neighbours who might be thought to be most like us.

◆

THE CENTRAL PUZZLE which has concerned me for much of my adult life has been the nature and origins of the strange 'modern' civilization within which I live. In most of my books so far I have tried to approach this question from one angle or another.

The quintessence of modernity lies in the necessary conjunction at a point in time of a number of historically unlikely features. One is an appropriate demographic structure – that is, a controlled mortality and fertility system. A second pillar is political. If we look around us, one of the conspicuous features of many successful modern nations is political liberty. The third necessity is a certain kind of social structure. The power of the family has to be reduced, rigid stratification based on birth has to be eliminated, and an open and fluid, relatively meritocratic system has to be established. The citizen needs to have his or her first loyalty to the State rather than any other birth-given group. This is dependent on a substitution of the individual for the group as the basic unit of society. Yet in order for the system to work, a rich array of intermediary associations which we term collectively 'Civil Society' needs to grow up, based on something more than pure contract, placed between the citizen and the State.

Yet if we think of the modern world there are two other features which are both a consequence of the above and also their under-pinning. One is the rise of a new mode of producing wealth. Many people would link modernity with a particular form of production, perhaps most essentially with a high degree of division of labour, applied through the use of machines which draw on non-human power. The 'industrial revolution' as it is now known gives liberty and equality its special flavour.

THE OTHER FEATURE which we associate with modernity is a certain way of knowing. Modernity is distinguished for its 'scientific' and 'secular' modes of thought. The ability to generate new ideas, to live in doubt and suspend judgment, to encourage challenges and to speed up evolution with experiments. It is roughly what we call the scientific revolution. Where and when did these five features emerge?

There is mystery enough in the reversal of the tendencies in any one of these five spheres. But that they should all happen simultaneously in one place at one time is incredible. Those who thought about these matters would have believed that simultaneously to sustain liberty, equality, demographic balance, and discover fabulous riches stored from the past action of the sun, as well as discovering a way of speeding up the evolution of reliable knowledge, would be beyond the wildest of possibilities.

All of the conditions needed to occur together. That place also had to develop these inter-locked parts very fast in order to gain critical momentum. If its influence was to change the world it needed to replicate itself. It looks impossible to achieve, and even as late as the generation of Adam Smith it was most unlikely that it could happen.

Yet much of the world is now 'modern'. The revolution has been successful. However that very success has made us forget the question. As Tocqueville wrote, 'great successful revolutions, by effecting the disappearance of the causes which brought them about, by their very success, become themselves incomprehensible.'[10] The modern world has become almost invisible to us – as have its causes – for it is all around us. This quasi-archaeological journey back into its origins will not be easy, but we need to dig down into our past in order to understand our future.

CHAPTER NOTES

PLEASE CONSULT THE BIBLIOGRAPHY FOR CITATION DETAILS.

1. Barrington-Moore, *Origins*; Jones, *European*; North and Thomas, *Rise*; Landes, *Prometheus*; Landes, *Wealth*; Mokyr, *Lever*; Diamond, *Guns*; Roberts, *Triumph*; Hall, Mann and Baechler, *European*.

2. Jones, *European*, 159.

3. Frank, *Re-Orient*; Blaut, *Colonizer*'s; Goody, *East* and other works.

4. Hodgson, *Venture*.

5. Pomeranz, *Great*; Wong, *China*; Goldstone, *Why Europe*. The arguments have recently been accepted by others, for example Morris, *Why West* and Jacques, *China*.

6. A good deal of his thinking has recently been summarized in Goody, *Eurasian*.

7. Gibbon, *Decline*; Toynbee, *History*.

8. A concept central to Elvin, *Pattern*.

9. Quoted in Stewart, Works, X, 68.

10. Tocqueville, *Ancien Régime*, 7.

CHAPTER 2

WAR, TRADE AND EMPIRE

WE START WITH brute force. The energy which projected what I shall argue was an unusual and early modernity through the world came through political, economic and imperial domination. For most of the most influential period of British history, the 'long' nineteenth century (about 1780-1914), the British Navy 'ruled the waves'. England had been a serious trading nation from the twelfth century. After the final victory over their main rivals, the Dutch, in the eighteenth century, and then over Napoleon at the start of the nineteenth, the British navy and merchant fleets were unchallenged until the early twentieth century.

This takes us into the curious history of British warfare. There are several significant features of the role of war in British history. One is that England has been almost constantly at war over the last thousand years. For example, in the 126 years between 1689 and 1815, when the industrial and agricultural revolutions were at their height, England was at war for 73 years.[1] Sorokin published a table which shows that England in the period 1100 to 1900 was at war for more than half the time.[2]

England was part of one of the most war-like civilizations in history. The constant warfare in Europe was different from the long periods of peace in Japan or China. The constant recurrent strife led to rapid technological and scientific evolution through a process of Darwinian selectionary pressures – the survival of the 'fittest'. Guns, boats, navigation, knowledge of physics and chemistry, all rapidly improved. The ships which crushed the Chinese in the Opium Wars in the nineteenth century were enormously different from the primitive medieval boats which would have been no match for a Chinese armada in the fourteenth century. So England benefited from the positive effects – but others paid the cost. Thus, at the battle of Omdurman, the British had six Maxim guns. The result was 28 British dead, and eleven thousand of their enemies were slaughtered.[3]

Being an island, England tended to fight her wars on other people's territories. From the medieval wars in Scotland, Wales and France, through to the eighteenth century wars in the Americas or India, she fought abroad – and brought the plunder home. Invaders did not periodically destroy the British cities and crops.

Even within the country the civil wars were relatively mild. The Wars of the Roses in the fifteenth century and the seventeenth century English Civil War were by European or Asian standards small affairs. There was nothing like the horrors of the Taiping or Boxer rebellions in England.

The English were exceptionally fortunate within Europe: France, Italy, Germany and Eastern Europe were constantly subjected to terrible warfare, for example in the Thirty Years War of the seventeenth century something like one third of the population of Germany was destroyed – and much of the infrastructure. Yet England, peaceful at home and guarded by its navy and mercenary soldiers, profited from the wars.

I shall come back to this under the heading of 'law and violence' when I describe a law-abiding, peaceful country with few weapons or forts, and no standing army and an unarmed police force. Yet it was also one of the most belligerent and confrontational of nations. The foundation of the British Empire was force – military and economic, based on superior technology.

EUROPE WITH ITS highly diverse ecology, economy and political units was long accustomed to widespread trade. And within this complex, the British Isles was particularly fortunate. In Britain itself, the micro-differences between different parts of the country, as well as the deeply indented coastline and hence the cheapness of water and sea transport made it particularly propitious for trading. It was also fortunate in that it was situated, like a northern Venice, as a fulcrum for trade from Scandinavia, much of continental Europe, and later the Americas and, by way of the Cape of Good Hope, the Far East.

Even in the Anglo-Saxon period, England was a serious trading nation and even more so in the medieval period. Yet it was from the sixteenth century with the opening up of the Americas and the Indies, that trade became the central thread of British wealth.

As Tocqueville put it in a note: 'For manufacture and trade are the best-known means, the quickest and the safest to become rich. Newton said that he found the world's system by thinking about it the whole time. By doing the same, the English have got hold of the trade of the whole world'.[4] It was a point which had also been made by Voltaire a century earlier: 'What has made the English powerful is the fact that from the time of Elizabeth, all parties have agreed on the necessity of favoring commerce. The same parliament that had the King beheaded was busy with overseas trading posts as though nothing had happened.'[5]

The great theorist of commercial empires was Adam Smith. Teaching in Glasgow, Smith discussed with the sea captains and merchants the mechanisms of trade in the great Atlantic trade with the West Indies. He described trade as the foundation of the richest commercial nation the world had ever known, synthesizing this in 1786 with the publication of *The Wealth of Nations*. His basic assumption, stated near the start of the book, was that human beings are traders and exchangers, socially contractual creatures. He believed that Britain had the good fortune to be a 'nation whose government is influenced by shopkeepers'.[6] The English were, along with the much smaller Dutch or Italian republics, the first to pioneer the idea of a whole country basing its wealth chiefly on trade rather than military predation.

This trade began to spread all over the world and some recent writers such as Pomerantz have argued that it was the colonial trade of the expanding British Empire which accounts for what they believe to be the sudden 'divergence' between the west and China after 1800. It is therefore worth reminding ourselves that most of the wealth from trade up until 1800 was derived from inter-European trade. The point has been made recently by Joseph Bryant. 'The revisionist position also misleadingly discounts the preponderant role of intra-European trade, which dwarfed in volume and value all colonial exchanges. Even for England, the world's foremost trading nation by 1800, commerce beyond the bounds of Europe contributed less than 10% to the English total … And as economic historians have extensively documented, it was not the comparative cheapness of colonial resources that provided Europeans with their decisive advantage, but the astounding productivity gains that came with mechanization and the factory organization of labour.'[7]

THIS TRADE WAS based on power, on an underpinning of military force and organization and it was when war and trade came together that one of the most distinctive of British contributions to world history, a new kind of Empire, emerged.

Most Empires in history have been military and ideological. The desire to conquer, pre-date, absorb peoples in pursuit of an ideology or as a source of power and wealth, or to prevent external attacks, are the main motives. The main oddness of the accidental Empire that emerged in Britain was that its primary goal was, as befits a nation ruled by shopkeepers, to make money. This switch from the military and religious empires of previous imperial powers, to the kind of Empire which has characterized the world in the twentieth century, American and now Chinese economic imperialism is one of the turning points in history.

Being an island with no wealthy continental neighbours to conquer, once the English had absorbed Wales and Scotland, it became evident, certainly after the defeats in France in the fifteenth century, that it was too expensive to hold onto large European territories by force. The costs would far outweigh the benefits. There were no military advantages, nor were there any particular ideological advantages. For a calculating shopkeeper it was a bad deal. So the overseas possessions in France, the first and only true military empire which England had owned, were abandoned in the fifteenth century.

Instead, the English let their trade find its own territories. They sucked in the wealth of the new equatorial crops particularly sugar, opium, cotton, tea, tobacco, coffee and later rubber. They found or forced markets for their manufactured goods. These products were particularly important as the industrial revolution proceeded from the later eighteenth century and profits could be made by mass production.

The first great step was in America. One part was in the colonization of North America and Canada. The deep structure of North America, its language, law, politics, class-structure, religion, kinship system, associational nature was all laid down by English colonists.[8] In the twentieth century America would then spread out these values and institutions to the rest of the world as the power of Britain waned.

The other part of the second, American, Empire, was in the West Indies, and particularly Barbados and then Jamaica. In combination with the three-way trade of slaves, the sugar, coffee and tobacco trade was part of the basis of the wealth which Smith saw throwing up new and prosperous businesses in southern Scotland and along the west coast of England.

Then in the early nineteenth century the pivot of the British Empire moved from the second, American, Empire to the Third, in India and later Burma. This was won by conquest and force of arms mixed with diplomacy. There the wealth derived from cotton and opium – forced onto China in exchange for tea and silk – was the heart of East India Company profits. This third Empire was supplemented by the white Empire of Canada, Australia and New Zealand and to a certain extent Africa.

THE BRITISH EMPIRE was huge – almost a quarter of the land surface of the world in the middle of the nineteenth century. It endured for a long period, over three and a half centuries from the first settlements in North America. What was particularly striking is the fact that such a relatively small island with a population of only a few million could hold together such a vast Empire. It could not do so by sending native troops from England to hold down the numerous races and peoples it held, for there was no standing army in England, and it was a tiny country with very few who could be sent, even when Scotland, Wales and Ireland made their contributions. It could only provide a few thousand trained individuals for the whole Empire so it could only supply the very top of any administrative organization. So England had to develop a different strategy.

The effectiveness of this alternative is shown in the musings of one administrator who wondered aloud, why the British needed only 500 men to rule India, with its population of 300 million, while the French were unable to get by with less than 200 *fonctionnaires* for one and a half million Cambodians.[9] Or, as George Orwell, who himself had been a policeman in Burma, wrote: 'The Empire was peaceful as no area of comparable size has ever been. Throughout its vast extent, nearly a quarter of the earth, there were fewer armed men than would be found necessary by a minor Balkan state.'[10]

So how was the Empire held together? The method was developed in India and then spread to the African colonies, namely the technique of indirect or delegated rule. Power is devolved down and the energies and skills of local rulers are harnessed. The skill was in accomplishing the 'difficult task of ruling without actually appearing to rule at all'. The essence, wrote a Lieutenant-Governor of Southern Nigeria, was 'authority combined with self-effacement'.[11] The archetype of this was the imperial hero, T.E.Lawrence, who 'was entranced by the conviction that he was controlling the Arabs without their even realizing it'.[12]

The philosophy was later summarized for Africa by Frederick Lugard in *The Dual Mandate* when he wrote that the theory was necessary 'when a few score are responsible for the control and guidance of millions.'

> 'His courage must be undoubted, his word and pledge absolutely inviolate, his sincerity transparent. There is no room for "mean whites" in tropical Africa... They lower the prestige by which alone the white races can hope to govern and to guide.' This would produce, for example, the ideal District Officer – 'permanently on tour, manfully resistant to bureaucratic interference from headquarters', and 'winning the trust and loyalty of [his] charges by [his] integrity, fairness, firmness, and likeableness'.[13]

Much of the military force comes from local troops, recruited either within the British Empire, for example Punjabis or Sikh regiments, or in neighbouring states, as with the Gurkhas of Nepal. They were used to police the system under the direction of British officers. They were also employed as sepoys to force opium onto China or to help fright off threats to the Empire.

Let us compare the success of large imperial adventures. The Portuguese, Spanish and French modelled their Empires on their own centralized bureaucracies – trying to create a culturally united system which included their colonies – based on one religion, language, educational system and national identity. The British model in India was not one of absorption but of tolerance of diversity, so that as long as British interests in making money were not threatened, people were allowed to retain their local customs and culture. The local inhabitants would never become 'British'.

In many ways the model of the British Empire, with a uniformity of laws and governing language and bureaucratic models, with a tolerance for huge diversity of cultures, is similar to the Chinese quasi-Empire, for example as described by Jacques.[14] The central Confucian order, now transmuted into the Communist Party, reaches into every area, but it allows considerable autonomy to the fifty-five officially recognized ethnic minorities. China now is roughly comparable to the British Empire at its height and is structurally quite similar.

WAR, TRADE AND Empire are an inter-connected package, all mutually supporting each other. Britain controlled the most powerful military and naval machine and became the largest trading nation in history by the nineteenth century. It was also the largest Empire in the nineteenth century when the full force of industrial civilizations in the west was giving a part of the world a huge lead in terms of military and other force. This conjuncture has shaped the possibilities of our world. Among other things it has flavoured the kind of trade, war and Empires that are now emerging.

It is also the essential context for much of what I shall write below. There I shall argue that the politics, social structure and ideology of the British, and particularly the English, are unusual and 'modern' in various ways. These features were unprecedented in the past but have now spread over much of the world so that we tend to take them for granted as both inevitable and somehow natural.

The set of characteristics spread so fast and so deeply because of the War-Trade-Empire complex. Firstly it gave birth to America, which in its imperial conquest in the second half of the twentieth century took much of its basic practice from Britain. Then the British Empire deeply influenced much of the rest of the world, particularly Asia and the Pacific and parts of Africa.

It was trade and Empire which carried forth the games, hobbies associations, language, arts and culture, politics and law and many other aspects of Britain which we consider to be part of the package of 'modernity'. They were partly adopted and accepted because of their intrinsic merit. They were also attractive because they were symbolically associated with 'modernity' and the overwhelming power located in one part of the world.

IN ONE SENSE the English and British part of this story is over. It was just as I was preparing to become an imperial ruler and carry on the family tradition in the 1950's that the British Empire withered away faster than almost any Empire in history. When I was six, India gained its freedom, when I was sixteen the Suez debacle dramatically showed the end of British power and the first parts of the Empire in Africa gained their independence. A half-century on, the British Empire is now just a ghost.

Yet ghosts, as the Chinese know well, continue to haunt us. The modern world lives on in the afterglow of a period of over a century or so when the force of history was channelled through a small island off the north west of Europe. Personally I was deeply shaped by this through my family and education. As I examine my life and thoughts I realize increasingly that war, trade and Empire have shaped my nation's history and through that my own identity. As I travel I see so many traces of a world made by way of the British Empire.

So we need to understand that central imperial phase – the worst of all Empires, except perhaps the rest which were even worse. The cost in terms of lives destroyed in slavery, opium and conquest is unbearable. Yet it was also the context which allowed the most massive material and economic transformation in human history since the discovery of agriculture to occur, namely the industrial revolution.

China's decision to turn away from navigation in the early fifteenth century, when it was well in advance of anywhere else in the world, closed off this whole route of development. Instead of the predatory, outwardly expanding type of seaborne Empire that Britain represents, hoovering up the assets of the rest of the world, China built walls and tried to keep out the barbarians, including the British, from the Middle Kingdom. It may have been a good strategy for a century or two, but despite the northern and southern silk roads, it became 'bounded and not leaky enough' (Gerry Martin). The enormous potentials of overseas raw supplies and markets were largely ignored because they were not needed. China had plenty to export – especially silk, tea and porcelain. But it let others do the transportation. And then those others arrived in their gunboats and humiliated China.

THE IMPERIAL PHASE of the British is over. Yet, in Huizinga's words, we can note its extraordinary nature. Without this Empire, the English 'would never have been able to spread the language and the way of life of the tight little island over half the world, found the greatest of all modern empires, rule the seas, amass vast wealth as well as knowledge, and sample and collect great treasures of art...During my travels in India and Pakistan I saw what tremendous things the British had done in this vast, teeming and fascinating continent. I saw the monuments, like the sombre vice-regal splendours of New Delhi, that testify to the immense imperial self-confidence which had enabled them, with a handful of administrators and a minimum of force, to subdue, rule and transform this Asiatic world. I discovered how strong and, in many ways, beneficent was the imprint left behind by their relatively short period of rule.' Huizinga was over-awed. 'The more I saw of what their empire-builders had done and how they had done it, the more I was inclined to agree that the British Empire, if only because of the disproportion between its vast size and the absurdly small number of those who had founded and run it, was indeed something little short of a miracle...'

And it largely achieved something even more astonishing – returning the Empire to its constituent peoples with relatively little resistance. The magnitude of gaining of a vast Empire and the proportionate difficulty of leaving it are described by Tocqueville. He wrote to Lady Theresa Lewis that 'Nothing under the sun is so wonderful as the conquest, and still more the government of India by the English. Nothing so fixes the eyes of mankind on the little island of which the Greeks never heard even the name. Do you believe, Madame, that a nation, after having filled this vast place in the imagination of the whole human race, can safely withdraw from it? I do not.'[15] Yet, after the experience of trying to hold on to its first Empire in North America and finding that it did even better by leaving it to run itself, the British looked as if they had learnt something.

After his second visit to Africa in 1948 Huizinga wrote that 'on second thoughts I was far from certain that the British schoolmaster had not acted wisely in starting to pack his bags even before his pupils grew so unruly as to be difficult to handle without a policy of open repression. For the more I saw of the colonial world the more I realised that in this democratic age its masters could hardly have retained sufficient courage of their colonial convictions to practice such a policy with success.'[16]

CHAPTER NOTES

1. Mokyr, *Industrial*, 219.

2. Sorokin, *Sociological*, 324.

3. Paxman, *English*, 64.

4. Tocqueville, *Journeys*, 105.

5. Quoted in Landes, *Wealth*, 234.

6. Smith, *Wealth*, II, 129.

7. Bryant, 'Divergence', 434.

8. Fischer, *Albion's*, Veliz, *Gothic*, Bennett, *Anglosphere*.

9. Tidrick, *Empire*, 110.

10. Orwell, *Lion*, 58.

11. Tidrick, *Empire*, 208.

12. Tidrick, *Empire*, 210.

13. Tidrick, *Empire*, 213, 216.

14. Jacques, *China*, chapter 7.

15. Tocqueville, *Memoirs*, II, 409.

16. Huizinga, *Confessions*, 240.

CHAPTER 3

MODERN TECHNOLOGY

IT IS USUAL to separate the industrial and agricultural revolutions, but in the short space here available, I shall treat them together and over a much longer time frame than is normal. The final breakthrough to steam power in the later eighteenth century is only one, if the single most significant, chapter in the story.

The importance of what happened hardly needs emphasizing. It is the reason why Britain's Empire ruled the world for over a century and why a set of peculiar developments on a small peripheral island changed the history of the human race. The British industrial revolution has conquered the world, allowing world population to grow to twenty times the absolute limits which Adam Smith thought possible with the energy available to humankind in the middle of the eighteenth century.

There is no sign that without the British Industrial Revolution there would have been such a revolution at all. It took between fifty and eighty years for any other nation, even with the example of England, to undergo this momentous change. Without England we can be almost certain that the modern industrial world would not have been born and we would still be living in an agrarian world.[1]

♦

LOOKED AT FROM the vantage point of the author of *The Wealth of Nations* in the middle of the eighteenth century, it seemed clear that after a tremendous burst of development, Europe had reached a threshold which it could not cross. Mediterranean Europe was in decline, France was static, even Holland was not developing. The reasons for this were fairly obvious to the Enlightenment thinkers and consisted of two central realities. Firstly the innate limits to the productiveness of the technology had been reached. Much more could not be squeezed out of plants, animals, wind, and water. Population had reached the maximum of what the surface of the earth could provide through photosynthesis of the sun's energy.

Secondly, the tendency towards predation and aggression had worked its usual effects so that the early promise of Italy and Southern Germany had been destroyed by war, and the tendency towards over-expansion and social hierarchies was sapping the energy of Spain, Portugal and France. The subtlest form of predation had afflicted Holland as it moved towards banking, trade, and mercantile wealth. Although Europe's weapons and science were now in advance of China, the continent was caught in the normal Malthusian trap, the law of diminishing marginal returns, increasing war, famine and disease. The benefits from the discovery of the Americas by Europe had been largely used up.

Apart from the English case, every other civilization in history had moved towards 'industriousness' (a concept introduced by Hayami Akira) – that is, harder work for humans – rather than industrialization. Continental Europe between the twelfth and eighteenth century de-industrialized in this sense: there were fewer animals, less machinery, less use of non-human power and no exploitation of the huge coal reserves of the continent. The same happened in an even more extreme manner in Japan, where even the wheel was largely forgotten and domestic animals became scarce – since all work being done by the human body.[2]

A form of what Clifford Geertz calls 'agricultural involution' was the normal course in history.[3] People threw their muscles at the job and the price of labour dropped. The results might be magnificent in terms of output per hectare of wet rice paddy, yet the trajectory is precisely in the opposite direction to the' industrial', labour-saving, path. The cost of human labour declines; people work longer hours and technology as we know it regresses. An immiserated peasantry fills the land – without much leisure, disposable income, education or public relief in times of hardship.

♦

IN RELATION TO the unusual path which England took, let us look first at some elements of agriculture and the application of better technologies in harvesting energy from the sun. The proliferation of mills driven by both wind and water in England was dramatic. As early as 1086 in England the Domesday Book lists 5,624 water mills for some 3000 communities.[4] There was roughly a water mill per 50 households 'medieval men and women were surrounded by water driven machines doing the more arduous work for them'.[5] This was something new in the world, something the Romans with their cheap slave labour had never developed.

These water mills were limited to areas with good water supplies. In the large flat plains in parts of France, Germany and even in the flat east coast of England, there was often little drop and hence less power from water. The next genuine macro invention, the windmill, apparently again unknown to the Romans and others, was allegedly invented in the 1180s at Weedon in the East Riding of Yorkshire in England. From there it rapidly spread all over England and much of northern Europe.

At the same time, an even larger amount of energy came from animals – especially draught animals. By the late eleventh century, it is estimated that seventy per cent of all non-human energy consumed by English society came from animals, the rest coming from water mills'.[6] The growth of the woolen industry was the backbone of England's wealth. England is rather too wet and cold to consistently produce wheat, except in certain regions. However, much of it is upland pasture with very good grass to sustain sheep and cows and horses. So the cows which produced milk, cheese, butter, meat and manure and gave England its famous national food – roast beef – as well as its characteristic landscapes, were also important.

Finally, and equally exceptionally, there were English horses, which from being of middling quality and quantity were developed by selective breeding into the largest, strongest, and most ubiquitous animals of their kind in the world. The importance of horses in agriculture was noted, for example, by Quesnay. They were much more powerful than the oxen which were the normal agricultural animal on the continent, and one horse could do the work of twelve men. Wrigley gives figures which show that between 1600 and 1800 the amount of oats available for consumption by animals went up more than four-fold, an increase of nearly 900,000 tons: 'This represents, in effect, a massive increase in the quantity of energy available for use on the farm, in transport, in industry, and for leisure.'[7] Right up to the nineteenth century much of the energy for early industrialism was supplied by horsepower in the mills and mines, and of course in supporting agriculture where they ploughed and carried.

By the end of the thirteenth century European agriculture, and particularly that of England and Flanders, was highly productive. It was increasingly 'mechanized', using animals, water and wind. It was a highly 'artificial' agriculture, in which large areas were deliberately kept for parks, grazing and pasturage. Above all it was based on labour–saving devices wherever they could be found.

The result was that agricultural productivity was extremely high. There are indeed grounds for thinking that medieval farming in the thirteenth or fourteenth century in England was as productive as it would be until the early eighteenth century. For example, Mokyr has recently written that 'There is now some evidence suggesting that the high levels of agricultural productivity in Britain around 1700 were nothing new and date back to the Middle Ages. The Ramsey manors in Huntingdonshire in the eastern Midlands, which have left us a great deal of evidence, show that labor productivity in agriculture in the first half of the fourteenth century was as high as it was to be in the early nineteenth century (Karakacili, 2004)... In a similar vein, however, Campbell and Overton (1993) have found that land productivity of the 1300s was not surpassed until about 1710 in Norfolk.'[8]

♦

THEN OCCURRED THE catastrophic set–back of the Black Death from the mid-fourteenth century, which destroyed at least one third of the population of Europe. In England, this emphasized a labour–saving approach since the cost of human labour rose even higher and the bonds of an already loose serfdom disappeared. The reaction to this was to increase the non–human elements in agriculture – for example the number of animals and in particular sheep. It was also an encouragement to improve productivity through new fertilizers, marling and lime, new crop rotations and new crops.

It is difficult to assess the effects of the new plants brought back by European penetration of South America, in particular, but also India, Africa and the Pacific. Potatoes, tomatoes and numerous new kinds of vegetables obviously had a considerable effect. Likewise sugar, tobacco, spices and later tea and coffee would profoundly change European diets, health and many other aspects of European life.

The effects were both mental and physical. Europe before Columbus had already developed a diverse and efficient agriculture. The sudden realization of the possibility of further improving production and consumption by using a range of tropical and semi−tropical plants must have been one of the factors behind the increasing pace of experiments in agriculture which we now call the 'agricultural revolution'. People who had watched what was grown in their gardens and fields being transformed, and who were experimenting with new stimulants and narcotics and sweeteners, were increasingly ready to try out new ways of improving their agriculture.

The great upsurge of activity in the seventeenth and eighteenth century consisted of a set of complex and inter−related changes. The increased use of fertilizers in the form of marl, lime and nitrogen−fixing plants such as clover; the increased use of winter feeds through root crops and hence the over−wintering of larger numbers of livestock; the greater amount of horse−power; new crop rotations which obviated the need for a third of the land to lie fallow; better transportation and storage of crops; experiments in improving the breed of sheep, pigs, cows and horses, all these together, particularly in England, raised the productivity of agriculture without adding to the labour input. Without these improvements it would have been impossible to feed the growing cities, or allow up to 40 percent of the population to engage in non−agricultural activities.

The increase in productivity can be seen in a number of statistics. For example, Wrigley has recently produced a table of cereal production which 'suggests that total net cereal output increased almost threefold between 1600 and 1800. The population rose from 4.16 million to 8.67 million between the two dates, suggesting that the amount of cereal food per head rose by almost 40 per cent.'[9] By 1800 one-third of the population were able to supply the rest with food, suggesting that output per person in agriculture expanded by at least three quarters between 1700 and 1800.[10] Putting these two facts together, Bryant summarized the position: 'Between 1600 and 1800, the English population grew from roughly 4 to 8.5 million, but the percentage of those engaged in agriculture actually fell by nearly one-half, from 70% of the total to 36% ...'[11]

♦

BY THE SEVENTEENTH century the English lived off the power of wind, water and animals in a way unequaled by any people in human history, and they did so by improving the harnessing of that power through increasingly complex machinery. Such machinery would easily adapt itself to mechanization using a new power source, and so the first steam engines – significantly called 'mules' – were developed.

Yet, there remains the question of why and how England achieved such an intensity of use of these natural resources. How could it produce so much iron and glass, how could it heat its vats for tanning and dyeing, and above all how could it not only afford to use half of its grains for beer, but over half of the land for animals? What was its secret?

At one level, the secret lay in the development of the coal industry. Basically agrarian societies have to use much of their land to provide wood for heating, cooking and craft activities. This sets a strict limit to the land available for agriculture. This rule inhibited all other civilizations. However, starting from as early as Anglo-Saxon times, and rising steeply from the later sixteenth century, the English increasingly used coal.

We all know that coal was at the heart of industrialization in the nineteenth century, yet we tend to overlook the fact that the exploitation of coal had been central, for heating, smelting and producing fertilizers, since the medieval period. The delightful ditty 'England's a perfect world! Has Indies too! Correct your maps: Newcastle is Peru' could have been written well before the later seventeenth century.[12] As Wrigley has documented, England was an animal-wind-water-coal economy several centuries before the efficient steam engine set the seal on this development.

In the 1560's, coal accounted for about ten percent of total energy consumption in England; by 1700 well before the 'industrial revolution', it was approximately half, by 1750 it was sixty-percent.[13] By 1700 the estimated output was about 2.2 million tons; to have provided the same heat energy from wood 'would have meant devoting 2 or 3 million acres to woodland. By 1800, on the same assumption, 11 million acres of woodland would have been needed. This would have meant devoting more than a third of the surface area of the country to provide the quantity of energy in question.'[14] By 1700, England's coal output is reckoned to be five times as large as the rest of world. By 1800 English coal production was still five times that of the rest of Europe combined.[15]

'The steam-pipe has added to her population and wealth the equivalent of four or five Englands', as Emerson was to write.[16] The English were increasingly using stored carbon energy. This released them gradually from the energy trap, for example allowing them to burn lime as fertilizer to increase agricultural productivity, heat and cook their food in their expanding cities, develop their semi-industrial manufactures of tanning, dyeing, iron and glass manufacture, salt production. Well before the great improvement of the steam engine, coal was being converted for many uses, and by the end of the seventeenth century, it was even being used in simple engines to pump water for London. The final evolution of the more effective steam engine is thus both a revolutionary change, but also just one stage in a long development.

Coal was important both in the several hundred years run-up to the 'industrial revolution' of the eighteenth century, allowing many other factors such as high agricultural productivity and high wages. It was equally important in sustaining the momentum. As Wrigley has recently pointed out '... the strategic significance of coal in the industrial revolution ... lay in the fact that it enabled expansion to continue rather than being brought to a halt by the energy constraints inherent in organic economies...' He believes that the key question regarding the industrial revolution is 'why it did not stop, the answer must lie in gaining access to a different source of energy.'[17]

England had already developed high levels of craft skills and reliable knowledge in relation to the manipulation of matter, and in particular the conversion of 'natural' energy through machinery (cogs, levers etc.) into something humans could use. The complex developments pioneered in Italy, Germany and France flooded into England and were linked together and supplemented by a few essential theoretical advances such as the discovery of the vacuum by Robert Boyle. The high level of metal technologies, particularly in iron, was also necessary. All the parts came together and fitted into a pattern which, like a complex key in a lock, had the right shape to release the population from the agrarian trap once and for all. This unlocking would, after an interval, be copied all over the globe in the following two centuries.

♦

WHAT HAPPENED IN England was truly amazing, admirable or shocking depending on one's taste. For Tocqueville, English agriculture in the nineteenth century was 'the richest and most perfect in the world'.[18] Yet for Heine around the same time,

> The perfection of machines, which are everywhere in use here and have taken over so many human functions

has for me something uncanny: this ingenious driving of
wheels and rods and cylinders and of thousands of little
hooks and pegs and teeth which move with a kind of passion, filled me with horror. The certainty, the exactness,
the madness, the precision of life in England fills me with
not less anxiety; for just as the machines in England seem
like human beings, so the human beings there seem like
machines.[19]

Already by the time of Adam Smith the English were a
semi-industrial nation. But what changed everything was the
ability through the steam engine and especially Watt's double
condenser, to turn coal into forms of energy to drive machines.
Suddenly a world which had been living largely off the trickle
of renewable carbon energy transforming the sun's rays through
plants and animals and could use millions of years of reserve
energy – first in the form of coal and later of oil. The machine,
urban, industrial, factory age was born on this small island, and
then, fifty years later, started to spread elsewhere.

The fifty-year advantage of England in its agriculture and
industry combined to make its Empire much more powerful,
and its imperial rule supplied the raw materials and the markets
for its goods – absorbing the sugar, tea, coffee, rubber, cotton
and much else which was processed and exported. The peculiar
social and economic structure, which had prevented England
from following the normal course, of moving towards industriousness, was now projected outwards as part of a set of features
which would conquer the world. Our world today is basically an
industrial one – originally made in England, even if over half of
the world's population still live off the land.

Yet, there still remains a puzzle. England clearly had coal
and this is one of the factors that made the escape possible.
Nevertheless, other countries, notably Germany and France
and, further afield, Japan and China, among others, had large
coalfields. Yet, none of these were exploited in anything but a

marginal way. Why was this? In some ways it was not a matter of coal creating the industrial revolution, but rather the industrial revolution created the need for coal. In other words, the rapid growth of the coal industry in England was a symptom of the already high level of wealth and technology. Therefore, we are left with the old puzzle of what was special about England that made it use animals, wind and waterpower so effectively and then, later, to exploit its coal.

◆

THE PICTURE I have painted is the conventional one. During the nineteenth and twentieth centuries economic historians believed that the industrial and agricultural revolutions of the eighteenth century were unique in world history. They documented in detail the developments over several hundred years which led to this momentous change. They showed that these revolutions were English in their first instance, and that apart from Holland, even in other parts of Europe – let alone further afield in India, China, America or elsewhere – nothing similar appeared to be happening. They showed that the great divergence between one society which was taking the industrial path of production and all others which were still or increasingly taking the industrious path of harder labour was something that happened well before 1800. Recently, however, this view has been challenged.

Some readers will be aware that in the 1990's a theory emerged, most notably in the work of Kenneth Pomeranz on *The Great Divergence*.[20] This argues that there was nothing special about either England or Europe. Parts of China, especially the Yangtze basin, Pomeranz argues, were at the same level of wages, productivity, expectation of life, and material wealth as England until about 1800. The 'Great Divergence' in economic production occurred after that date. Hence the contrast after 1800 was not caused by such factors as social, religious, political or economic differences, but rather by two 'accidents', the widespread presence and use of coal in England, and the fact that Europe had colonized parts of Asia, Africa and the Americas and could suck wealth out of them.

This viewpoint goes against the argument of this chapter. It is therefore necessary to acknowledge its presence and to comment very briefly on whether it has substance. It is worth drawing attention to the work of a number of scholars who have looked closely at the material and arguments of the revisionists and argue that they are largely incorrect. There is a burgeoning literature of anti-revisionist criticism, so I shall confine myself to a few recent statements in articles and books.

LET ME START with two scholars who have done detailed comparative developments in the main areas upon which Pomeranz draws most heavily on, namely the most advanced parts of China (the Yangzi basin) and Europe (namely England). One of these is Robert Allen, an Oxford economic historian, whose work is frequently cited in support of the Pomeranz thesis.

In an article published in 2006 by Allen and others on 'Agricultural Productivity... in England and the Yangtze Delta', they write that 'Real male wages and female textile earnings were significantly lower in the Yangtze than in England in the early nineteenth century ... The real wage comparisons push the start of the Great Divergence back from the nineteenth century to the seventeenth. ...In addition, all of the income measures in the Yangtze Delta were trending downward from the mid seventeenth century onwards. The rising population is the obvious explanation.... The Yangtze Delta looks more like an economy becoming increasingly involuted rather than one on the brink of take-off. This analysis suggests that the Yangtze's golden age was in the seventeenth century and that its future prospects were poor.'[21]

A year later Allen and others published an article on 'Wages, Prices and Living Standards in China...' They conclude that

Adam Smith's views on China seem correct. 'Money wages were in accord with his view: In China, they were certainly lower than wages in the advanced parts of western Europe in the eighteenth century. Chinese wages were similar to those in the lagging parts of Europe... The upshot of the wage and price comparisons is that living standards were low in China. In the eighteenth century, advanced cities like London and Amsterdam had a higher standard of living than Suzhou, Beijing or Canton. The standard of living in the Chinese cities we have studied was on a par with the lagging parts of Europe, the Ottoman Empire, India, and Japan...Wages seemed to be slipping in China in the eighteenth century.' They conclude that 'newly discovered data would have to be very different from what is currently at hand to convince us that pre-industrial Chinese living standards were similar to those in the leading regions of Europe. In this regard, Adam Smith's pessimism looks closer to the truth than the revisionists' optimism.'[22]

Allen's views, in line with the above argument, have been spelt out in much greater detail in his recent book. The general theme of the book is that it was the uniquely high price of labour and goods in England which encouraged the spread of labour saving inventions and provided a large consumer market for the new manufactures. All this happened from at least the seventeenth century. For example, one chapter 'emphasizes that north-western Europe's ascent began in the century before the American and Asian trades became important. This emphasis extends the work of historians like Davis (1954) and particularly Rapp (1975), who have noted that the commercial revolution began in the seventeenth century before the Atlantic trades became significant and was an intra-European reorganization in which north-western Europeans out-competed Mediterranean producers in woollen textiles.'[23]

A SECOND SCHOLAR who has worked for much of his life on the economics of Chinese agriculture is Philip Huang. He has written a long review of Pomeranz's book in which he notes that 'in further contrast to the growing capitalization of eighteenth-century English agriculture, the Yangzi delta was moving in the opposite direction of ever greater labor intensification.'[24] The difference in trajectory of labour intensity in the agricultural systems 'make understandable the difference in average farm sizes between England and the Yangzi delta in the eighteenth century: The difference would be 125 acres to 1.25 acres, a difference of 100 to 1.... The above differences in labor intensity, farm size, and agricultural land per capita tell crucially about involution and development not only in farming but also in rural industry, rural incomes, and consumption. But this basic information is not discussed anywhere in Pomeranz's book.'[25]

In relation to Pomeranz's claim that China did not have the coal which gave England its advantage after 1800 Huang writes,

> His assertions about coal supplies in China and for the Yangzi delta are also highly questionable. Tim Wright's detailed study of the coal industry in China shows China to be one of the best-endowed countries in the world in terms of coal deposits (1984, 17). .... Obviously, those same mines could as easily have supplied the Yangzi delta. China's (or the Yangzi delta's) delayed industrialization, in other words, cannot be explained by the lack of availability of coal as Pomeranz asserts; rather, it is the lack of industrial demand that explains the non-development of China's coal industry. Pomeranz's argument, in short, places the cart before the horse.'[26]

He concludes, 'It is ironic that Pomeranz should have chosen to use a comparison between pre-1800 Britain and the Yangzi delta to anchor down his argument of no economic difference between Europe and China until after 1800. England and the delta in the eighteenth century, we have seen, were in fact virtually at opposite poles in a continuum from development to involution across Europe and China.' In eighteenth-century England there were a set of intersecting features, 'an agricultural revolution, proto-industrialization, new demographic patterns, new urbanization, new consumption patterns, and large coal output. But none of these was present in eighteenth-century China or its Yangzi delta. What was present were not the roots of a nine-teenth-century Industrial Revolution but rather the roots of a massive nineteenth-century social crisis.'[27]

THERE ARE NOW numerous other detailed critiques. Stephen N. Broadberry and Bisnupriya Gupta, in 'The Early Modern Great Divergence: Wages, Prices and Economic Development in Europe and Asia, 1500-1800' (2005), write in their abstract that 'Contrary to the claims of Pomeranz, Parthasarathi and other "world historians", the prosperous parts of Asia between 1500 and 1800 look similar to the stagnating southern, central and eastern parts of Europe rather than the developing north-western parts....The "Great Divergence" between Europe and Asia was already well under way before 1800.'

Peer Vries in a short book in *Via Peking back to Manchester (2002)*, writes,

> I think the thesis can indeed be defended that China had fallen into a "high-equilibrium trap": from which it could only escape by external impulses from industrialised countries. There is no indication whatsoever that China in the eighteenth century, or even at the beginning of the First Opium War (1839-1842), was on the brink of having an industrial revolution of its own. There simply are no indications whatsoever that technological breakthroughs of the kind that were at the heart of Britain's industrialisation were imminent. The Industrial Revolution in Britain was a miracle; an industrial revolution in China would have been super-miraculous.[28]

Later, Vries notes, 'Broadly and comparatively speaking, China's pre-industrial agriculture in the eighteenth and nine-teenth centuries can be characterised as land-, labour-, and resource-intensive. Britain's agriculture can be characterised as land-extensive, energy-intensive and resource-extensive. As a matter of fact these qualifications can be applied to their entire economies.'[29]

There is a wide-ranging 2006 article by Joseph M. Bryant on 'The West and the Rest', surveying the work of Jack Goody and Pomeranz. He summarizes a number of arguments and then writes,

> Given all these pronounced differences in social orga-
> nization and in economic practices, is it sociologically
> plausible that the advanced regions of China and Western
> Europe were trending along a comparable developmen-
> tal course, a shared trajectory that would have yielded
> similar outcomes, but for the "accidents" of geography.
> How can a society that remained overwhelmingly agrar-
> ian, increasingly overpopulated relative to resources and
> technologically stationary, and whose key social players
> were peasants, rentier landlords, merchants, and a stratum
> of governing officials whose training was literary rather
> than technical, have been open to the developmental pos-
> sibilities of a society that was increasingly urban-based,
> effectively harnessing new scientific knowledge to tech-
> nologies that were revolutionizing the means of produc-
> tion, and whose key social players were, as these changes
> unfolded, capitalistic farmers, proletarians, industrialists,
> and parliamentary representatives?[30]

Another critique is by Robert Brenner and Christopher Is-
ett. After detailed surveys of the evidence, they conclude, 'In marked contrast with developments in the Yangzi delta, the secular trend in England toward rising agricultural labor productivity constituted the basis for a transformed relationship be-
tween agriculture and industry and between country and town, what was indeed a classically Smithian pattern of growth via the gains from trade.' They add, 'Pomeranz believes that the

developmental trajectories pursued by the Yangzi delta and the English economy were basically similar through around 1800. In fact, the Yangzi delta's Malthusian path made for decline and crisis, while the English economy followed a Smithian trajectory during the same time period.'[31] And they conclude,

> It has been our central argument, in contrast, that between roughly 1500 and 1750, the developmental paths of the two economies had already led them in radically divergent directions, with the result that by the second half of the eighteenth century, England had, by world-historical standards, become a developed economy and a relatively quite wealthy one, while the Yangzi delta had become ever poorer.'[32]

Bozhong Li and Jan Luiten van Zanden have made a detailed comparison between one of the most advanced parts of China, the Hua-Lou area of the Yangzi delta, and the Netherlands, in the early nineteenth century. 'On average, labour productivity in the 1820's [in the Netherlands] is about double the level found in Hua-Lou,' they write, '…and GDP per capita is circa 86 percent higher in this part of Western Europe…' And they conclude that Chinese per capital GDP as a whole was only a little over half that of Europe as a whole. 'These results appear to confirm the view that there existed large differences in GDP per capita between these two parts of Europe.'[33]

Furthermore, they show in all kinds of production, such as printing, oil-pressing, spinning and weaving, the level of mechanization was very low in this most advanced part of China; it was far behind that in the Netherlands. For example, 'the Dutch developed a highly capital intensive windmill-technology to press their oilseeds, the Chinese version of this was driven, again, by humans or oxen.' Chinese junks were inefficient in terms of the need for labour so that there was a ratio of a ton per man ratio of about 5 or 6. In Dutch shipping, a ton per man ratio of 15 to 25 was already usual in the 18th century.'[34] If we remember that England was already fully richer than the Netherlands by the early nineteenth century, its use of non-human energy was well in advance of the Netherlands, then we see that there must have been a considerable divergence between the most advanced parts of China and Europe well before the start of the nineteenth century.

There are other interesting contributions to the debate – for example those made by Ricardo Duchesne in several articles and his recent book, *The Uniqueness of Western Civilization*. The general conclusion of these writers is that while England moved towards industrialization and growing productive efficiency in terms of agriculture and industry in the period 1500-1750, there is no sign of this in southern or Eastern Europe, India and China before 1800. There is no sign that China was moving toward the kind of trajectory to be found in England. The 'Great Divergence' debate has strengthened the previous interpretation that there was something unique happening in one part of the world. Yet it has also emphasized that this is not a matter of 'the west', but of England.

All the measures show that Adam Smith was right: England was significantly different even from France, let alone other parts of southern and eastern Europe. It was not a 'European Miracle' as it used to be called– though it was developed out of features from across Europe. Instead, it was an *English* (or perhaps a British) miracle. As Joel Mokyr concludes in his latest book, *The Enlightened Economy: Britain and the Industrial Revolution, 1700-1850*, 'It was a remarkable confluence of circumstances that led to the events described here, and one of the irrepressible sentiments of the economic historian studying the Industrial Revolution is a sense of amazement that it occurred at all.'[35]

CHAPTER NOTES

1. For useful tables of other countries, see the diagram in Rostow, *Stages*, 1; Landes, *Wealth*, table 16:1, 231.

2. For a detailed analysis, see Macfarlane, *Savage*, ch. 3.

3. Geertz, *Agricultural.*

4. White, *Technology*, 84.

5. Mokyr, *Lever*, 34.

6. Mokyr, *Lever* 38.

7. Wrigley, *Energy*, 75, 83.

8. Mokyr, *Enlightened*, 173.

9. Wrigley, *Energy*, 80.

10. Huang, 'Great', 502.

11. Bryant, 'Divergence', 434.

12. Quoted in Vries, *Economy*, 167.

13. Wrigley, *Energy*, 37.

14. Wrigley, *Energy*, 39.

15. Wrigley, cited in Huang, 'Great', 532.

16. Emerson, *English*, 124.

17. Wrigley, *Energy*, 101, 207.

18. Tocqueville, *Ancien*, 34.

19. Heine quoted in Wilson, *Strange*, 179.

20. Pomeranz, *Great*; see also Blaut, Frank, Goody, Goldstone, Bin Wong cited earlier.

21. Allen, 'Yangtze', 15.

22. Allen, 'Wages,' 30-1.

23. Allen, *British*, 128.

24. Huang, 'Great', 506.

25. Huang, 'Great', 510-1.

26. Huang, 'Great', 533.

27. Huang, 'Great', 533-4.

28. Vries, *Peking*, 32.

29. Vries, *Peking*, 47.

30. Bryant, 'Divergence', 432.

31. Brenner and Isett, 'England's', 636.

32. Brenner and Isett, 'England's', 650.

33. Li and van Zanden, 'Before', 24-5.

34. Li and van Zanden, 'Before', 22-3.

35. Mokyr, *Enlightened*, 487.

CHAPTER 4

THE ORIGINS OF CAPITALISM

THE INDUSTRIAL AND agricultural revolutions were part of something even bigger – namely market capitalism, a complex set of attitudes, beliefs, institutions and networks within which economy and technology are situated. The quintessential features of this system have often been described. At its heart is the separation out of the economy into a special domain, dis-embedded from society, religion and politics. Such a process can be seen in various key areas.

One of these is in attitudes to property. The privatized and individual nature of property in English Common law is a very old feature, dating back over a thousand years. Property in England is owned by an individual. He may own a horse, a coat, a house, a field, the right to fish, the right to cut down a tree.

The powerful principle of law-protected private rights in property which John Locke saw as underpinning English freedom, and which was transmitted as one of the defining features of individualistic capitalism to the U.S., is present in English law and society from very early. In terms of ownership, the unit is the individual – neither family, religious or political authority can forcefully (lawfully) deprive a person of these rights. This is unusual in the world until recently.

AT THE HEART of capitalism there is an attitude towards profit maximization and the saving or spending of wealth. Max Weber pointed out that while the great cities of Italy, Spain or France in the fifteenth to seventeenth centuries were full of wealth, luxury, money, consumerism, yet they were in their essential spirit 'pre-capitalist'. Meanwhile, in the rural backwoods of America, Benjamin Franklin and his friends showed in their attitudes to time, money, investment and saving, a capitalist ideology.

England was like backwoods America. Until the middle of the eighteenth century, England was a rather rural place – filled with smallish towns and small cities, less urbanized than most of the rest of Europe, seemingly filled with country people. Yet when we start to investigate the mentality of those villagers, we find little, if any, difference between their basic attitudes to time, saving, re-investing of profits and anxieties about consumption and status to those seen in England today. The mentality of the seventeenth century country clergyman Ralph Josselin whose diary I have analysed is as 'capitalist' as any modern farmer or businessman.[1] We can trace similar attitudes through the numerous letters, diaries and other sources which survive from the later middle ages.

In other words, the Weberian 'Protestant Ethic' is there in England, certainly after the Protestant Reformation, but also well before. The legal cases, the literary sources, the village records, none of them indicate a sudden watershed or move from a pre-capitalist ethic to a capitalist one. The acquisitive, wealth-pursuing, rational and dis-embedded accumulation is there in Chaucer and the legal records of England from the fourteenth century onwards.

It is this ethic which found its expression in the austere, saving, calculating world of English Puritanism, but it was also there much earlier. And it is, as Weber noted, the engine that drives that capital accumulation, the re-investment for profit, which gradually leads a country to become richer.

In most societies, temporary success in accumulation is normally used for consumption, display and gifts, for fear that it will be grabbed by the powerful or destroyed through war. On the contrary, the 'Protestant Ethic' enjoined hard work, time and labour saving, re-investment for profit. All of this is a feature which distinguished England from most countries, though the Dutch, as Simon Schama points out in *Embarrassment of Riches*, had the same tendency. It was not just the forms but also the spirit of capitalism which was early present in England.

The outcome was a constant striving for more – as my school motto put it, 'Striving for the sun'. There was not, as in most cultures, a fixed limit. There was always extra profit to be made, or fears of ruin to be allayed.

FRENCH VISITORS NOTED these traits in England. Hippolyte Taine wrote in the middle of the nineteenth century that 'The mind becomes narrower, men grow hot after gain, work too much, acquire too many needs….Everybody becomes plebeian, proletarian or shop-keeperish, sharp, hard, anxious and unhappy. To make money – such, nowadays is the daily concern, the all-absorbing idea – and in this country more than any other.'[2] Poverty, he writes, is generally degrading. 'It is to some extent to avoid falling into such degradation that the English strive so fiercely after riches. They prize wealth so highly because it is, in their eyes, the accompaniment to, sustenance for and condition of morality, education and all the attributes which make a gentleman. It is under this unremitting lash that every man goes forward, drawing his load after him. And use turns into a need: even when he has reached his goal, he still goes on pulling and, in default of a load of his own, harnesses himself to that of his parish, his association, or the State.'[3]

Taine gives a portrait of a model life. 'Here, then, is an admirable specimen of an English life: left early to fend for oneself; marriage to a woman with no fortune; a large family of children; income all spent, no savings; work very hard and place one's children under the necessity to do likewise; constant acquisition of facts and positive knowledge; find relaxation from one task in another task, and rest in travel; produce constantly and consume as much.'[4] Or as Max O'Rell put it, 'Poverty is no vice in France. It is in England. But everything has its redeeming point. This thirst for wealth, this adoration of the Golden Calf, has made the English nation a nation of bees. Everyone works. The heir of a millionaire does not dream of a life of idleness.'[5]

Another Frenchman who noted the same characteristic which had been transferred even more forcefully to America, was Tocqueville. He wrote that 'Intelligence, even virtue, seem of little account without money. Everything worthwhile is somehow tied up with money. It fills all the gaps that one finds between men, but nothing will take its place'.[6] Everything was about money. 'In a nation where wealth is the sole, or even the principal foundation of aristocracy, money, which in all society is the means of pleasure, confers power also. Endowed with these two advantages, it succeeds in attracting towards itself the whole imagination of man; and ends by becoming, we may almost say, the only distinction which is sought.'[7]

◆

IT IS ALMOST always the case that in agricultural societies, co-operation in, and command of, labour is obtained through real or manufactured kinship links. Those who herd the animals, work the farm, run the estate, are recruited on the basis of kin ties. In such a system, to increase the level of production, the central mechanism is to increase the family labour force, either by marriage strategies which bring in wives and children, or through the creation of fictive kinship ties such as god-parent-hood or adoption. There is little incentive to devise 'labour-saving' devices. This overlap between the unit of reproduction and production continued in much of Europe until quite recently. 'The decline of the family as a productive unit…reached the European peasant and working classes only during the nineteenth century, and, in some areas like Southern Italy, rural Ireland, and rural France, not until the twentieth century'.[8] It is easy to assume that this was also the case in England. Yet what is striking is that from at least the fourteenth century, the family does not seem to have been the basic unit of production.

What emerges from the detailed study of manorial and taxation documents is that we are not dealing in English history with a familistic, subsistence, economy, but with one where from the medieval period most of the labour that is recruited is contractual labour, that is work provided by servants, apprentices, day−labourers and full−time labourers. Hired labour was no oddity in the system but a central feature of it. Whether we look at the large medieval estates or the small copyholdings, we find that they were not, on the whole, run by groups of parents and children, but by people who have a non−family relationship. Of course, it was possible for small family firms and partnerships to develop; but this was a matter of conscious choice, not of automatic organization. Only husband and wife acted as a joint unit.

♦

THE GAP WHICH had emerged between people and the land, the flexibility of property concepts, the non−familistic use of labour, all of this was only made possible by various symbolic instruments, the most important of which was money. Monetized values, whether in the form of actual currency or credit, are usually held on the edge of the community in most traditional societies. Tribal societies keep money right outside the system, only engaging in exchange on the boundaries. Peasant societies are linked to the market and to money but also refuse to allow the medium of money to penetrate too deeply into the local community and into the operation of daily life. Money and all its stands for, it is realized, will destroy the inter-blending of social and economic which is of their essence. While money is essential in such societies, principally to pay taxes, rents and to purchase some luxuries and perhaps even necessities from the outside world, it is something which is kept out of most daily relationships.

The situation which is evident to any historian who has contemplated the English records from the fourteenth century is different. The penetration of cash and money values appears almost complete and spectacular from the earliest documents. The detailed account rolls, manor court rolls, rentals and other materials would not make sense unless we realize the importance of monetary values in all parts of life. Almost everything was given a monetary value, and almost everything could be bought and sold for cash.

Just to give one example, the agricultural treatise of Walter of Henley written in about 1280 as a work to help the management of estates carefully works out how much each agricultural cost is in cash. A horse costs 13s 6d a year to keep; one sixth of a bushel of oats costs a half penny; shoeing the horse one penny. The cost of sowing an acre of wheat is also worked out carefully with cash values, as are many other items.[9]

The centrality of kinship is often best indicated when people need help. In most societies, it is to kin that an individual will turn in sickness, old age, flood or fire. When money is needed for a wedding or a funeral, it is kin who are asked first. What is therefore significant about the impression from the English documents is that it was ultimately not kin who were a person's main resource for help. When people borrowed, as we can see from lists in inventories taken of a person's possessions at death, and from account books and diaries, the majority of the loans were not from kin.

In times of poverty, resulting from accident, old age, unemployment or other calamity, it does not seem to have been the wider kin group that acted as the insurance group. Poor relief was based on residence, not on kinship; it was fundamentally institutions other than kin – the church, the manor, the parish, which had taken on the problems of poverty, disaster and old age, and it is out of this tradition that England developed the first Welfare State. Just as there was, ultimately, no legal right of the children in their parents' or siblings' property, so, reciprocally, the parents had no legal right in their children's good fortune.

This is not to say that the family would never help out in emergencies. Just as today, it is probably the case that a good deal of informal help was given by close kin. Yet the difference between the past in England and in much of the rest of the world is considerable. A situation where kin are the only people one can trust, the only people who help, who carry all the burden of sickness, accident and old age, where elder siblings will automatically help their younger ones is not one we find in England.

♦

THAT ENGLAND WAS a capitalist country from the middle ages is mirrored and expressed in a number of other features which it is worth briefly noting. In my book on *English Individualism* I documented the widespread use of wage labour and high social and geographical mobility in the thirteenth to fifteenth centuries as further evidence of the early penetration of the market.[10] For example, by the later fourteenth century in East Anglia over half the adult male population were listed as servants and labourers.

Another feature is that land was conceived of as a commodity – not as something intertwined with the family. 'Keeping the name on the land', a central value in all peasantries from Ireland to China, was largely absent, except perhaps to a small degree with aristocratic families. Land is like everything else, a commodity – something to buy, sell, and speculate in. In France, as Tocqueville observed, the French 'peasant's love for property in land was extreme, and all the passions born in him by the possession of the soil were aflame.'[11] On the other hand, 'habits and instincts of the English peasant are…totally unlike those of our own. If he possesses more intelligence or more capital than his neighbours, he turns his advantages to account in trade; the idea of becoming a landowner never enters his head. With the English, therefore, land is a luxury; it is honourable and agreeable to possess it, but it yields comparatively little profit. Only rich people buy it.'[12] In France from the twelfth century or earlier many peasants, as families, held absolute property in their land.[13] In England there was never peasant allodial land – all land in England was ultimately held of the Crown and was something that could and would drift away from a particular family.

This makes the holding of land seem at first sight somewhat insecure – especially if it was rented. But here again, there was a peculiarity. In share-cropping or similar regimes, there is little or no incentive for the tenant to make improvements – the landlord would take the improved assets the following year. Yet in England from early on the sub-letting of land for lengthy periods was secure. And the tenant kept the value of the improvements. Consequently, as Laing observed, 'we do see tenants in England, such is their reliance on the moral principle, laying out money, and largely too, in draining, manuring, obtaining fine breeds of cattle and sheep, and in all the most expensive farm improvements; and doing so as freely and confidently, under their no-tenure, as the Scotch tenant under his nineteen years' lease duly registered and in form of law complete.'[14] The same applied to all property, including, housing, factories or other leased property. It was in the tenants' interest to improve the yield from the asset, for which they would be compensated.

ANOTHER FEATURE WORTH considering is money lending. As we have seen, in embedded peasant civilizations of the world, from China to Italy, money is on the periphery of the village economy. When a peasant needs money – for a wedding, funeral, harvest failure, he or she has to borrow the cash from a professional moneylender, usually at very high rates of interest, up to a hundred percent a year or more. This is an almost universal feature of peasant civilization. Yet medieval records in England do not suggest that there was a class of professional money-lenders at the village level in recorded English history.

Most people had access to money from informal networks or savings. The widespread pawning of rice and other assets which most peasantries had to undergo in order to last through the difficult parts of the year is hardly to be found in England.

Indeed the process was the opposite. The problem was what to do with surpluses of cash, in other words how to save profitably. Hence there grew up one of the great banking traditions of the world. People saved cash, and were paid interest by institutions which held their money. This flowered in the age of Barclays, Lloyds and above all the Bank of England, but its roots are in the medieval period. These banks in turn lent at fixed and low rates of interest, at 5-15 percent. rather than the 30-100 percent. one would characteristically find in most pre-industrial societies. Money was unusually available and country wills and inventories show that most people held or had access to cash.

A further indication of an unusual situation lies in the practice of share-cropping, called by various names around the world – *mezzadria* in Italy, and *adé lava* in my village in Nepal. The idea is that land is let by the owner to a cultivator who gives in return a half or more of the harvest to the owner. Share-cropping was neither recognized in English law nor is there any evidence that it was ever practised. By the middle of the eighteenth century Adam Smith wrote of this institution that it was called 'Metayers' in French and in Latin *Coloni Partiarii*. He gave these names because, he wrote, 'They have been so long in disuse in England that at present I know not a name for them.' He noted that in France 'five parts out of six of the whole kingdom are said to be still occupied by this species of cultivators.'[15]

Adam Smith was right, there is no evidence in any of the manorial documents or other local and legal cases of the medieval period or in the treatises on land law that share-cropping was ever practised in England. If one let a piece of property to another person, one would expect to receive a fixed amount, not a share of the harvest. This payment would be in cash, equivalent to a modern rent, and not in crops. Money intervened in the transaction. The extortionate share-cropping systems which consigned millions to back-breaking work and poverty in Asia and Europe were absent.

Another indication of the difference concerns bargaining and barter. Where economic transactions are on the edge of a modern market, objects do not have a fixed price – they are subject to local laws of supply and demand and to the power relations and social nexus of the individuals involved. So bargaining, the attempt to raise or lower prices on the spot is almost universal in peripheral markets.

Yet in England bargaining seems to have been largely absent, to the astonishment of foreigners. As Count Pecchio observed in the early nineteenth century 'In England there is no bargaining. The price of every article is fixed. This custom is not the product solely of competition and confidence, but also of the necessity of saving time. Thus a child may go to buy without being cheated.'[16]

Or as Laing, in his *Observations* based on travels in nineteenth century Europe, wrote:

> A shopkeeper with us, even in the lowest class, would feel it to be a degradation of himself to ask more at first than the just price, and his customer would feel it was a gratuitous insult, an implied doubt of the man's veracity and honesty, if he were to beat down the demand and offer less. On the Continent the most respectable man in trade will begin with asking a price one half higher than he will be content to take, and will tell half-a-dozen falsehoods to make you believe that the price he asks is fair and moderate.[17]....The English are a nation of shopkeepers; but these shopkeepers are gentlemen in their feelings of self-respect, and of honourable dealing with their customers, compared to the same class in the countries claiming

a higher education and more chivalrous spirit. In Paris, and a few other cities of the Continent, the shopkeepers begin now to place in their windows the announcement that they sell *au prix fixe*, and to do homage to the principle of fair dealing so universally acted upon for generations in England.'[18]

Examination of local documents from the medieval period onwards in England shows that a great deal of time was taken in fixing the price of various commodities, particularly the most important such as bread and ale. Those who sold above or below these prices were liable to be punished.

♦

THE ENGLISH HAVE a strange attitude to cities. In the end they created the most urban civilization known to man in the nineteenth century, yet there is a basic anti-urbanism in their mentality. 'The country is England's poetry, the town her prose, which is just the reverse of the position in Latin countries – one has but to think of the towns of Italy, for instance.'[19] Or as Taine observed, 'Here and in Liverpool, as in London, the English character can be seen in their way of building. The townsman does everything in his power to cease being a townsman and tries to fit a country house and a bit of country into a corner of the town'.[20]

There was no great difference in terms of social, mental or moral structures between the city and the country. There was *rus in urbe* – that is, the country in the towns – with an attempt to make the towns country-like with trees, parks, and small gardens. And there was *urbs in rure* – that is to say the countryside was inhabited by people whose values were urban: obsessed with time, with calculation, with social mobility.

In most civilizations until recently there were the bourgeois, the town dwellers, often literate, with a particular mentality and morality, living behind their city walls and despising the sea of illiterate and hard-working 'peasants' who surrounded them. The late adoption of the French term 'bourgoisie' in England is an indication that there was no native separate estate or class of 'bourgeois' in England. Townsmen spent much time in the country, and by the seventeenth century a fifth of the English population had spent some time living in London.

Foreigners were astonished at the love of the English gentry for rural life. Taine noted that 'As long as three centuries ago the traveller Poggio could write of this country... "Among the English the nobles think shame to live in the towns; they reside in the country, withdrawn among woods and pastures; they consider him the most noble who has the greatest revenues: they give themselves to the things of the fields, sell their wool and their cattle, and do not consider such rustic profits shameful."'[21]

In the middle of the fifteenth century, Sir John Fortescue, who had lived in France for some years described how the English countryside 'is so filled and replenished with landed men, that therein so small a Thorpe [village, hamlet] can not be found wherein dwells not a knight, an esquire, or such a householder, as is there commonly called a frankleyn, enriched with great possessions: And also other freeholders and many yeomen able for their livelihoods to make a Jury in form aforementioned. For there be in that land diverse yeomen which are able to dispend by the year above a hundred pounds...' This was very different from the Continent as he had experienced it.[22]

In essence, England was one large town in its values, and the wall round it was the sea. Not only did the 'bourgeois' not constitute a separate 'estate' in Parliament, or a recognizable separate social category, not only were any walls that had once existed around some of the older cities allowed to crumble, not only were towns not islands in a peasant sea, not only was there great mobility between the merchants and the 'aristocracy', but the barriers between trade and other activities did not really exist.

Just as Pirenne has described the Netherlands as a suburb of Antwerp, so one could describe England as a suburb of London. This is implied in many of the earlier travelers, who move in and out of London and other cities and then into the countryside with no sense of shock or surprise that they were moving into another world – which they certainly would have felt in China, India, and Russia or Continental European countries.

If one follows Braudel and agrees that 'Money was the active and decisive element...Money is the same as saying towns', then England is one large town, for it has been fully integrated into a money economy very early on.[23] Curiously there was no distinct 'bourgeoisie' in this ancient nation of shopkeepers because everyone was in one way or another a member of the bourgoisie.

♦

TO PUT ALL this in another way, England has never been a peasant society. The early monastic institutions and the agricultural treatises of the thirteenth century, for example, show an attitude towards making money, investing, banking, rational profit calculation, the flow of capital, which would have delighted Adam Smith.

The wealth that created many of the greatest cathedrals in medieval Europe was derived from this early market system and the immense wealth of the wool trade. Basically England was all one 'market' with few barriers, good water communications, widespread wage labour, carefully regulated and supervised pricing mechanisms, extensive guilds and craft organizations. The world we see portrayed in Chaucer's fourteenth century *Canterbury Tales*, not only in its occupations, but also in its attitudes, is a recognizably modern, capitalist, one. There is not a peasant amongst them, nor are there recognizable peasants in the stories which the pilgrims told.

This is also related to a complex legal underpinning with its mortgages, banks, loans and financial dealings. Almost everyone, we can see, is out to make money. This was the background to the development of the great institutions which carried the weight of British expansion in later centuries – the Bank of England, the East India Company, the Stock Exchange. All this, as Weber noted, was based on a system of Germanic legal devices, of law and trusts and legal fictions of various kinds. By the time of the industrial revolution, Britain was already becoming the Banker of the World.

CHAPTER NOTES

1. Macfarlane, *Josselin*.

2. Taine, *Notes*, 190.

3. Taine, *Notes*, 62-3.

4. Taine, *Notes*, 60.

5. In Wilson, *Strange*, 227.

6. Tocqueville, *Journeys*, 78.

7. Tocqueville *Memoir*, I, 230-1.

8. Scott and Tilly in Rosenberg, *Family*, 176.

9. Oschinksy, *Walter*, 319, 325.

10. See Macfarlane, *Individualism*, chapter 6.

11. Tocqueville, *Ancien*, 29.

12. Tocqueville, *Memoir*, II, 7.

13. Bloch, *Feudal*, I, 248.

14. Laing, *Observations*, 291.

15. Smith, *Wealth*, I, 413, 414; he probably based the estimate on Quesnay.

16. Wilson, *Strange*, 178.

17. Laing, *Observations*, 267.

18. Laing, *Observations*, 268.

19. Cohen-Portheim in *Wilson*, 250.

20. Taine, *Notes* 220.

21. Taine, *Notes*, 141.

22. Fortescue, *Governance*, fols. 66v-67.

23. Braudel, *Capitalism*, 397.

CHAPTER 5

MATERIAL LIFE

I REMEMBER VIVIDLY the occasion when I visited a barren region to the north of Beijing in 1996. When we asked through an interpreter about the people's lives they spoke with enthusiasm of a recent dramatic improvement. Since the liberalization of Deng Xiao-Ping, they had seen their material comfort increase rapidly. No longer did they live on inferior grains and little meat, their clothes and houses were rapidly improving, they were starting to buy televisions and fridges. This massive transformation to a 'modern', modestly affluent, material world is one of the strongest ways we express and judge 'modernity'. I have seen its effects in the remotest parts of China on numerous visits and its origins add interest to our exploration.

In all agrarian civilizations there have been some fabulously rich families. In India, China, France and elsewhere, with their splendid food, clothing, palaces and treasures, the tiny group of extremely rich have long existed. Yet normally an immiserated peasantry who eat the worst grains surrounds them, living in hovels and dressed in rags. This was the case over much of Europe in the early modern period and lasted up to the spread of the affluence revolution of the later nineteenth century which is a major sign of 'modernity'. In 1788 Edward Gibbon completed his great work on *The Decline and Fall of the Roman Empire*. The following year he surveyed the world around hum. There seemed little improvement over the last two thousand years. 'The far greater part of the globe is overspread with barbarism or slavery: in the civilized world, the most numerous class is condemned to ignorance and poverty.... The general probability is about three to one that a new-born infant will not live to complete his fiftieth year.'[1]

What was the situation in England over the centuries? Here are some general observations of observers who visited England. In the 1590's Paul Hentzner from Brandenburg, a jurist and counsellor, visited England and commented that 'the soil is fruitful and abounds with cattle, which inclines the inhabitants rather to feeding than ploughing, so that near a third of the land is left uncultivated for grazing.' Upon the hills 'wander numerous flocks' of sheep. This, he thought, was the 'true Golden Fleece, in which consist the chief riches of the inhabitants, great sums of money being brought into the island by merchants, chiefly for that article of trade.' The inhabitants consumed less bread and more meat than their French counterparts, and 'put a great deal of sugar in their drink'; 'their beds are covered with tapestry, even those of farmers ... their houses are commonly of two stories ... Glass-houses (i.e. with glass windows) are in plenty here.'[2]

A German, Henry Meister, in an account of his travels in England declared, 'I do not impose upon you when I say that though the English labourer is better clothed, better fed, and better lodged than the French, he does not work so hard. You will wonder at this the less, when you consider that the wages of the former are higher, and his diet more substantial; consequently that he has greater strength and activity in the performance of his tasks'.[3]

Particularly interesting are the comments of those from the Netherlands, one of the richest parts of Europe in the fifteenth tand sixteenth centuries. Emanuel van Meteren was an Antwerp merchant who lived in London throughout the reign of Elizabeth and travelled through the whole of England and Ireland. He noted the high standards of living.

The English 'feed well and delicately, and eat a great deal of meat... The English dress in elegant, light and costly garments, but they are very inconstant and desirous of novelties, changing their fashions every year, both men and women. When they go abroad riding or travelling, they don their best clothes, contrary to the practice of other nations...' He believed that the wealth came from sheep, rather than from hard labour. He noted that people did not have to work as hard as in other nations: 'the people are not so laborious and industrious as the Netherlanders or French, as they lead for the most part an indolent life ... They keep many lazy servants, and also many wild animals for their pleasure, rather than trouble themselves to cultivate the land.'[4]

Another Dutchman, the physician Levinus Lemnius, visited England in 1560 and gives an account of affluence. He wrote of 'their populous and great haunted cities, the fruitfulness of their ground and soil, their lively springs and mighty rivers, their great herds and flocks of cattle, their mysteries and art of weaving and clothmaking ... the multitude of merchants exercising the traffic and art of merchaundise among them.'[5]

The *Relation, or rather a true account, of the island of England* of 1497 by the Venetian Ambassador to England, Andrea Trevisano, was written as a report to one of the richest governments in Europe. It was a description of Trevisano's impressions from a country which had had a difficult century, with the Wars of the Roses and the loss of its French empire. It is a country which is often described by recent historians as poor and marginal in Europe, yet this is not the impression Trevisano gave Instead, he was struck by the great wealth of the country: '... the riches of England are greater than those of any other country in Europe, as I have been told by one of the oldest and most experienced merchants, and also as I myself can vouch from what I have seen.' He thought that this was due to their 'great fertility of the soil,' the 'sale of their valuable tin,' and 'from their extraordinary abundance of wool.' Whatever the cause, 'everyone who makes a tour in the island will soon become aware of this great wealth'.

The wealth, he observed, was widely distributed: 'there is no small innkeeper, however poor and humble he may be, who does not serve his table with silver dishes and drinking cups; and no one, who has not in his house silver plate to the amount of at least £100 sterling, which is equivalent to 500 golden crowns with us, is considered to be a person of any consequence. They also 'all from time immemorial wear very fine clothes.' But above all are their riches displayed in the church treasures; for there is not a parish church in the kingdom so mean as not to possess crucifixes, candlesticks, censers, patens, and cups of silver...' This magnificence came to a peak in the wealth shown in Westminster Abbey and the magnificent tomb of St Thomas the Martyr at Canterbury 'which surpasses all belief'".

Even when the English were involved in a military campaign, 'when the war is raging most furiously, they will seek for good eating, and all their other comforts, without thinking of what harm might befall them.' Trevisano noted that money and trade were widespread. 'The common people apply themselves to trade, or to fishing, or else they practice navigation; and they are so diligent in mercantile pursuits, that they do not fear to make contracts on usury.' He believed that 'there is no injury that can be committed against the lower orders of the English, that may not be atoned for by money.'[6]

The impressive wealth noted by foreign visitors to England in the late fifteenth and sixteenth centuries was an even more dramatic feature two centuries later. The French, who were now in many ways the leading nation in Europe, were among those who noted this. In the later eighteenth century La Rochefoucauld wrote '...I am inclined to think that the English must be richer than we are; certainly I have myself observed not only that everything costs twice as much here as in France, but that the English seize every opportunity to use things which are expensive in themselves.' Even more emphatically, he wrote 'there is no interference whatever with their business, and, in the eyes of an impartial traveller, England has the appearance of being a hundred times richer than France.' He thought that 'In the eyes of a foreigner Flanders is the province in France which gives the greatest impression of wealth. But, compared with England, it is nothing...'[7]

♦

WHAT DID THE English themselves think? The Franciscan Friar Bartholomaeus Anglicus, in his encyclopedia on *The Properties of Things* compiled in the middle of the thirteenth century, wrote that 'England is a strong land and a sturdy, and the plenteowest [most plentiful] corner of the world, so rich a land that unneth [uncompelled] it needeth help of any land, and every other land needeth help of England...' It 'is full of mirth and of game and men oft times able to mirth and game, free men of heart and with *tongue*...'[8] It fits well with the world depicted a century later in Chaucer's *Canterbury Tales*, even though they were written after the catastrophe of the Black Death.

Sir John Fortescue paints a particularly detailed comparative picture. He was Lord Chancellor to King Henry VI and fled into France with the young King in 1461. During the next ten years of exile he wrote his book comparing the system of government in France and England. He gave his comments on the material conditions of the two countries. In France, he found:

> The people being with these [pillage by soldiers, salt taxes etc] and diverse other calamities plagued and oppressed, do live in great misery, drinking water daily. Neither do the inferior sort taste any other liquor saving only at solemn feasts. Their shamewes [a gown cut in the middle] are made of hemp, much like to sack cloth. Woolen cloth they wear none, except it be very coarse, and that only in their coats under their said upper garments. Neither use they any hosen, but from the knee upwards: the residue of their legs go naked. Their women go bare foot saving on holy days. Neither man nor women eat any flesh there, but only lard or bacon, with a small quantity whereof they fatten their potage and broths. As for roasted or sodden meat of flesh they taste none, except it be of the innards sometimes and heads of beasts that they killed for gentlemen and merchants.[9]

In England, on the other hand, the position of rural inhabitants was very different. The absence of heavy taxation, of billeted soldiers, and of internal taxes, meant that 'every inhabiter of that realm useth and enjoyeth at his pleasure all the fruits that his land or cattle beareth, with all the profits and commodities which by his own travail, or by the labour of others he gaineth by land or by water.'

The result was that 'the men of that land are rich, having abundance of gold and silver and other things necessary for the maintenance of a mans life. They drink no water, unless it be so that some for devotion, and upon a seal of penance do abstain from other drinks. They eat plentifully of all kinds of fish and flesh. They wear fine woollen cloth in all their apparel. They have also abundance of bed coverings in their houses, and of all other woollen stuff. They have great store of all hustlements [utensils, tools] and implements of husbandry, and all other things that are requisite to the accomplishment of a quiet and wealthy life according to their estates and degrees.'[10]

Fortescue thought people lived easily in England at this time in a wealthy country so that people 'are scant troubled with any painful labour.' He believed that 'In deed England is so fertile and fruitful, that comparing quantity to quantity, it surmounteth all other lands in fruitfulness. Yea it bringeth forth fruit of it self scant provoked by man's industry and labour.' It is an elegant description of a paradise, where 'the lands, the fields, the groves and the woods do so abundantly spring, that the same untilled do commonly yield to their owners more profit than tilled, though else they be most fruitful of corn and grain.' The livestock grazed safely in the absence of wild animals, so that 'their sheep lie night by night in the fields unkept within their folds, wherewith their land is manured.'[11] Nor did Fortescue believe that the rich and free land he was describing in the middle of the fifteenth century was new. His explanation for its existence – a combination of natural fertility, limited monarch, and Common Law – made him believe that the differences were very ancient.

IN SHAKESPEARE'S AGE there are many descriptions of the state of England. One of the best known is that of John Aylmer which has echoes of Fortescue's account. Aylmer had been the tutor of Lady Jane Grey and was later to become Bishop of London under Elizabeth. He was exiled to Europe during the reign of Mary and lived abroad, like Fortescue, for ten years. He had visited France and Germany and clearly gleaned information about Italy. As with Fortescue, he made an explicit comparison of England and its neighbours. It is clearly a polemical piece, warning of the dangers of Catholicism and continental absolutism, yet it fits with other observations at the time, and some of the minor details, which we can check, ring true. I shall only quote a part of his lengthy exhortation:

> In Italy they say it is not much better [than France], the husbandmen be there so rich: that the best coat he weareth is sacking, his nether stocks of his hose, be of his own skin, his diet and fare not very costly, he cometh to the market with a hen or two in one hand, and a dozen eggs in a net in the other, which being sold and told, he buyeth and carrieth home with him, no Beef or Mutton, Veal or sea fish, as you do: but a quart of oil to make salads of herbs, wherewith he liveth all the week following. And in Germany though they be in some better case than the other: yet eat they more roots than flesh...Now compare them with thee: and thou shalt see how happy thou art. They eat herbs: and thou Beef and Mutton. They roots: and thou butter, cheese, and eggs. They drink commonly water: and thou good ale and beer. They go from the market with a salad: and thou with good flesh fill thy wallet. They lightly never see any sea fish: and thou hast they belly full of it. They pay till their bones rattle in the skin: and though layest up for thy son and heir...Thou livest like a Lord, and they like dogs...'[12]

Around the same time, the Essex clergyman William Harrison was gathering material for his detailed *Description of En-*

gland, published in 1577, which gives a detailed portrait of the material wealth of England, for example in its furniture, housing and clothing.[13] Likewise in the early seventeenth century, when Fynes Moryson made extensive travels for many years over much of the Continent, his published reports showed the great wealth of England in comparison to most of the places he visited.[14]

By the end of the seventeenth century there could be no doubt in Englishmen's minds that, along with Holland, they were living in the wealthiest land in the world. 'The working manufacturing people of England eat the fat, and drink the sweet, live better, and fare better, than the working poor of any other nation in Europe; they make better wages of their work, and spend more of the money upon their backs and bellies, than in any other country'.[15]

The gap was even greater in the eighteenth century and obvious to travellers such as Arthur Young or Thomas Malthus. Malthus wrote:

> Now it is generally agreed that the condition of the lower classes of people in France before the revolution was very wretched. The wages of labour were about 20 sous, or tenpence a day, at a time when the wages of labour in England were nearly seventeenpence, and the price of wheat of the same quality in the two countries was not very different. Accordingly Arthur Young represents the labouring classes of France, just at the start of the revolution, as "76 per cent. worse fed, worse clothed, and worse supported, both in sickness and health, than the same classes in England."[16]

♦

RECENT SCHOLARS ALSO have commented on the differences, though I shall only give a few examples here. Colin Clark estimated that French wages in 1700 were the equivalent to 2.6 kg. of wheat per day, whereas in England some fifty years earlier the wages had been almost twice this with 4.8kg. of wheat per day, which in turn was 'only half what it had been in the fifteenth century.'[17] Joel Mokyr guessed that in 1788 British GNP per capita was about thirty percent. higher than that of the French– and this presumably included Scotland and Wales.[18]

France was not the extreme, for it was part of the relatively rich western European complex. If we compare these figures to the Third World until recently they are even starker. De Vries estimates that the figures reported in 1688 by Gregory King set per capita income as two or three times as high as contemporary modern Asia or Africa.[19] David Landes suggests that in the eighteenth century the English income, equivalent to about £100 per head, was four times higher than that per head in India in the 1960's.[20] In other words, even before the industrial revolution, England was over the threshold of poverty, 'modern' in its affluence, different from most of its neighbours – except the Dutch, who were even richer for a short while – and far away from the Third World.[21]

♦

IN MOST *ANCIEN RÉGIME* societies, perhaps up to three-quarters of the population were forced to live on low quality foods, inferior grains, little or no meat and few vegetables. What was the situation in England? In the sixteenth century, Harrison wrote, 'It is no marvel therefore that our tables are oftentimes more plentifully garnished than those of other nations, and this trade hath continued with us even since the very beginning'.[22] A century earlier, as we have seen, Fortescue had described this contrast. In the eighteenth century, Saussure wrote of the English:

> They are all well fed and well dressed, and the coarse black bread our peasants eat is unknown to them. On Sundays they always have a good piece of beef before the

fire, and all the year round a cask of ale in the cellar; in a word, there is plenty everywhere...[they] are large eaters; they prefer meat to bread, some people scarcely touching the latter.[23]

Arthur Young, in the same century, described a suitable diet for a labouring man:

On the first day he was to eat two pounds of bread made of a mixture of wheat, rye and potato, two ounces of cheese and two pints of beer. Next day he was to have three messes of soup made of lean beef, peas, mealy potatoes, ground rice, onions, celery and salt and water.[24]

Emerson describes the contrast between well-fed English and the scarcity of good food on the continent right up into the later nineteenth century:

They use a plentiful and nutritious diet. The operative cannot subsist on water-cresses. Beef, mutton, wheat-bread, and malt-liquors are universal among the first-class labourers. Good feeding is a chief point of national pride among the vulgar, and, in their caricatures, they represent the Frenchman as a poor, starved body.[25]

In particular, from the medieval period at least, the best and most expensive of grains – wheat – had been the staple even of the poor in England. Thus, Thorold Rogers wrote, 'From the earliest times the staple food of the English people has been wheaten bread, and wheat is the costliest, and on the whole the most precarious of our corn crops.'[26] The Scotsman Kames noted in the middle of the eighteenth century that 'Not a person in London who lives by the parish-charity will deign to eat brown bread; and in several parts of England, many who receive large sums from that fund, are in the constant custom of drinking tea twice a-day.'[27] In Kames' home country, the staple was oats; as Adam Smith commented, 'The common people in Scotland, who are fed with oatmeal, are in general neither so strong nor so handsome as the same rank of people in England who are fed with wheaten bread',[28] putting in a matter-of-fact way Dr Johnson's gibe that the English fed their houses with the oats which the poorer Scots ate themselves.

In sum, the transition to a 'modern' high protein and carbohydrate diet only occurred in the later nineteenth century on much of the Continent, and after the Second World War in parts of East Asia. It is only now occurring in China and India. But the 'modern' diet, seems to have been a perennial feature of England, from the top to very near the bottom of society and from the medieval period onwards.[29]

♦

WHAT YOU DRINK has always been important for the English. As we show in *Green Gold*, the English, unlike all continental countries, would not, if possible, drink water over the centuries up to the nineteenth.[30] For example, 'In 1726 a Swiss visitor to London, M. de Saussure is astonished at the amount of water used. He says that absolutely none is drunk; that the lower classes, even the paupers, do not know what it is to quench their thirst with water'.[31]

The English favoured expensive alternatives. For a number of centuries, they drank half of their grain harvest as beer and ale. Later they turned to tea imported from China, supplemented by sugar from Jamaica. Saussure commented, 'Throughout the whole of England the drinking of tea is general. You have it twice a day and, though the expense is considerable, the humblest peasant has his tea twice a day just like the rich man; the total consumption is immense.' He later wrote, 'I have already remarked the universal consumption of tea in England from the lowest peasant to the highest of the nobility and in such large quantities that it is reckoned that in the course of the year every single person, man or woman, on the average consumes four pounds of tea. That is truly enormous.[32]

This consumption of ale, beer and then tea with sugar and milk, had immense effects on the health and working capacity of the English. It gave them a drinking regime which is in effect 'modern' – in other words it consisted of cold and hot drinks produced through human intervention, rather than highly polluted and dangerous water which most other peoples have endured. Without this drinking pattern, it is difficult to see how the English could have broken out of the Malthusian trap of larger cities like London growing to a size where polluted water would cause high mortality.

One outcome of the difference in nutrition lies in the history of famines. Apart from the famine of 1315-9 there is no evidence of any national famine in the country between the Norman Invasion and the present day. In the rest of the world, famine with massive deaths continued until the later eighteenth century in the rest of Europe (Scandinavia and continental Europe), the later nineteenth century in Japan, the 1930's in the Soviet Union and the middle of the twentieth century in China and India. Thus the English effectively escaped famine five hundred years before most of the rest of the world's population.[33]

◆

TURNING FROM WHAT we eat and drink to the way in which we protect our bodies, we can first investigate clothing. The essence of modern clothing is that in cold periods it protects and preserves body heat and in the summer it keeps us cool. Many of us take such a 'modern' clothing regime for granted. In most *ancien régime* countries clothing was and still remains for many skimpy and cheap and often the majority of the population wear no shoes or hats. We can see this in the traditional clothing in Japan, China or India until the twentieth century and even in the Highlands and Islands of Scotland as well as in many parts of Europe until the later nineteenth century.

Observers noted that the English wore expensive and substantial clothes from early on. Aided by the fact that they had many livestock – and hence animals skins – they wore leather shoes, they often wore hats, and they had warm, well-made woollen clothing coming from their abundant sheep, later added to by cotton from the eighteenth century.

The sumptuous clothing of the English is described in the *Canterbury Tales*. Many railed against the 'fantastical' and the lavish clothing of the ordinary people.[34] In the sixteenth century, Thomas Becon wrote:

> I think no realm in the world, no, not among the Turks and Saracens, doth so much in the variety of their apparel, as the Englishmen do at this present. Their coat must be made after the Italian fashion, their cloak after the use of the Spaniards, their gown after the manner of the Turks: their cap must be of the French fashion; and the last their dagger must be Scottish, with a Venetian tassel of silk.[35]

The English constantly changed their clothing according to fashion at least in the middling groups and all this led to comfort, conservation of energy, and an encouragement to manufacturing.

In the early eighteenth century the Swiss observer Saussure noted that the 'lower classes are usually well dressed, wearing good cloth and linen. You never see wooden shoes in England, and the poorest individuals never go with naked feet'. With the middling sort, 'Englishmen are usually very plainly dressed, they scarcely ever wear gold on their clothes; they wear little coats called "frocks", without facings and without pleats, with a short cape above. Almost all wear small, round wigs, plain hats, and carry canes in their hands, but no swords. Their cloth and linen are of the best and finest'. As for the women, 'They pride themselves on their neatly shod feet, on their fine linen, and on their gowns, which are made according to the season either of rich silk or of cotton from the Indies. Very few women wear woollen gowns. Even servant-maids wear silks on Sundays and holidays, when they are almost as well dressed as their mistresses'.[36]

A particular oddity was the English love of hats. A nineteenth century American, Oliver Wendell Holmes, described this: 'As for the Englishman's feeling with regard to it, a foreigner might be pardoned for thinking it was a fetich, a North American Indian for looking at it as taking the place of his own medicine-bag. It is a common thing for an Englishman to say his prayers into it, as he sits down in his pew.'[37]

♦

THE SUBSTANTIAL NATURE of English housing is still visible to anyone who travels through the Cotswolds, East Anglian wool towns, the Yorkshire dales or in the older parts of country towns. As far as I know, England is the only country in the world which still has many thousands of houses whose basic structure and building materials date back to over five hundred years ago.

Let me just again quote two French observers.[38] The first is Rochefoucauld: 'In a word there is always a marked superiority in the houses of the common people of England over those of the poor peasants of France, which it often pained me to observe.'[39] The second is Saussure: 'I must own that Englishmen build their houses with taste; it is not possible to make a better use of ground, or to have more comfortable houses'.[40]

Again the contrast, for example, between an eighteenth or nineteenth century Japanese peasant's house and that of poorer people in England was immense. The former were, in Lafcadio Hearn's delightful phrase, 'floating lanterns' made of cheap materials without foundations and only lasting a few years. The latter are substantial and expensive buildings, often of two floors, built of brick or stone, particularly from the seventeenth century, with chimneys, separate rooms, perhaps a cellar and probably a garden. Karamzin in the early nineteenth century noted that 'England is a realm of bricks; in towns and villages all the houses are of brick, covered with tiles and unpainted.[41]

The result of all this was another positive feedback to economic activity in the building and furnishing of these dwellings, as well as many other aspects of life. This was well summarized by Defoe, who observed, 'This...causes a prodigious consumption of the provisions and of the manufactures ... of our country at home and this creates what we call inland trade,'[42] This process was one of the key ingredients of the industrial revolution. A rich and large middle class was actively consuming manufactured goods and hence stimulating further production. This 'consumer revolution' had, in fact, started in the middle ages, but it increased in strength through the centuries until by the eighteenth it was a central feature of English economic development.

It would be possible to find much further evidence of the extraordinary wealth of England from the twelfth and thirteenth centuries onwards in its communal buildings, particularly the amazing cathedrals and churches which still cover England. The presence of the beautiful and expensive churches in many English towns and villages, whether in my own King's College Chapel and the chapels of Oxford and Cambridge, or in the Suffolk and Norfolk wool towns or elsewhere is a testament to the spread of affluence in the later medieval period when many of these were built. Many countries have a few of these medieval buildings– great French cathedrals for example. Yet even the French cathedrals pale beside their English equivalents. 'English Cathedrals are, most of them, larger than any other cathedrals in Europe, except St. Peter's.'[43]

♦

THE EFFECTIVENESS OF the production system also meant that the patterns of work were different. This is another key feature of modernity. The considerable time for leisure and hobbies was already present in England in the fourteenth century as we can see from Chaucer's pilgrims. Many considered the English to be less hard-working than their neighbours; a study comparing English with Japanese work patterns certainly shows how incredibly hard the Japanese worked as compared to all Europeans, but especially the English.[44]

Sorbière wrote, 'The speed [the English] make on horseback appeared so much the more remarkable to me, because of its being used in a country where the people are very lazy, which I can very well affirm without offence; for they do perhaps glory in their sloth, and believe that true living consists in knowing how to live at ease…'[45] More precisely, La Rochefoucauld commented:

> For this wage, which is enormous, they do not do nearly as much work as our people. I have been at close enough quarters to follow some of them and to watch their work throughout the day, and I can assure you that, whatever may be the opinion of some of the English who have travelled in France and disagree with this view, the English labourers do their work in a very casual way, taking frequent rests and talking a great deal. I am convinced that a French workman does nearly a fifth more work in a day than an Englishman.[46]

The relative amount of leisure and the good diet of the English is the background of many of the oddities of the culture. The English on the whole were not exhausted at the end of work and hence engaged in and developed energetic sports and games – from football and rugger to bell ringing and mountain climbing – to absorb their surplus energies. To fill in the long hours of leisure, they invented the ultimate time-user, cricket.

While others were constantly busy when away from the fields trying to keep up with work-related chores, Peter Kalm noted with amazement in the middle of the eighteenth century that the

rural English labourer was able to devote time to his own pleasure, observing of farm servants that 'as soon as they entered the
cottage in the evening, they did not apply themselves to the least
work more than that they ate, sat and talked till eleven o'clock in
the evening. They never troubled themselves to make waggons
or agricultural implements'. He was puzzled at the time they
spent in the local pubs with friends and often 'wondered over
this, that folk who could only provide food for themselves, their
wives and children out of daily wages, could spend time and
money in this way.'[47]

The English obsession with time-filling hobbies – including
flowers and gardening – and with energetic sports and games,
all fit within this pattern. The effects on nature and the countryside – the prevalence of song birds (usually eaten in peasant
societies) or of often-neglected wild fruit, is an old feature.

The result in England was a countryside in which much valuable land was not put to agricultural production; it was used for
leisure or conspicuous consumption. Laing describes this well:

> Woods and groves planted and preserved for ornament,
> parks, pleasure-grounds, lawns, shrubberies, old grass
> fields of excellent soil producing only crops for luxury,
> such as pasture and hay for the finer breeds of horses,
> village greens, commons, lanes between fields, waste cor-
> ners and patches outside of the fences or along the roads,
> hedges, ditches, banks, walls, all which together occupy
> perhaps as much land in England as the land under crops
> of grain, are very rare on the Continent.[48]

In general, England is a country which has long afforded the
luxury of much spare time, much spare land and much material
well-being of a kind which is only now becoming common in
many countries. It is one of the main fruits and signs of modernity.

CHAPTER NOTES

1. Gibbon, *Autobiography*, 217.

2. Rye, *England*, 109-11.

3. Marshall, *People*, 160-1.

4. Quoted in Rye, England, 70-1.

5. Rye, *England*, p.79.

6. *Italian Relation*, 28-30.

7. Rochefoucauld, *Frenchman*, 30, 198, 116.

8. *Property of Things*, I, 734 (modernized).

9. Fortescue, *Governance*, fols. 81-81v.

10. Fortescue, *Governance*, fols. 84v-85v.

11. Fortescue, *Governance*, fols. 66-66v.

12. In Orwell, *Pamphleteers*, I, 30-1.

13. For example, Harrison, *England*, 200ff.

14. For example, Moryson, *Itinerary*, IV, 233.

15. Daniel Defoe, quoted in Allen, *British*, 25.

16. Malthus, *Population*, I, 230-1.

17. Clark, *Subsistence*, 109.

18. Mokyr, *Industrial*, 45.

19. Vries, *Economy*, 211.

20. Landes, *Prometheus*, 13.

21. For recent work see Mokyr, *Enlightened*.

22. Harrison, *Description*, 124.

23. Saussure, *Foreign*, 221.

24. Marshall, *People*, 173.

25. Emerson, *Traits*, 56.

26. Rogers, *Industrial*, I, 59.

27. Kames, *Sketches*, III, 83.

28. Smith, *Wealth*, I 179.

29. For more evidence, see Macfarlane, *Savage*, chapter 6.

30. Macfarlane, *Green Gold*.

31. Quoted in Wright, *Decent*, 93.

32. Rochefoucauld, *Frenchman*, 23, 26.

33. For an account of famine and some reasons for its early disappearance in England centuries before most other countries, see Macfarlane, *Savage*, chapter 5.

34. For example, see Harrison, *Description*, 145-6.

35. Becon, *Works*, 438.

36. Saussure, Foreign, 113, 112, 204.

37. O.W. Holmes in Wilson, *Strange*, 231. For clothing, see Macfarlane, *Savage*, chapter 13.

38. There is a detailed description in Macfarlane, *Savage*, chapter 12.

39. Rochefoucauld, *Frenchman*, 158.

40. Saussure, *Foreign*, 68.

41. In Wilson, *Strange* 129.

42. Quoted in George, *London Life*, 264.

43. Betjeman, *English*, 16.

44. Macfarlane, *Savage*, 42-8.

45. Sorbière in Wilson, *Strange*, 45.

46. Rochefoucauld, *Frenchman*,77-78.

47. Marshall, *People*, 193.

48. Laing, *Observations* 147-8.

CHAPTER 6

CASTE AND CLASS

IT WAS TOCQUEVILLE who first brought home to me the importance and peculiarity of the English class system. As a French nobleman who had watched the Revolution in France, visited America, and married an English lady, he saw something which was almost invisible to most Englishmen. 'Wherever the feudal system established itself on the continent of Europe it ended in caste; in England alone it returned to aristocracy. I have always been astonished that a fact, which distinguishes England from all modern nations and which can alone explain the peculiarities of its laws, its spirit, and its history, has not attracted still more than it has done the attention of philosophers and statesmen and that habit has finally made it as it were invisible to the English themselves...'

He then expands on the idea. 'It was far less its Parliament, its liberty, its publicity, its jury, which in fact rendered the England of that date so unlike the rest of Europe than a feature still more exclusive and more powerful. England was the only country in which the system of caste had been not changed but effectively destroyed. The nobles and the middle classes in England followed together the same courses of business, entered the same professions, and, what is much more significant, inter-married. The daughter of the greatest noble in England could already marry without shame a "new" man.' This system, and particularly the widening of the middle class, 'with the English passes finally to America ... Its history is that of democracy itself.'[1]

It was an observation made by many others. 'The gentry, the squires, barons, feudal chiefs… kept in touch with the people, opened their ranks to talent, recruited to their number the pick of the rising commoners…' The traditional integration of English social ranks, was 'the very reverse of the situation in France where burgess and artisan, noble and peasant are separated by distrust and discord, where broadcloth and corduroy do, indeed, live cheek by jowl but with fear and rancour in their hearts…'[2]

This is a feature going back more than a thousand years. The outcome was confusion and competition. 'The labourer is a possible lord. The lord is a possible basket-maker. Every man carries the English system in his brain, knows what is confided to him, and does therein the best he can. The chancellor carries England on his mace, the midshipman at the point of his dirk, the smith on his hammer, the cook in the bowl of his spoon; the postilion cracks his whip for England, and the sailor times his oars to "God save the King!" The very felons have their pride in each other's English staunchness.' Everything is possible – but at a price. 'English history is aristocracy with the doors open. Who has courage and faculty, let him come in. Of course, the terms of admission to this club are hard and high.[3] It was the insecurity and competition which drove the system – as it still does. 'This peculiar national spirit nourished by our social system, in which the lowest may rise to the highest station and importance, is the true source of our national prosperity and greatness.'[4]

♦

THE MODEL *ANCIEN régime* social structure has four legally separate strata: the blood *nobility* are the rulers and warriors, the *clergy* are the religious and literate group, the *bourgeois* are mainly town-dwellers who trade and manufacture and the *peasants* are illiterate workers in the fields. The English social structure from Anglo-Saxon times had none of these.

Nobility as it grew up over Europe was based on legal differences acquired by birth. The nobility were treated as a separate legal estate. Tocqueville as a nobleman noted the difference when he visited England. 'The English aristocracy in feelings and prejudices resembles all the aristocracies of the world, but it is not in the least founded on birth, that inaccessible thing, but on wealth that everyone can acquire, and this one difference makes it stand, while the others [i.e. nobility in other countries] succumb either to the people or to the King.'[5]

The situation in England was analysed by Maitland for the medieval period. 'Our law hardly knows anything of a noble or of a gentle class; all free men are in the main equal before the law.'[6] The only legal privilege, which they shared with the rest of the population, was that they had the right to be judged by their peers – in their case other lords.

The French historian Marc Bloch describes how by the thirteenth century a true nobility, based on hereditary blood and legal differences was established in most of continental Europe (but not in England). There may have been some parallel development in the eleventh to twelfth centuries, but then England took 'a very different direction in the thirteenth century'. Bloch gives an account of the peculiarity of the aristocratic system in England, for 'in the French or German sense of the word, medieval England had no nobility; that is to say that among the free men there was no intrinsically superior class enjoying a privileged legal status of its own, transmitted by descent. In appearance English society was an astonishingly egalitarian structure.' 'In short, the class of nobleman in England remained, as a whole, more a "social" than a "legal" class'. Although, naturally, power and revenues were as a rule inherited, and although, as on the continent, the prestige of birth was greatly prized, this group was too ill-defined not to remain largely open' Status was based on wealth and land, not on blood and law as in France.[7]

♦

UNDER THE ARISTOCRACY there was another status group – the gentry. As the bridge between the large 'middling sort' and the non-exclusive aristocracy, they were in many ways the most important, distinctive and exceptional feature of English social structure. Again for purpose of brevity we can draw on French observers.

Tocqueville realized that the word 'gentleman' was a central key to a vast difference in England and France. He wrote 'there is none more pregnant, nor containing within it so good an explanation of the difference between the history of England and that of the other feudal nations in Europe.' He was puzzled by what caused the difference. 'How is it that the word *gentleman*, which in our language denotes a mere superiority of blood, with you is now used to express a certain social position, an amount of education independent of birth; so that in the two countries the same word, though the sound remains the same, has entirely changed its meaning?'[8] He muses further on the difference of words with a common derivation but which developed such different meanings. '"Gentleman" and "gentilhomme" evidently have the same derivation, but "gentleman" in England is applied to every well-educated man whatever his birth, while in France *gentilhomme* applies only to a noble by birth. The meaning of these two words of common origin has been so transformed by the different social climates of the two countries that today they simply cannot be translated, at least without recourse to a periphrasis.'[9]

Likewise Taine wrote, 'I have been trying to get a real understanding of that most essential word "a gentleman"; it is constantly occurring and it expresses a whole complex of particularly English ideas. The vital question concerning a man always takes this form: "Is he a gentleman?" And similarly, of a woman "Is she a lady?" ... In France we have not got the word because we have not got the thing, and those three syllables, in their English sense, sum of the whole history of English society'. He describes some of the radical differences between English gentleman and French *gentilhomme*. He believed that the essential nature of the English gentleman lies in his character. But for real judges the essential quality is one of heart. Speaking of a great nobleman in the diplomatic service, B— told me "He is not a gentleman." ... For them a real "gentleman" is a truly noble man, a man worthy to command, a disinterested man of integrity, capable of exposing, even sacrificing himself for those he leads; not only a man of honour, but a conscientious man, in whom generous instincts have been confirmed by right thinking and who, acting rightly by nature, acts even more rightly from good principles.'[10]

The essence was that the gentleman had no special legal status. As Maitland wrote, 'Below the barons stand the knights; the law honours them by subjecting them to special burdens; but still knighthood can hardly be accounted a legal *status*'. Thus he argues that 'In administrative law therefore the knight is liable to some special burdens; but in no other respect does he differ from the mere free man.'[11]

So how does one come to be known as a gentleman? Saussure simplified it when he said 'The term gentleman is usually given to any well-dressed person wearing a sword.'[12] In fact if we look at William Harrison's sixteenth century definition of a gentleman we can see how he gets this position. 'Whosoever studieth the laws of the realm, whoso abideth in the university giving his mind to his book, or professeth physic and the liberal sciences, or, beside his service in the room of a captain in the wars or good counsel given at home, whereby his commonwealth is benefited, can live without manual labor, and thereto is able and will bear the port, charge and countenance of a gentleman, he shall for money have a coat and arms bestowed upon him by heralds (who in the charter of the same do of custom pretend antiquity and service and many gay things), and thereunto being made so good cheap, be called master, which is the title that men give to esquires and gentlemen, and reputed for a gentleman ever after.' He continues that there is no loss to the

Crown in this promotion 'the gentleman being so much subject to taxes and public payments as is the yeoman or husbandman, which he likewise doth bear the gladlier for the saving of his reputation.'[13]

Thus you could tell an English gentleman by the outward marks, the house, the clothes, the education, the accent, self-confidence and general wealth and particularly by the fact of his profession and his earning a living without manual labour. My whole education in boarding schools was founded on the effort to train me in the habits or *habitus* of a gentleman – so that one day I would be called 'sir' (the modern equivalent of 'Master') by my pupils and the College Porters at King's College, Cambridge. If you lost these outward marks, if your wealth failed or you could no longer live as a gentleman, you sank.

♦

WHEN WE MOVE to the 'middling sort', a host of different occupations and situations were muddled together, comprising perhaps nearly a half of the inhabitants of England in the five hundred years between the fourteenth and nineteenth centuries. These were not illiterate labourers, but small tradesmen, small landowners, small manufacturers. To select out of these another peculiar non-legal but important status, again pivotal in government and the social structure, let us look at the yeomanry.

The importance of this estate was clear to Adam Smith. He believed that 'Those laws and customs so favourable to the yeomanry, have perhaps contributed more to the present grandeur of England, than all their boasted regulations of commerce taken together'. He believed that they provided the step between gentry and labourers. He talks of various advantages, geographical and other, which England enjoyed, 'But what is of much more importance than all of them, the yeomanry of England are rendered as secure, as independent, and as respectable as law can make them.'[14]

Once again Harrison gives a useful description of the nature of this group. 'Yeomen are those which by our law are called *legales homines*, freemen born English, and may dispend of their own free land in yearly revenue to the sum of 40*s*. sterling, or £6 as money goeth in our times.... This sort of people have a certain pre-eminence and more estimation than laborers and the common sort of artificers, and these commonly live wealthily, keep good houses, and travail to get riches. They are also for the most part farmers to gentlemen... or at the leastwise artificers; and with grazing, frequenting of markets, and keeping of servants... do come to great wealth, insomuch that many of them are able and do buy the lands of unthrifty gentlemen, and often, setting their sons to the schools, to the universities, and to the Inns of the Court, or otherwise leaving them sufficient lands whereupon they may live without labor do make them by those means to become gentlemen...'[15]

You became a yeoman through wealth which was then manifested in education, taste, house, food and clothing. Again it is clear that it is a fully 'modern' status, roughly 'middle middle class' in recent terminology. As with the aristocracy and gentry, we have a status group which is dependent on material success for esteem. They gain and keep their position through their relatively strong control over the means of production by landholding, manufacture and trade. The wealth from this activity is converted into status for their sons.

◆

WHEN WE TURN to what we would now call the 'lower middle class and working class' – and was for long called 'artificers and labourers' – Harrison describes them as follows. 'The fourth and last sort of people in England are day laborers, poor husbandmen, and some retailers (which have no free land), copyholders, and all artificers, as tailors, shoemakers, carpenters, brickmakers, masons etc.....This fourth and last sort of people, therefore, have neither a voice nor authority in the commonwealth, but are to be ruled and not to rule other; yet they are not altogether neglected, for in cities and corporate towns, for default of yeomen, they are fain to make up their inquests of such manner of people. And in villages they are commonly made churchwardens, sidemen [assistants to the churchwardens], aleconners [inspectors of ale] now and then constables, and many times enjoy the name of headboroughs.'[16]

Small craftsmen and shop-keepers were significant in number, but more numerous were the husbandmen and labourers. The peasant bound to his holding and the soil is unknown in England. What we have are people who have only a very little of their own land, or none at all, and work for others – husbandmen and labourers. The history of this group is one of the most intriguing developments in England

Anglo-Saxon society had known slaves, but from at least the thirteenth century English law did not recognize the status of slave – that is of a human being who was totally without legal rights in relations to others, to be bought and sold as a chattel, or even maimed or killed.

The classic account is by F.W.Maitland, drawing on both his studies of medieval court records, court rolls and legal treatises. He notes that villeinage or serfdom means both a type of landholding and a personal status and that in relation to everyone except his lord, a villein or serf is legally like any other. He writes that 'The same word *villeinagium* is currently used to denote both a personal status and a mode of tenure'. 'Villeinage' is a tenure as well as a status. 'It is very possible, as Bracton often assures us, for a free man to hold in villeinage…'[17]

Maitland describes how. 'The serf's position in relation to all men other than his lord is simple: – he is to be treated as a free man. When the lord is not concerned, criminal law makes no difference between bond and free, and apparently the free man may have to do battle with the bond. A blow given to a serf is a wrong to the serf.' Furthermore, 'in relation to men in general, the serf may have land and goods, property and possession and all appropriate remedies.' Serfs own chattels and can make wills and contracts – their condition even in relation to their particular lord is 'unprotected, rather than rightless.'[18]

Maitland describes the ease with which serfs may gain liberty and notes that 'Even the great distinction between bound and free is apt to appear in practice rather as a distinction between tenures than as a distinction between persons'. By the thirteenth century 'freehold and villeinhold' were already becoming difficult to ascertain. In fact, many people may not have been certain whether they were serfs or not. Extents and surveys are not very careful to separate the personally free from personally unfree, it is highly probably that large numbers of men did not know on which side of the legal gulf they stood.[19]

Thus English serfs 'are unfree, but we must not call them slaves, they are not rightless; the law does not treat them as things, it treats them as persons'.[20] 'As regards mankind at large the serf so far from being a mere thing is a free man', and 'We hesitate before we describe the serf as rightless even as against his lord'.[21]

The position is anomalous. A serf was like an indentured or permanent servant – a condition from which a person could not escape without release, but as much a contract as a status. When the troubling problem of slavery in the New World came up-,when they were brought to England they were treated in a similar way to the medieval serf. It was generally agreed that 'Slaves cannot breathe in England, if their lungs receive our air, that moment they are free; they touch our country, and their shackles fall'.[22] Or as Chamberlayne wrote in the later seventeenth century, 'Foreign slaves in England are none, since Christianity prevails.' Yet what happened if foreign slaves were brought to the country? The same ambiguous status was found – free but bound. Foreign slaves automatically become 'free', but were bound as perpetual servants to the master.[23]

In such an ambiguous category, where the serf or villein had been free in all relations except to his master, it was possible for the master to end the contract, just as he might dismiss a servant. The extraordinarily rapid disappearance of serfdom in England in the fifteenth century, which has long puzzled historians, is explicable only if we realize that it was a contractual, inter-personal, tie, not a status. After the labour shortages caused by the Black Death in the middle of the fourteenth century, lords found it impossible to hold onto their serfs, who were desired and protected by other lords, and either let them go or allowed the serf condition to vanish and their workers to become 'free' labourers.

By the time Harrison wrote in the middle of the sixteenth century he could say 'As for slaves and bondmen, we have none; nay, such is the privilege of our country by the especial grace of God and bounty of our princes that if any come hither from other realms, so soon as they set foot on land they become so free of condition as their masters, whereby all note of servile bondage is utterly removed from them...'[24]

♦

MOST SOCIETIES HAVE a sharply tapered social structure, with a tiny elite and a huge mass of the poor. England had a different shape, more like a bell, with a small aristocracy, a large 'middling class' and then a working class of about the same size. Gregory King estimated that nearly half of the population in 1688 were above the level of workers and the poor.[25] As we see in India or China today, the growth of a large, prosperous, middle class is both a cause and consequence of capitalist modernity. It is a feature of England as we can see it in Chaucer's *Canterbury Tales*, back as far back as the fourteenth century and well before. As Freeman put it in relation to the thirteenth century 'the great middle class of England is rapidly forming; a middle class not, as elsewhere, confined to a few great cities, but spread, in the form of a lesser gentry and a wealthy yeomanry, over the whole face of the land.'[26]

Since it was wealth alone, rather than birth-given blood ties and legal privilege, which ensured prestige and respect, the English, like the Americans, were obsessed with making money. Emerson from America noted that 'There is no country in which so absolute a homage is paid to wealth. In America, there is a touch of shame when a man exhibits the evidences of large property, as if, after all, it needed apology. But the Englishman has pure pride in his wealth, and esteems it a final certificate.'[27] Or as Saussure commented earlier 'A sign that they are very fond of wealth is that as soon as you mention anyone to them that they do not know, their first inquiry will be, "Is he rich?" In this country one is esteemed for one's wealth more than for anything else. It is true that riches are accounted happiness everywhere, but more particularly here'. The women were equally interested in money: 'I have told you that I find men interested in money matters; the women are just as much so.'[28]

It was obvious that climbing the social ladder required wealth. Defoe had written 'Wealth, howsoever got, in England makes Lords of mechanics, gentlemen of rakes. Antiquity and birth are needless here. Tis impudence and money makes a peer'.[29] As a result, as Tocqueville noted 'In all countries it is bad luck not to be rich. In England it is a terrible misfortune to be poor. Wealth is identified with happiness and everything that goes with happiness; poverty, or even a middling fortunes spells misfortune and all that goes with that. So all the resources of the human spirit are bent on the acquisition of wealth. In other countries men seek opulence to enjoy life; the English seek it, in some sort, to live.' Tocqueville believed that the desire for wealth helped explain English success. 'Take into account the progressive force of such an urge working for several centuries on several millions of men, and you will not be surprised to find that these men have become the boldest sailors and the most skillful manufacturers in the world'.[30]

As Adam Smith also put it 'Every individual is continually exerting himself to find out the most advantageous employment for whatever capital he can command. It is his own advantage, indeed, and not that of the society which he has in view'.[31] The aim was superiority – to feel higher up the ladder than others. 'The French wish not to have superiors. The English wish to have inferiors. The Frenchman constantly raises his eyes above him with anxiety. The Englishman lowers his beneath him with satisfaction.'[32]

In order to gain and retain that notoriously slippery substance called wealth, no barriers of law could be allowed to be an obstacle. As Voltaire noted in relation to commerce in England '… and indeed a Peer's Brother does not think Traffic beneath him. When the Lord Townshend was Minister of State, a Brother of his was content to be a City Merchant; and at the Time that the Earl of Oxford govern'd Great-Britain, his younger Brother was no more than a Factor in Aleppo, where he chose to live, and where he died.'[33] However, around the same time, Montesquieu writing of France noted that 'It is contrary to the spirit of monarchy to admit the nobility into commerce. The custom of suffering the nobility of England to trade is one of those things which have there mostly contributed to weaken the monarchical government.'[34] Saussure wrote, 'Merchants come after the clergy, and in England commerce is not looked down upon as being derogatory, as it is in France and Germany. Here men of good family and even of rank may become merchants without losing caste. I have heard of younger sons of peers, whose families have been reduced to poverty through the habits of extravagance and dissipation of an elder son, retrieve the fallen fortunes of their house by becoming merchants and working energetically for several years.'[35]

The result is a paradox. English social structure was and still is very hierarchical, in the sense that distinctions of 'class' matter a great deal and much of most people's life is concerned with minor differences in food, drink, housing, cars and education, which will elevate them or their children, in the constant game of 'keeping up with' or even surpassing a neighbour: 'Apparent equality, real privileges of wealth, greater perhaps than in any country of the world.'[36]

So it is noticeable that much of English satire from Shakespeare to Oscar Wilde has been founded on this competitive game of class. Yet the game is so fascinating and absorbing only because England had a modern, open, system based on merit, ability and a good deal of strategy and chance – a meritocracy of sorts.

As Roy Porter put it describing the eighteenth century '... though the social hierarchy was inegalitarian and oozing privilege (some of it hereditary), it was neither rigid nor brittle. There was continual adaptiveness to challenge and individual mobility, up, down and sideways. More than in other nations, money was a passport through social frontiers'.[37]

Thus while it is arguable as stated by George Orwell that 'England is the most class-ridden country under the sun. It is a land of snobbery and privilege, ruled largely by the old and silly'. Yet he can also write 'The whole English-speaking world is haunted by the idea of human equality, and though it would be simply a lie to say that either we or the Americans have ever acted up to our professions, still, the *idea* is there, and it is capable of one day becoming a reality.'[38]

It is a tough game. 'An Englishman shows no mercy to those below him in the social scale, as he looks for none from those above him; any forbearance from his superiors surprises him, and they suffer in his good opinion.' It is also a game of pretence – the invention of status through a conjuring trick. 'All the families are new, but the name is old, and they have made a covenant with their memories not to disturb it.' There was constant re-invention to fit the mobility. 'But the analysis of the peerage and gentry shows the rapid decay and extinction of old families, the continual recruiting of these from new blood. The doors, though ostentatiously guarded, are really open, and hence the power of the bribe. All the barriers to rank only whet the thirst, and enhance the prize.'[39] The game of invention of ancestry with the selling of coats of arms, which Harrison had noticed the heralds playing in the middle of the sixteenth century, has been going on for many hundreds of years.

There is always the danger of slipping since nothing is permanently guaranteed. There is much about this in English novels. Yet there is also the chance of scrambling up – nicely described by Stendhal. 'Society being divided as by the rings of a bamboo, everyone busies himself with trying to climb into the class above his own and the whole effort of that class is put into preventing him from climbing.'[40]

There was above all a belief in the 'from log cabin to White House', or from coal-mining grandparents to marrying the heir to the throne in the contemporary saga of Prince William, the heir to the throne of England. This is the 'American dream' and now the dream in India and China. It has been a long dreamt in England, as in the story of Dick Whittington and his cat, or Jack and the Beanstalk. Nowadays it is 'Slumdog Millionaire' who epitomizes this dream.

The aspirations and reality are described in the nineteenth century. 'Every weaver's son strives to be a Peel, or a father of Peels; every grocer's, a Gladstone; every operative's, a Cobden. In our social and political system there is nothing to make such a dream impossible or extravagantly improbable, and therefore he dreams it, and lives in a struggle to realise it.' Laing believed that 'The Continental man in the same class and position, would be mad indeed if he expected, by his utmost efforts and good luck to attain a higher social position, or greater social influence than what belongs to his original calling.'[41]

This was based on reality. 'With us in every village and town how many instances we see of men rising by industry and good conduct, from very small beginnings, from a very low place in the social body, to such wealth, influence, and importance, that government employments or any situations the Church or the learned professions could offer, are inconsiderable objects in comparison! We hear every day of common labourers becoming great manufacturers or opulent merchants ... this principle of progress from the lowest to the highest rank, is wanting in the Continental structure of society.'[42]

The effect of this is that the ruling groups, basically the upper middle class, were constantly being refreshed. This is described by Huizinga. The ruling class never disappeared but was reincarnated: 'a process which had taken place over and over again in the history of this country, where not blood but success, usually though not always measured in money, had always been the qualification for membership of the ruling class. Not that just any kind of money constituted an acceptable entrance fee; it had to be what Belloc called "cooked money" and not "raw money", its owners had to have had it long enough to learn to adapt themselves to the aristocratic style of the blood. But only this style of the English ruling class was hereditary; its personnel had been constantly renewed and its economic basis reinforced by the absorption of new generations of the socially successful, men who possessed sufficient economic power really to be able to rule and sufficient modernity of spirit to preserve the policy of this class from fossilisation and thus to safeguard its prestige.'[43]

The central fact is that there are no formal legal statuses, but an innumerable set of small gradations which make it possible to move up and down. Yet it is impossible to be quite certain where one is or who is above or below. Is a poor clergyman higher or lower than a middle farmer? Is a middling lawyer low-

er or higher than an army officer? Is a butcher higher than a baker? Is someone who 'comes home' from Jamaica or Australia or
India with a considerable fortune fit to be absorbed into polite
society? Is someone who joins some dissenting church to be
spurned? It goes on forever.

The excellent accounts of the numerous ladders, and especially the importance of the large middle class are given by
Laing. 'It is the common theme of foreign travellers who visit
England, and of many superficial observers among ourselves,
that the social state of the English nation is a monstrous junction
of boundless wealth, extravagance, and luxury above, and of
utter destitution, misery, and suffering below. They look only
at the upper and lower strata of the social mass, and do not perceive that all between the two is densely filled up with incomes
and earnings of every amount and every fractional difference,
from the highest, the thousands or tens of thousands a year,
down to zero. There is no vacuum in the mass between the top
and the bottom, as in the social state of the Continent.'[44]

The result is constant discontent – or at least striving, sometimes called the protestant ethic by Weber and interestingly
linked to wider anxiety by Michael Walzer, not so much anxiety
about religious salvation as social salvation.[45] 'In English life,
men are never contented and happy unless in the struggle to attain some higher social position than they are in, and which the
public confers. The merchant, the tradesman, the working-man,
however easy in his circumstances and prospects according to
his position in life, could not sit down, like the amiable contented German in the same station, to talk, and sip, and puff away
three or four hours daily…'[46]

◆

THERE IS A danger of being too optimistic. The English
may have been unusually affluent and middle class, but the difference, as in India today, between the aristocrats with their huge

houses and parks, and the burdened labourer – especially during
the industrial revolution - was immense. One should never forget accounts of the working class by Engels in Mnchester, or the
searing account of Taine when he visited Liverpool.

> In the neighbourhood of Leeds Street there are fifteen or
> twenty streets with ropes stretched across them where
> rags and underwear were hung out to dry. Every stairway
> swarms with children, five or six to a step, the eldest nurs-
> ing the baby; their faces are pale, their hair whitish and
> tousled, the rags they wear full of holes, they have neither
> shoes nor stockings and they are all vilely dirty. Their fac-
> es and limbs seemed to be encrusted with dust and soot. In
> one street alone there must have been about two hundred
> children sprawling or fighting. You draw near a house,
> look in, and in the half-light of a passage, see mother
> and grown daughter crouching, wearing little more than
> a chemise. What rooms! A threadbare slip of oilcloth on
> the floor, sometimes a big sea-shell or one or two plaster
> ornaments; the old, idiot grandmother crouches in a cor-
> ner; the wife is engaged in trying to mend some wretched
> rags of clothes; the children tumble over each other. The
> smell is that of an old-clothes shop full of rotting rags....
> A really horrible detail is that these streets are regular and
> seem to be quite new: the quarter is probably a rebuilt
> one, opened up by a benevolent municipality: so that this
> was an example of the best that can be done for the poor.[47]

The system was Darwinian and merciless, a struggle for survival and hence there is something in Marx's observation that
Darwin projected onto nature the social struggle he witnessed
around him. Yet it was in this class structure, as in other things,
that the marked modernity of England flowered. The English
working class, as Edward Thompson noted, is very unusual,
scarcely believable to others, one peculiarity of a peculiar history. The working class was surprisingly open, often self-confi-

dent, and did not see itself, much to Marx's irritation, as united in its consciousness of itself as a class.[48]

◆

THERE IS ONE final oddity worth noting. This was an apparent absence of strongly enforced 'codes of honour' amongst the bulk of the population. Although people wanted to be honoured for what they had achieved and for what they were, the respect was diffused over the society as a whole and did not have to be shown in a highly deferential face–to–face relationship. As compared to those societies in Mediterranean Europe and elsewhere known to anthropologists as 'honour and shame' cultures, there is in fact a curious lack of emphasis on 'respect' on 'honour' and on 'deference'.

Leaving on one side the possible exception of a few courtiers and the highest aristocracy, the constant competition for the maintenance of personal honour, with its ramifications of wounded pride, duelling, taunts, gossip, the flaunting of male power, the insidious danger of the undermining of honour through assaults on the women attached to men, all this is largely missing in the majority of the population through most of English history. Even at the level of Jane Austen's novels, it is difficult to speak of an 'honour and shame' culture, and certainly it is little in evidence for the villages about which we know. It does not seem that this is a society held together by those face–to–face competitions for honour, the equality of honourable men and their superiority over their weaker clients, which is characteristic of so many societies. For example, I know of no instances, as one would find in many societies, of families killing or maiming men who have courted their daughters or sisters and hence dishonoured them.

The honour that is present is not of a familistic nature. It is the kind of honour that is needed in a commercial society. It is basically concerned with behaving honourably, that is to say being truthful, just, uncorrupt, keeping one's contracts and pledges, not being deceitful, being fair—minded. The honourable Magistrate or Judge, the honourable merchant, the honourable clergyman, is not one who jealously guards an internal store of a precious commodity which is constantly under threat. Rather, an individual appealed for recognition of his (or her) character to a wider public. He showed himself to be sincere and trustworthy, for these were the characteristics which both won respect and gave people confidence needed in the numerous contracts on which the society and economy depended. Destroy a man's reputation, and he was likely to spiral downwards. But the way to do this was not to suggest that he was not brave, aggressive, virile, but rather that he could not be trusted – a liar or a cheat. Likewise, to destroy a woman' reputation was better achieved through attacks on her probity, intelligence and cultural performance than to attack her sexual status.

CHAPTER NOTES

1. Tocqueville, *Ancien*, 88, 89, 90.

2. Taine, *Notes*, 144, 162.

3. Emerson, *English*, 80, 134.

4. Laing, *Observations*, 462.

5. Tocqueville, *Journeys*, 43.

6. Maitland, *History*, I, 408; Freeman, *Growth*, 92ff, is a strong statement of the total absence of a '*nobilité*' of the continental type.

7. Bloch, *Feudal*, II, 326, 329, 330-1, 331.

8. Tocqueville, *Memoir*, II, 224.

9. Tocqueville, *Journeys*, 52.

10. Taine, *Notes*, 144-5.

11. Maitland, *History*, I, 410-1.

12. Saussure, *Foreign*, 212.

13. Harrison, *Description*, 113-4.

14. Smith, *Wealth*, I, 415, 443.

15. Harrison, *Description*, 117-8.

16. Harrison, *Description*, 118.

17. Maitland, *History*, I, 231, 359.

18. Maitland *History,* I, 419, 419, 417.

19. Maitland, *History,* I, 417, 408, 374, 431.

20. Maitland, *Consitutional*, 33.

21. Maitland, *History*, I, 415, 430.

22. William Cowper in *Quotations,* 124.

23. Chamberlayne, *Present*, 339, 182.

24. Harrison, *Description*, 118.

25. The table is in Allen, *Industrial*, 50.

26. Freeman, *First Essays*, 43.

27. Emerson, *English*, 118.

28. Saussure, *Foreign*, 207-8.

29. Quoted in McLynn, *Crime,* 56.

30. Tocqueville, *Journeys*, 105.

31. Smith, *Wealth*, I, 475.

32. Tocqueville, *Journeys*, 60.

33. Voltaire, *Letters*, 55.

34. Montesquieu, *Spirit*, I, 327.

35. Saussure, *Foreign*, 215-6.

36. Tocqueville, *Journeys*, 79.

37. Porter, *Eighteenth*, 341.

38. Orwell, *Lion*, 52, 119.

39. Emerson, *English*, 231, 150, 151.

40. Stendhal in Wilson, *Strange*, 164.

41. Laing, *Observations*, 462.

42. Laing, *Observations*, 308.

43. Huizinga, *Confessions*, 105.

44. Laing, *Observations*, 296.

45. Walzer, *Revolution*.

46. Laing, *Observations*, 461-2.

47. Taine, *Notes*, 225-6.

48. Thompson, 'Peculiarities', 312, 347.

CHAPTER 7

CULTURE

ONE SIGN OF 'modernity' is the importance of competitive games and sports. Here we find one of the earliest and most important of British exports, including the games which can claim to be the new world religion – cricket and football. India is united by cricket, and Brazil by football. Games both teach competition and channel it at the same time, express similarity and difference, sharpen the wits, teach team spirit and the joint pursuit of a common goal. Playing games of all kinds was a hugely important and old phenomenon in Britain – we see it in art, literature and other sources from the Middle Ages. To a very considerable extent, the 'imagined Empire' of Britain was held together by games.

Games, sport and hobbies are an essential mirror of capitalism. In Britain there are large areas which are fenced off from the direct intrusion of competitive consumer capitalism – sport, leisure, nature, love – in which commercial pressures in theory should not dominate. These provide excitement and relaxation, but in a way that is different from the daily grind of 'work'.

Such relaxation cannot be 'afforded' for the majority of people in most societies. Most people have been too hard-worked and ill fed to be able to devote much time to purely leisure activities of no economic benefit, except on special holidays. When I arrived in a mountain village in Nepal, I remember my surprise that the Gurungs had no indigenous sports or games – apart from running and throwing a rock. Nor were there any obvious hobbies.

So one of the distinctive features of modernity is that games, sports and hobbies are widespread and highly valued. We just have to think of what is on international television – the obsession with football, cricket, baseball, snooker, the wide range of sports represented in the Olympics and the vast scale of sports accessories. Modern society is saturated with aspects of *Homo Ludens*. Where did all this come from?

Many have observed that the English are particularly obsessed with games playing and have been for many centuries. In terms of games, it is well known that many of the world's competitive team games were either invented, or perfected and institutionalised in England. Paxman gives a good overview:

> The word "soccer", *the* world sport, is public-school slang for Association Football. Baseball is a form of the English children's game rounders, American football a version of rugby ... Tennis was redeveloped by the Marylebone Cricket Club (i.e. Lord's) and the first of the world-famous tournaments was held in 1877. Englishmen set the standard distances for running, swimming and rowing competitions and developed the first modern horse-races. Contemporary hockey dates from the codification of rules by the Hockey Association in 1886, competitive swimming from the formation of the English Amateur Swimming Association in 1869, modern mountaineering can be dated from the 1854 attempt on the Wetterhorn by Sir Alfred Wills. The English invented goalposts, racing boats and stopwatches and were the first to breed modern

racehorses. Even when they imported sports from abroad, like polo or skiing, the English laid down the rules.[1]

And this does not even include the most characteristic, namely cricket, about which Paxman writes at length. Nowadays England has some very good computer games companies (e.g. the makers of *Grand Theft Auto*) and also excellent board games (for example, the very capitalist game *Monopoly*).

IN THE EARLY eighteenth century, for example, Saussure wrote:

> Another amusement which is very inconvenient to passers-by is football. For this game a leather ball filled with air is used, and is kicked about with the feet'. And on the next page he described the other national sport: 'The English are very fond of a game they call cricket. For this purpose they go into a large open field, and knock a small ball about with a piece of wood. I will not attempt to describe this game to you, it is too complicated; but it requires agility and skill, and everyone plays it, the common people and also men of rank. Sometimes one county plays against another county. The papers give notice of these meetings beforehand, and, later, tell you which side has come off victorious. Spectators crowd to these games when they are important.' Furthermore 'square lawns are kept for this purpose, and are called bowling-greens.[2]

Saussure also noted another characteristically English pasttime which he felt distinguished it from elsewhere – and again it is one that requires a good deal of leisure and spare energy. 'Another great pleasure of the people is the ringing of bells, and it is a source of great delight to them whenever an opportunity of doing this presents itself. I do not suppose there is a country where bell-ringing is brought to such an art as it is here, where bells are always in chime and in harmony.... A good bell-ringer can ring out more than a thousand different peals and chimes

… and the people are so fond of this amusement that they form societies among themselves for carrying it out.'[3]

The English gentleman was above all distinguished by and dedicated to outdoor sports – shooting, hunting for fox or hare, horse-riding. Much of the history of the English countryside is written in the privileged hunting and fishing of animals.

♦

I REMEMBER JAPANESE friends noting as a major difference between the English and Japanese the English obsession with hobbies. 'We are a nation of flower-lovers, but also a nation of stamp- collectors, pigeon-fanciers, amateur carpenters, coupon-snippers, darts-players, cross-world-puzzle fans'. This is 'another English characteristic which is so much a part of us that we barely notice it, and that is the addiction to hobbies and spare-time occupations, the *privateness* of English life'. He suggests that 'All the culture that is most truly native centres round things which even when they are communal are not official – the pub, the football match, the back garden, the fireside and the "nice cup of tea."'[4]

I know all this from my personal experience. The boarding schools I attended were obsessed with games, sports and hobbies. Games were, and are for many people functionally analogous to religion; they give a meaning to existence, an explanation of misfortune and a set of rituals to link people together. A.C. Benson, who had taught at a boarding school, implies that in the later nineteenth century games had become the unifying religion of the British people. 'It requires almost more courage to write about games nowadays than it does to write about the Decalogue, because the higher criticism is tending to make a belief in the Decalogue a matter of taste, while to the ordinary Englishman a belief in games is a matter of faith and morals.'[5]

Claudio Veliz notes that in the places most deeply influenced by English culture, whether in Boston, Winnipeg or Auckland, the suburbs are inhabited by great numbers of 'enthusiastic and well-organized amateur astronomers, cat fanciers, train spotters, country-style dancers, pigeon fanciers, bush trekkers, cake decorators, bird-watchers, gardeners, and vintage car enthusiasts than have ever gathered anywhere and at any time to devote so much time and attention to what are, by definition, characteristically non-profitable "hobbies".'[6]

Veliz also suggests that games, sports and hobbies have provided that solution to the break-up of 'community', in societies previously held together by religion and kinship. He writes that 'it is possible, with few and heavily qualified exceptions, to assert that modern sports are a by-product of an English Industrial Revolution that created a need for new community arrangements, a substitute for the proximity, the intimacy, and the *Gemeinschaft* displaced by advancing industrialism.'[7] In fact, the games and hobbies and sports were there well before industrialism.

Furthermore games and hobbies fit perfectly with the class system. Different strata have different games, sports and hobbies. There is an aristocratic set, a middle class set, a labouring set – for example public schools play rugby union, other schools enjoy rugby league. Only the wealthy hunt foxes with hounds, only the working class, on the whole, race pigeons. The upper classes fish for edible 'game' fish like salmon and trout; the working class fish for inedible 'coarse' fish.

◆

THE QUALITIES WE were meant to learn at school were exactly those which it was thought would fit us for success as entrepreneurs, lawyers, teachers, soldiers – bravery, self-confidence, independence of thought, risk-taking, skills of co-operation, enthusiasm, ability to lose with good grace and the concepts of fair play. We were to learn, through simulation in a context where money would not be won or lost, the cunning and other necessities of a capitalist nature. Taine notes the close association between the obsession with competitive money making and sport through betting on horses. 'As for the reasons which make horses and horse-racing into a universal national passion, it seems to me that we must look for them in the rustic, athletic life they lead. The rich, and the well-to-do spend a great part of the year in the country ... all these attributes of their way of living (*moeurs*) culminate in the Derby, which is their special festival'.[8]

Law cases were another form of competitive game – trying to outwit and vanquish the opponent – but with words rather than with a bat or ball. Likewise many have noted that confrontational politics as practised most overtly in the debates in the House of Commons is like a game. Tocqueville noted: 'No people carry so far, especially when speaking in public, violence of language, outrageousness of theories, and extravagance in the inferences drawn from those theories. Thus your A.B. says, that the Irish have not shot half enough landlords. Yet no people act with more moderation. A quarter of what is said in England at a public meeting, or even round a dinner table, without anything being done or intended to be done, would in France announce violence, which would almost always be more furious than the language had been'.[9]

The competitive underpinning of western, particularly English and American, capitalism was particularly apparent to those who encountered it in the middle of the nineteenth century. One of these was the Japanese philosopher and modernizer, Fukuzawa Yukichi. When he came to translate a basic treatise on western market capitalism, he was faced with a problem which he describes in his *Autobiography* – and solved it by using the words for competitive racing and warfare.

Fukuzawa described his difficulties with translation: 'when I came upon the word "competition" for which there was no equivalent in Japanese, and I was obliged to use an invention of my own, "kyoso", literally, "race-fight". When the official saw my translation, he appeared much impressed. Then he said suddenly, "here is the word 'fight'. What does it mean? It is such an unpeaceful word".' Fukuzawa tried to explain, but the official refused to take the translation to his superior because the word fight was not conducive to peace. Fukuzawa then commented acidly. 'I suppose he would rather have seen some such phrase as "men being kind to each other" in a book on economics, or a man's loyalty to his lord, open generosity from a merchant in times of national stress, etc. But I said to him, "if you do not agree to the word 'fight,' I am afraid I shall have to erase it entirely. There is no other term that is faithful to the original."'[10]

Yet alongside this very unpeaceful 'race-fight' with which Fukuzawa translated the quintessence of capitalism, there was another more peaceful and co-operative side. Competitive capitalists when trying to catch the largest fish, grow the largest vegetable, collect the largest set of stamps or race the fastest sailing boat, need people to be competitive with. They need to collaborate and share and compare, so all these activities were centred round friendships, groups, clubs and mutual recognition of skills and achievements.

◆

THE MULTIFARIOUS CLUBS, associations, hobbies and sports were given extra strength by the presence of those quintessentially English phenomena, the English inn and pub. The inn and the public house where a person could meet 'friends' are both an expression and a cementing of the patterns of association.

The prevalence of large inns throughout English towns and countryside, where people could stay the night and find food and drink, is a central feature of English social history, much celebrated, for example, in the novels of Charles Dickens. As I know from my own experience, if one travels around England, even if there are kin living near one's route, one often goes to stay in an inn or 'bed and breakfast' rather than 'putting the family to trouble'.

At the next level was something equally notable, the ubiquity and centrality of the alehouse and pub where drink could be bought and conversation with friends or strangers was possible. This was supplemented from the middle of the seventeenth century as the new drinks of coffee and tea became popular by the tea and coffee houses found in cities and towns.

Harbison notes the oddness of a 'public place' which yet feels exclusive, cosy and intimate, where strangers can become temporary friends, where a semi-family atmosphere can emerge.:

> There is a remarkable English institution more homey than any home can sensibly be and more old-fashioned, an institution public in a way peculiar to itself. Americans, who forget that *pub* comes from *public*, take it for a special sound signifying coziness and contentment, and it becomes an idea so potent no single embodiment can live up to it... Though every European country had village inns, elsewhere they have become gleaming cafés, while in England they are more villagy than ever, more like burrows.[11]

People with a relatively large disposable income and spare time, not basing their lives on exclusive kinship or caste groupings, needed places to meet and associate. Close friends might come into one's house. But having a bounded, protected, half-public, half-private space in another person's house gave people who were unrelated a chance to meet and chat. In effect, every village and town had for many centuries one or several 'community centres' at its heart – the village inn, tavern or alehouse.

In the late eighteenth century Rochefoucauld noted the importance of inns as a place for club meetings. 'The third kind of club is of greater advantage to the class of small labourers whom we call peasants. Here again the meeting-place is an inn, but a village inn or the smallest inn in a town. There the club meets for dinner once a year... These clubs are to be found in every part of England; every country district derives some benefit from them. In the inn in which meetings are held there is a box locked with two keys, with a little slot into which the club members put their money.'[12]

Burke notes their importance.

The taverns have been and still are centres of political debate, of argument on technical developments in literature and painting, of discussions on moral philosophy and religion, of gossip (and no doubt slander) and of all that piquant or pungent and always extravagant pleasantry which the most staid Englishman can release in his hours of ease. And they still are a part of the social life of a large section of the community, not only as rendezvous for recreation but as Lodges of the various Friendly and benevolent Societies and of Slate Clubs [a group of people who save money in a common fund for a specific purpose – usually distributed at Christmas], and as the headquarters of clubs covering all manner of interests from angling and pigeon-fancying to chrysanthemum-growing and archaeology and bowls.

The inn or pub was also used for legal and political meetings. 'It was regularly used, and sometimes still is, as a Coroner's Court, as a Churchwardens' Court, as a Court for the election of borough officers, and even Quarter Sessions have been, as late as mid-Victorian times, held at the inn ... the election of borough officers was almost always held at the inn, and was always followed by a dinner debited against the town's rates.'[13]

♦

THE ENGLISH ARE widely known as a nation of pet-keepers, as well as shopkeepers.[14] Kate Fox writes,

> Keeping pets, for the English, is not so much a leisure activity as an entire way of life... An Englishman's home may be his castle, but his dog is the real king.... They get far more attention, affection, appreciation, encouragement and "quality time" than our children, and often better food.... We had the Royal Society for the Prevention of Cruelty to Animals long before the establishment of the National Society for the Prevention of Cruelty to Children...'[15]

This tradition of pet-keeping seems to go back a long way. Keith Thomas points out that 'pet-keeping had been fashionable among the well-to-do in the Middle Ages'.[16] We learn of lapdogs, birds, rabbits, hounds, caged birds, squirrels and monkeys, for instance.[17] About the rest of the population we have little evidence, but as soon as they become visible in the records, pets are widespread. Thus Thomas concludes that 'it was in the sixteenth and seventeenth centuries that pets seemed to have really established themselves as a normal feature of the middle-class household'.[18] Thomas Ady in 1656 listed rats, mice, dormice, rabbits, birds, grasshoppers, caterpillars and snakes, as both 'lawful and common among very innocent and harmless people' as pets. He even told of a Gentleman who 'did once keep in a Box a Maggot that came out of a Nut, till it grew to an incredible bigness'.[19] The range was very wide, therefore, and it may be mistaken, as Thomas argues, to believe that taste in pets grew more catholic in the eighteenth century.[20]

It is more difficult to obtain some idea of the incidence of pets, but two indications of the extent of the keeping of domestic animals can be given. In his seventeenth century pictorial encyclopaedia for children, Comenius gave a picture of a house and its animals; these included the dog, cat, and squirrel, ape and monkey which 'are kept at home for delight'.[21] Defoe in his

Journal of the Plague Year describes how almost every house in London had a dog and several cats,[22] though here, as elsewhere, we face difficult problems of defining what exactly a 'pet' is. If it is regarded as non-utilitarian, like a flower garden, we nevertheless find that by the sixteenth century in the large middling ranks of society many had rabbits, weasels, ferrets, monkeys, parrots, squirrels, muskrats, toy dogs, and other pets.[23] If it is certainly the case that by '1700 all the symptoms of obsessive pet keeping were in evidencs',[24] it could well be argued that strong indications of such an obsession were present several centuries earlier, as soon as we have sufficient documentation to be able to note pets. It is clear from this that the phenomenon developed well before urbanization and industrialization could have had much effect. Widespread pet keeping is a by-product of something deeper than the changes of the eighteenth century.

At one point Thomas links the psychological function of pets to their attractiveness within a modern, atomistic, kinship system.[25] This intriguing suggestion could be broadened. In the majority of societies, a combination of early marriage, constant childbearing, the close physical and emotional presence of numerous kin, together provide the emotional satisfactions which many people now find in their pets. As we shall see, this individualistic kinship and marriage system is old in England, probably dating in its central features to at least the thirteenth century if not before. It is not difficult to see that pet-keeping and a fondness for nature are early and related phenomena. Just as English children were luxuries, regarded as superior pets,[26] so English pets were luxuries, regarded as alternative children. Another theory is that they give members of 'the lonely crowd' some warmth and a simple uncomplicated relationship: 'for many of us, they represent our only significant experience of open, unguarded, emotional involvement with another sentient being.'[27]

The boundaries between the animal and the human, and between the exploitation and preservation of species are complex. We see in England over the centuries that through a careful classification of the world into tame and wild, edible and inedible, it was possible for our ancestors, as it still is for us, to be meat-eaters, bear-baiters and fox hunters and yet greatly devoted to particular animals and concerned with animal cruelty.

♦

IF WE TURN from animals to plants, we may consider the 'Gardening Revolution'. It is indeed true that the English are unusually enthusiastic domestic gardeners. Fox suggests that 'Gardening is probably the most popular hobby in the country – at the last count, over two-thirds of the population were described as "active gardeners",'[28] It is also true that the content of their gardens altered dramatically over the centuries. We are told that 'in 1500 there were perhaps 200 kinds of cultivated plant in England. Yet in 1839 the figure was put at 18,000'. But because there were few cultivated species to choose from before 1500, this does not mean that flower gardening was uncommon. There were commercial plant sellers from at least the thirteenth century and we are assured that 'more flower-gardening had gone on in the Middle Ages than is sometimes appreciated', even though the 'repertoire seems to have been fairly limited'.[29]

This repertoire was limited by what was native to England and Europe, but it is symptomatic of the innate enthusiasm that as soon as it became possible to vary the plants by importing exotic species from newly discovered America and the widening contacts with Africa and Asia, people enthusiastically did so. William Harrison in the later sixteenth century marvelled at the English garden which had been 'wonderfully' increased in its beauty not only with flowers but also with 'herbs, plants, and annual fruits' which 'are daily brought unto us from the Indies, Americas, Taprobane (Ceylon), Canary Isles, and all parts of the world'. As a result 'there is not almost one nobleman, gentleman, or merchant that hath not great store of these flowers'. Harrison, an Essex vicar, concluded by boasting a little of his own garden 'Which is but small and the whole area thereof little above three hundred foot of ground, and yet, such hath been my good luck in purchase of the variety of simples, that, notwithstanding my small ability, there are very near three hundred of one sort and other contained therein, no one of them being common or usually to be had'.[30]

The enthusiasm for gardening, from the small cottage garden to the large garden of the gentry house, which is such a striking and characteristic feature of England even up to the present, was clearly indicated from the earliest detailed records of the sixteenth century. We are told that 'Elizabethans did not spend any more time indoors than necessary, for they were lovers of gardens if they loved their homes', and Pearson provides extensive accounts of the gentry and merchant gardens of the time.[31] Contemporary treatises on gardening began to be published as soon as printing became common, for instance, Thomas Hill's *A Most Briefe and Pleasaunt Treatyse, Teachynge Howe to Dress, Save and Set a Garden* in 1563. The poetry of the Elizabethans, and in particular Spenser and Shakespeare, as well as the central motif of the Garden of Eden as the fount of innocence and pleasure, all indicate the widespread absorption with natural beauty in the shape of flowers and trees. As the philosopher Bacon argued in his essay 'Of Gardens' in the early seventeenth century, 'God Almighty first planted a garden. And indeed it is the purest of human pleasures. It is the greatest refreshment to the spirits of man, without which, buildings and palaces are but gross handiworks'.[32]

Such appreciation was not limited to the wealthy. There is evidence that middling folk were keen gardeners. Writing of the English yeoman in the later sixteenth and early seventeenth century, Mildred Campbell concluded that 'already gardens, that happy result of the Englishman's climate and his skill, added beauty and colour for a part of the year to the farm and village scene'. She alludes to the record made by a neighbour of all the flowers that were in bloom in the garden of a certain 'Goodwife Cantrey', a Northamptonshire yeoman's wife, on 28 July

1658. These included 'double and single larkspurs; double and single Sweet Williams; three kinds of spiderwort; lupin in four colours; purple and white "scabious"; marigolds; Life Everlasting; London pride; "hollioakes" (hollyhocks); and many other well-known favourites.' She also had a wide range of medicinal plants like fennel, camomile, rue and white lilies.[33]

It is, of course, difficult to know how widespread gardening and the love of flowers was, but Thomas gives several pieces of evidence to suggest that it was indeed spread down to very ordinary people in the seventeenth century. He quotes John Worlidge who in 1677 wrote that 'in most parts of the southern parts of England', there was scarce a cottage' which was without 'its proportionable garden, so great a delight do most of men take in it'. A few years earlier, a book on flower gardening intended chiefly for 'plain and ordinary countrymen and. women' had been published and the first impression was sold out in three months.[34] We can be sure that the widespread and enthusiastic interest in flowers and gardens is present well before the growth of cities and industrialism in the second half of the eighteenth century. Again, we must try to explain it by something that is present in England before the seventeenth century.

As for the aesthetics of the English garden, this also expresses something special. Pevsner devotes part of one of his lectures on the *Englishness of English Art* to English landscape gardening. 'The English Garden... is asymmetrical, informal, varied, and made of such a parts as the serpentine lake, the winding drive and winding path, the trees grouped in clumps, and smooth lawn... The English garden is English in a number of profoundly significant ways not yet touched upon. First the simplest way: formally the winding path and the serpentine lake are the equivalents of Hogarth's Line of Beauty, that long, gentle, double curve... Hogarth ... says that they "lead the eye a wanton kind of chase."'[35] It is full of surprises and concealments, whereas 'On the Continent neither naturalness nor surprise in gardening appeared before the great invasion of the mid eighteenth century.'[36] I have found in my own experience that the pattern of irregular, concealed, natural garden, with surprises, winding paths an irregular pond, all give me special delight.[37]

◆

I HAVE SUGGESTED that England was not characterized by sharp divisions or oppositions in its geography, class, urban-rural, or other aspects. Rather there was a strong overlap or continuum between different parts. It is worth examining this in relation to the anthropological idea of the 'Great' and 'Little' traditions, or the high and low culture discussed by historians such as Peter Burke.[38] Strong oppositions or gaps occur in peasant societies, where there is a great difference between an urban, literate, upper-class culture and that of the oral village community. So you find a thriving 'folk' culture in many parts of China, India, Latin America and much of continental Europe, including parts of the Celtic fringe.

The richness of local traditions of song and dance, of local costumes, of regional foods and drinks, of customs concerning courtship, weddings and deaths, of material culture such as furniture and tools, and of folklore as shown in myths, legends, stories and proverbs, as well as local dialects, can be seen in many books on oral cultures, and physically manifested in the great 'Folk' museums of France, Italy, Portugal, Austria and Scandinavia.

In England, however, there does not seem to have been such a sharp separation between high and low. England was from at least the medieval period a geographically unified, stratified society, with an interweaving of the country and the town, with widespread penetration of writing, money, national language and laws into all of the countryside. This explains why the mentality, morality and material culture that has survived does not show a strong difference between a high and a low culture or a Great and a Little tradition.

Of course there are small elements of local particularity. There are people singing 'folk songs' in some Suffolk pubs, a difference in the way a house is thatched or decorated, a certain local accent, a way of making eel traps, a local cheese, a local dance (often relatively recently invented, as was Morris dancing in the seventeenth century). Yet these are mild and relatively small variations compared to what we find in classic peasant or tribal cultures.

For if we look through the list of features of oral, 'folk' culture noted above, from dancing to folklore, and check these against English evidence, we draw an almost complete blank. An English 'folk' museum, such as that in Cambridge, is in reality a museum of working class life, with an entirely different feel to the continental museums of rural culture. English folk song, as one of its major analysts, A.L. Lloyd, writes, 'is the musical and poetic expression of the fantasy of the lower classes – and by no means exclusively the country workers.'[39] If we examine the work of the British folklorists, we find that it is almost entirely concerned with Celtic, Continental or non-European tribal folklore.[40]

CHAPTER NOTES

1. Paxman, *English*, 194.

2. Saussure, *Foreign*, 294-5.

3. Saussure, *Foreign*, 295.

4. Orwell, *Lion*, 39.

5. Benson, *College*, 266. The Decalogue is the Ten Commandments, the central text of Christianity.

6. Veliz, *Gothic*, 108.

7. Veliz, *Gothic*, 131.

8. Taine, *Notes*, 35.

9. Tocqueville, *Memoir*, II, 353.

10. Fukuzawa, *Autobiography*, 190.

11. Harbison, *Spaces*, 27-8.

12. Rochefoucauld, *Frenchman*, 245.

13. Burke, *English Inns*, 44.

14. This is based on Macfarlane, *Culture*, chapter four.

15. Fox, *Watching*, 234.

16. Thomas, *Natural*, 110.

17. Salzman, *English*, 100-2.

18. Thomas, *Natural*, 110.

19. Ady, *Candle*, 135.

20. Thomas, *Natural*, 110.

21. Comenius, *Orbis*, 55.

22. Defoe, *Journal*, 137.

23. Pearson, *Elizabethans*, 19.

24. Thomas, *Natural*, 117.

25. Thomas, *Natural*, 119.

26. Macfarlane, *Marriage*, 54-6.

27. Fox, *Watching*, 235.

28. Fox, *Watching*, 129.

29. Thomas, *Natural*, 226.

30. Harrison, *Description*, 265, 270-1.

31. Pearson, *Elizabethans*, 58ff.

32. Bacon, *Essays*, xlvi.

33. Campbell, *Yeoman*, 241.

34. Thomas, *Natural*, 228.

35. Pevsner, *Englishness*, 174.

36. Pevsner, *Englishness*, 176.

37. See Macfarlane, *Letters*, 276-7.

38. Burke, *Popular*.

39. Lloyd, *Folk*, quote on back cover.

40. See Dorson, *Peasant*.

CHAPTER 8

FAMILY, FRIENDSHIP AND POPULATION

THE HOUSEHOLD ACTS as a joint economic, social, religious, and political unit in most peasantries. The head of the household is simultaneously a mediator with the ancestors, the political head, the economic boss. A woman is subservient, first to her father, then to her husband, then, as a widow, to her son. The individual has no political, economic or other rights.

The ritual, economic and other worlds overlap for a person in the household. Hence a political act is also a religious one. It is impossible to conceive of individuals apart from the groups of which they are members; they are only parts with meanings in relation to a whole. The family is the basic organizational unit of a society; through the family an individual reaches redemption, wealth and power. This kind of society finds its archetype in Eastern Europe, India and China.

Turning to the other end of the continuum, the central and principal feature of the modern family is that it does not act as infrastructure, that it does not organize politics, economics and religion. The family and society have become separated. Put in the words of sociologists, it has lost many of its functions − it is just stripped down to what is primarily a socializing agent.

The essence of 'modern' society is that each of the spheres has become separate, hence the disappearance of the religious household and the domestic mode of production. Instead of the group being primary, whether a family, caste or community, the individual becomes a microcosm of the society as a whole, with individual rights and duties. He or she becomes a legal, political, religious and economic entity in his or her own right, not merely insofar as he or she is a member of a wider group.

This atomistic system is one where wider ties of blood and territory are weak and integration is through money, citizenship, paper, law and sentiment. People, in Marx's ironic words, have been 'set free', not only in relation to the market, but also in relation to God and the State.

The spread of the modern family system was noticed as something that was happening all over Western Europe in the nineteenth century and since then has spread over the world.[1] For long it was believed that the 'modern' family system with its bundle of characteristics was a product of the disruption of the industrial and urban revolutions – with the entire world having an *ancien regime* system before that.

◆

PROBABLY FROM ANGLO-SAXON times – and certainly from the thirteenth century – children had no automatic rights in a parent's property. A child could be disinherited; there is no 'family property', *nemo est heres viventis* (no one is the heir of a living person). Maitland documents this in detail, showing that from at least the thirteenth century parents could leave their property to whom they liked – and by gift, sale or will disinherit all their children if they so wished.[2] For example, Bracton in the early thirteenth century shows that 'an heir is one who claims by descent what has been left undisposed of by his ancestor;

what his ancestor has alienated he cannot claim.'[3] The claims of kindred were destroyed in England at just the time they were protected elsewhere on the Continent.[4]

All property is individual, except that husband and wife have some shared rights and after a man's death a widow may have some automatic rights, once called 'free-bench and courtesy'. Otherwise a person has to earn his or her way in the world from birth. The 'restraint of the line', which operated all over Europe, where the lineage can prevent the holder of a family estate from selling it off – or demand shares – is totally absent. In England alone there was no restrait lignager.[5] There is a great deal of evidence of this in Maitland and other sources.

The reverse is also true. A child can hold property rights against his or her parents and can even sue them. A woman can hold property and sue her husband. Each person can have separate property and the only 'jointness', to a certain extent, is that of husband and wife. Just as there is no obligation in law for parents to leave anything to their children, there is no legal obligation for children to support their parents in old age. Indeed, it is unlikely that they will do so, for the absence of a joint holding means that early in life the children will have been sent away to be trained to enter the capitalist market.

The effect of family insecurity was magnified by another peculiarity only found in England and Japan, namely the custom of primogeniture, or single-heir inheritance of the main family holding by the first-born male. Where property is family property, all heirs have equal rights, including women through the dowry system. Yet in England and Japan many properties were considered as indivisible. The farm or family firm should not be subdivided between all the heirs. Among the effects of this was that, unlike most countries, where, as population built up, capital was constantly divided and sub-divided with smaller and smaller holdings, in England the main holding or business was often passed to one heir. This allowed capital to be maintained.

A second effect was that while all children could be effectively disinherited and hence were insecure, younger children were particularly insecure. Much of the vigour of English expansion in the imperial period, and the way in which successful gentry and aristocratic families sent their children off into the professions and trade, arose from the younger son syndrome. As Taine put it, younger sons who 'awake from earlier youth, to the fact that they can count on nobody but themselves. They are accustomed to well-being and luxury and have the memory of the paternal "country seat" always before them: what sharper spur to achievement could there be? It is like a sword at their backs, pricking them on to work. Not to attain to their father's level is to fail.... Considered from this point of view the law of primogeniture combined with the habit of living well is a system of training. They hasten away to the Indies, to China and Australia, skim the cream off the world and return home to found a family. There is, in London, a whole quarter which is qualified as "Australian", inhabited by people who made their fortunes in Victoria or Melbourne.'[6]

♦

ONE AREA TRADITIONALLY the preserve of the family is that of childrearing and socialization. The child grows up within the kin universe and learns how it works. He (or she) gains his skills and his prestige from his family, either from wider kin or parents. Often a parent acts as teacher employer and father all rolled into one. If we look at the pattern of English childrearing as far back as the records go, that is at least back to the thirteenth century, we appear to have a situation where the family is not the only or even the main unit of socialization.

As foreigners noted, many English children from a very early age were taken out of their family of birth and were reared by non-kin through the institutions of servanthood, apprenticeship, and, for the wealthy, through formal educational channels such as schools and universities. The nineteenth century boarding school was just one stage in this centuries–long tradition. These institutions converted the person from a dependent member of unit created by birth, a 'status' relationship in Maine's usage, to a free–floating individual who entered into contractual relationships to establish his or her position. It turned a person into someone who had to compete as a 'free' and equal citizen.

A classic account of this pattern is by the Venetian Ambassador Trevisano in 1497. He wrote that 'the want of affection in the English is strongly manifested towards their children; for after having kept them at home till they arrive at the age of seven or nine years at the utmost, they put them out, both males and females, to hard service in the houses of other people, binding them generally for another seven to nine years. And these are called apprentices...' He felt that if the parents had taken their children back when their apprenticeship was over 'they might, perhaps, be excused' but noted that 'they never return'. Instead, they have to make their own way in the world, 'assisted by their patrons, not by their fathers, they also open a house and strive diligently by this means to make some fortune by themselves.'[7]

If poor, the children went off as servants at between six and ten, if middling as apprentices, if rich to the households of richer families or to boarding schools and universities. Here they would be treated as separated individuals, cut off from their families, expected to make their own way.

♦

AS SEPARATE INDIVIDUALS it is not surprising that they should be expected to initiate their own marriages. I have documented in considerable detail the history of romantic love in England.[8] Using moralists and philosophers, poetry and novels, letters and autobiographies, wills and village histories, I have shown that the unusual tradition of basing marriage on 'love' is very old. For example, Chaucer's verse is filled with such assumptions about the prevalence of love as a basis for marriage.

We can go back to Anglo-Saxon poetry such as 'The Lover's Lament' and much more to the same effect.

Throughout all social classes, a person would meet the person they wanted to marry, they would court each other, and they would announce their love. If their parents tried to block the marriage, after a struggle the parents would usually have to give in. The presence of romantic love as the institutional basis for marriage is largely unique in the world, largely being confined to England and America before the nineteenth century, yet it is widely documented in England from Anglo-Saxon times.

Outsiders saw this as strange and even obscene – particularly because it made the relationship with the marriage partner more important than that with parents. As Rochefoucauld observed in the eighteenth century:

> As soon as a young man marries, he takes a house in which he lives alone with his wife, he avoids living even in the same town as his father – I could produce a score of examples of this. If the father lives in the country, the son will go to live in the town; each will live his own life in his own household, father and son seeing little of each other in the course of the year.' Rochefoucauld was clearly rather shocked. 'Thus the Englishman would rather have the woman he loves than preserve the love of his parents. This is part of the national character, which is quite foreign to ours, and strikes me as being in some way contrary to Nature.[9]

The relationship which husband and wife set up after a number of years away from home and based on 'love' and companionship was stronger than any other. The Japanese and other nations were shocked to find that the English put love of a spouse, a lateral relationship, before love of parents, a vertical relationship. Lafcadio Hearn, who married a Japanese wife and lectured on English novels at the end of the nineteenth century,

FAMILY, FRIENDSHIP AND POPULATION

reported that ' Our society novels do not strike them as indecent because the theme is love. The Japanese have a great deal
of literature about love. No; our novels seem to them indecent
for somewhat the same reason that the Scripture text, "For this
cause shall a man leave his father and mother, and shall cleave
unto his wife," appears to them one of the most immoral sen-
tences ever written.'[10]

One of the great explorations of the clash between conjugal and filial love is in Shakespeare and one particularly illuminating discussions is that between Brabantio and
his daughter Desdemona. Brabantio says to Desdemona:

> Come hither, gentle mistress:
> Do you perceive in all this noble company,
> Where most you owe obedience?

Desdemona replies:

> My noble father I do perceive here a divided duty:
> To you I am bound for life and education;
> My life and education both do learn me How to respect
> you; you are the lord of duty, -
> I am hitherto your daughter: but here's my husband;
> And so much duty as my mother show'd To you, prefer-
> ring you before her father,
> So much I challenge that I may profess
> Due to the Moor, my lord.'[11]

This move from upward directed to sideways-directed obligation is now widely recognized to be one of the hallmarks
of 'modernity'. Yet it is clearly present in England from the
Anglo-Saxon period onwards. It is connected with the fact that
English law did not uphold the power of the parents, and particularly the father. In Roman Law and indeed in most legal and
moral systems around the world – Islam, Confucianism, Hindu-

ism, the parents have absolute authority over their children for life – *patria potestas* or patriarchal power.

◆

TALK OF PATRIARCHAL power takes us to the wider topic of gender relations. The changing role and position of women in England over the period from the Norman Conquest to the late nineteenth century is a large and complex subject about which I can only say a little. Firstly, contrary to many people's assumptions, it appears that over most of the period the legal position of women did not gradually improve, but, if anything, declined. At the start Maitland paints a picture of considerable equality. He gives many examples of the mulitfold and high legal status of medieval women. Women were almost immediately capable of inheriting military fiefs. Unmarried women, that is both before marriage and as widows, were 'on the same level as men'.. They could bring legal actions against their husband for derelictions of conjugal duties.[12] Unlike Roman Law, there was never any concept of patriarchal power in English Common Law – the innate right of fathers, husbands or men to dominate women.

As the Equity Courts developed from the fourteenth century the protection of women's property was strengthened and they could bring actions against their husbands for cruelty or neglect. There was never anything equivalent to the continental concept that a woman's property was merged with that of her husband. Here husband was conceived of, Maitland says, as a guardian of her property while they were married and he needed her consent if he made large decisions about it.[13] The husband was not allowed to use force on his wife, he must consult, cajole, persuade her into a course of action.

Thus many accounts of medieval women, from the contemporary sources such as Chaucer or collections of letters (such as those of the Pastons), as well as the world portrayed in Shakespeare's plays, show the independence and general equality of women. The one area where they were largely absent was in relation to public offices, though even here the forceful behavior of a number of royal and aristocratic women, most notably Queen Elizabeth I, shows the power of women even in the public realm. After the sixteenth century, however, the relatively high status of women in law declined somewhat until it was revived again in the later nineteenth century.[14]

While the legal position was, compared to almost all other parts of Europe, very high, many people observed that in practice, de facto, women's position was even higher than the law implied. For example, in the later seventeenth century Chamberlayne stressed the difference between the subject status of wives under Common Law and their actual freedom, the former being de jure weak, but 'their condition de facto is the best in the world.'[15]

Those who compared the position of English women to those in other continental countries seemed convinced of their superiority in status. There was, of course, the famous proverb: 'England is a prison for men, a paradise for women, a purgatory for servants and hell for horses.[16] English women were seen by foreigners to be in a very favourable position.[17] When Fynes Moryson traveled round much of the continent in the early seventeenth century, he found that despite their legal disabilities, women had a much higher status in England than almost anywhere else.[18] Or when Burt traveled to Scotland in the middle of the eighteenth century he suggested that English women were given much more financial freedom than their Scots counterparts, and their reputation was much less vulnerable than their Scottish contemporaries So Scots women that 'that the English are the kindest husbands in the world.'[19]

We may wonder, beyond the legal background, what made for what seems an unusually modern set of gender relations. One factor suggested by Tocqueville was Protestantism. This may have reinforced the situation, but, as we have seen, the high legal status seems to have existed in England well before the Reformation. Another approach would be to link it to the wider nature of English society, especially the nature of the family, economy and in particular the way in which values were not dependent on preserving male honour and female chastity.

There appears to have been an unusually relaxed attitude between the two genders in England, and this is clearly related to the fact that the family and society are no longer integrated. In the majority of societies, where the family and family links constitute the basis of society, mating and sex, which bring together the sexes, have to be carefully supervised. When directed correctly, marriage furnishes allies, produces heirs, contributes to the labour force. But women's sexual and procreative powers are both an immensely powerful, but also a desirable and dangerous asset. In order to protect this asset, familistic system usually emphasise the opposition between males and females.

Gender is used as a major principle of organizing social life in the majority of societies and there is usually a very sharp opposition between the ideals and behaviour of the two sexes, as we find in Hindu, Islamic and, to some extent, Catholic cultures. In the extreme cases, the worlds of men and women overlap very little. There is often a strong emphasis on the threat and hostility between the genders and on the inferiority and subservience of women. Men have honour, women bring shame. Women should be dressed in an unprovocative way, be kept out of sight and in purdah, wear veils and hats.

Against such a background what is striking in the evidence we have examined is the absence of such a marked gender opposition in English culture. English women were, in their clothing, their freedom, their openness, "shameless" by the standards of many cultures. There is a striking similarity between men and women, a relaxed and friendly attitude which is marked in many of the documents, a mutual and affectionate sparing of almost equals, an absence of most of the stress on male virility, machismo, and on female shame and virginity. Women were not hidden away by dress, by etiquette or by architecture; they were not vulnerable, weak, possessions of men. The relatively relaxed and open relationship which existed from early life passed through unchaperoned courtship into companionate marriage.

◆

RETURNING TO THE family, how did parents who were deprived of their children's labour manage? The answer seems to be another peculiarity of the English. For many centuries, if they were in the middling class upwards, the English hired paid servants, who often lived in the house. The 'servant mode of production' as some have called it, has been analysed by Peter Laslett, John Hajnal and others, who through their study of English listings and other sources have shown that servanthood, with both males and females as servants, was present on a large scale from at least the thirteenth century.[20]

It was a very widespread institution in England, replacing kinship with paid labour at the heart of the family. It is a peculiar and particular feature of England, not to be found elsewhere except in it the peripheries of English culture such as America. There were numerous different kinds of servants – indoor, outdoor, specialized, and general.

Now with modern labour-saving devices and the expansion of nursery schools and primary and secondary schools, the need for household servants has declined, starting quite rapidly in the early nineteenth century. Yet for a long time the presence of servants was a sign of the replacement of kin by unrelated wage labour. The same happened with farm servants.

◆

WHAT IS NOT easy to explain is why and how the English family system became so different. In basic structure the English system has the same roots as the family systems of most of North West Europe. So if one had looked at northern France, Germany, Scandinavia and England in the tenth century, for example, one would not have found any clans (unlike the Celtic system), but rather ego-centred networks. Yet somehow from the twelfth century at least, there was a growing divergence so that by the fifteenth century, at least, England's family system struck foreigners as extraordinary. The divergence then grew even greater so that from the seventeenth century, when the system was carried throughout the British Empire and North America, it was very different from that in most continental countries.

Nowadays the idea that a parent does not have to leave his property to his children, that children do not legally have to look after their parents, that a person can marry whoever they love, that women and children have separate rights which they can maintain against their families, is basic not only to America and Europe but to wherever the Empire spread. In India and increasingly in China and elsewhere, these ideas have spread. The English family system, like its games, has infiltrated much of the world.

Yet the absence of kinship as a way of organizing economics leaves a gap. Most activities require strong, trusted, bonds with others in order to achieve good results. In most societies it is only the family one can trust, or family-like patrons. What replaced this mechanism in England?

♦

MANY PEOPLE WHO live in modern societies look on friendship as their most important type of relationship. The central place of 'friendship' in modern civilizations is taken for granted. We may therefore be surprised at how unusual it is.

The majority of relationships in ancien regime societies are given by birth. One is close to people who are of the same kinship group, the same caste, the same village. One does not choose these people; they remain with you all your life and the relationship has little flexibility. It is not really about emotions – of course you may love an aunt, or hate a cousin. But the important thing is the set of expected roles and relationships given by the structure.

The strength of the status-given patterns is so great that if one wants to extend one's contacts, one turns non-kin into quasi-kin. Very widespread in most of the world have been such mechanisms as adoption, 'spiritual' kinship including blood brotherhood, milk brotherhood, godparenthood and other formal methods of setting up friends. Beyond this there were long-term manipulative and calculative exchange relationships, such as *afno manche* in Nepal, *guanxi* in China. These relationships are often unequal and merge into exploitative, a–symmetrical, non–kin relationship which have to be contractually set up to fill gaps in personal contacts in certain societies. They are labeled patron–client ties.

Historically in most societies people liked certain kin and neighbours more than others and will seek them out. But the idea of forming a relatively deep, shared, relationship with an unrelated person based on nothing more than mutual liking, is unusual. The idea of such 'friends' being of the opposite sex is almost impossible after childhood.

We have seen that in England effective blood kinship was restricted. Nor was 'fictive' or constructed kinship much relied on. Adoption was not recognized in English law until the twentieth century. God-parenthood was, on the whole, rather unimportant, particularly compared to the Catholic societies of the Mediterranean. Blood or milk brotherhood was unknown. Even 'patronage' in the full patron-client sense of the literature on the Mediterranean was relatively unimportant in England.

Instead one made 'friends', a word of Anglo-Saxon origin and so powerful a relationship that it was often applied to the most important emotional tie in one's life – people became 'married friends'.

After moving out of the home at an early age, often a strong personal bond would arise from being members of the same institution – school, university, company, church, or playing the same games or enjoying the same hobbies. Through these mechanisms one discovered people whom one liked and with whom one could share and co-operate. The relationship had to be fairly equal – mutually beneficial exchanges were fine, but they must balance out over time otherwise it would turn into the 'lop-sided friendship' which is better described as patron-client relations. The relationship had to have effective content; people should enjoy each other's company, enjoy conversations, have a shared sense of humour, cultural preferences, in short, like each other. Once all these features were present the friendship could flourish – as it had done at school where one shared confidences and activities.

Friendships are usually based on a mutual interest, whether in literature, religion, leisure or business. They are imbued with sentiment, with 'liking' which can move into love, and they endure over a long period. Such permanent relationships were the extreme end of a continuum in England, while at the other end were very fleeting, fragmentary relationships. In this situation, people treated each other as potential partners or opponents in endless little games of exchange and contract. People were constantly doing deals – buying, selling, hiring, borrowing, promising, agreeing, both within the economic sphere and in the social, political and religious one. A sort of 'car–boot sale society', with endless short–term relationships. Such a system of fragmentary and daily negotiation is the opposite pole from the durable kinship world of true 'Community'. It can only operate in a world protected by an elaborate legal and customary code of law and a great deal of trust.

♦

IN MOST CIVILIZATIONS in history, the major check on population is mortality. Here there are two main variants. Either perennial diseases and high infant mortality keeps population more or less in balance – or, in another variant, the population is moderately healthy, numbers build up quite rapidly, and then periodic crises caused by war, famine and epidemic disease occur. In these two cases, humans have experienced the threat of high mortality in one form or another and tend to be anxious to have many children in order to combat the dangers. This is the pattern observed through much of Chinese, Indian or European history.[21]

The 'modern' pattern is one where it is lowered fertility which keeps population in check, rather than high mortality. Different mechanisms are used, late marriage and high rates of non-marriage, various forms of controls on the numbers born alive through infanticide and abortion, and nowadays high levels of contraception. These are what Wrigley calls 'low pressure' regimes. Until quite recently it was widely believed that this 'low pressure' regime is the product of some 'demographic revolution', perhaps caused by improvements in contraceptive technology in the nineteenth century.

It is now quite clear from the work of Tony Wrigley and other that in England a combination of late age at first marriage (often over twenty-five for women), plus selective marriage (with up to a quarter of women never marrying) was enough to keep population more or less static for some centuries.[22]

Putting it simply, in an embedded peasant economy, when the unit of production and consumption is the family household, it is sensible to have as large a family as possible, to work the land and to protect against risk in sickness and old age. To increase reproduction is to increase production. Yet as Jack Caldwell and others have shown, when the individual becomes integrated into the market, when wealth flows down the generations, when the cost of education and leaving for an independent economic existence on an open market occurs, children become a burden rather than an asset.[23] In other words, capitalistic relations combined with individualism knocks away the basis of high fertility, and if this is combined with a political and legal security so that one does not have to protect oneself with a layer of cousin, the sensible strategy is to have a few children and to educate them well.

A low-pressure demography means that a society avoids the situation where extra resources are automatically absorbed by population expansion. As Malthus argued, the only force strong enough to stand against the biological desire to mate and have children, was the even stronger social desire to live comfortably and avoid poverty. This is exactly what seems to have happened in England from at least the late medieval period.

It was until recently thought that before the nineteenth century England must have been filled with young marriages and large families, a pre-modern demography. Now thanks to Wrigley and his colleagues we know that the modern demographic pattern of relatively low fertility and mortality goes back to at least the early sixteenth century. Literary and other evidence suggests that, in fact, the English have always had this 'modern' demography. In the absence of any familistic production system since the Anglo-Saxon period, there seems to have been a 'modern' marriage system. There was an institutionalized individual choice pattern which encouraged people to wait for marriage, rather than a system of arranged marriage at an early age as in India, much of China or in Islamic civilizations.

The effect has been immense. For example, between the mid fifteenth and mid seventeenth centuries, when national wealth was growing at an average of about 0.25% a year, the population did not grow. So at the end of the period the country was twice as rich as at the start. The normal tendency is to invest any economic gains in extra moths – which kept an increasing population at the same economic level – as happened in China in these centuries.

As Malthus noticed, England was not the only 'modern' demography for he found something similar in Norway and Switzerland and we can see it also in seventeenth century Holland. Yet this pattern was very early present in England, with its foundation of a separation between the head (rational calculation) and the heart (biological imperatives), a separation of the society (family) from the economy. It was an essential feature of the peculiar trajectory of this small island. If England had had the normal high-pressure regime, it could never have industrialized, for the infrastructure and large consumer middle class would have been absent.

People had to be able to 'afford' to marry and have children. When economic conditions changed dramatically and called for a huge burst of extra labour, in other words with the early labour-intensive phase of the industrial revolution, then the age at marriage dropped and a larger proportion of the population married. Population grew rapidly as jobs became available.

Demography is a sensitive index to the presence of modernity. Where, as in most civilizations, the family is the basic unit of the economic, social, political and religious world, to expand the family is the ultimate goal – people want as many children as possible. But where a modern division between the spheres of economy, society, polity and religion has taken place, so that it is the individual alone who links the separated spheres, the individual's interest are not served by large families.

The extraordinary spread of the 'modern' demographic regime throughout Europe and then to many parts of the world in the nineteenth and twentieth centuries has puzzled specialists. For it does not fit with any usual indicators such as education, literacy or wealth. I suspect that if one plotted these falls against the change from an ancien regime integrated, family-based, world to the growth of individualistic, modern, separated, capitalist relations, one would find a fit. So demography is both an effect of modernity, but also a potent reinforcer, by leading to the positive feedback loops of putting extra comfort for the individual before extra hands and mouths for the family.

CHAPTER NOTES

1. See Goode, *World*.

2. Maitland, *History*, II, 12-13, 308-9.

3. Maitland, History, II 19.

4. Maitland, History, II, 344.

5. Maitland, *History*, II, 313.

6. Taine, *Notes*, 154.

7. *Italian Relation*, 24-6.

8. Macfarlane, *Marriage*, especially chapter nine.

9. Rochefoucauld, *Frenchman*, 88-89 .

10. Hearn, *East*, 72-3.

11. Shakespeare, *Othello*, Act I, Scene 1 .

12. Maitland, *History*, I, 484; II, 262; II, 485;II, 381.

13. Maitland, History, II, 411.

14. Maitland, *History*, II, 403.

15. Chamberlayne, *State*, 18; see also 33ff.

16. Thomas Fuller, quoted in McLynn, *Crime*, 83.

17. For example, Campbell, *Yeoman*, 261.

18. Moryson, *Itinerary*, III, 451; IV, 324.

19. Burt, *Letters*, I, 107-8, 192ff, 109.

20. Laslett, *Illicit*, 47; see also Kussmaul, *Servants*.

21. There has recently been an attempt by Lee, Wang and Cameron to suggest that Chinese and European demography were very similar. For a summary and critique of their arguments, see Huang, 'Great' and Bryant, 'Divergence'.

22. The evidence is surveyed in Macfarlane, *Marriage and Love*, part 1.

23. Idem.

CHAPTER 9

CIVIL SOCIETY

THE ESSENCE OF modernity is the elimination of all three traditional means of enforcing co-operation – kinship, an absolutist State and an absolutist Church. Yet modern societies, if anything, need more self-sacrifice of the individual for the general good than ever. How can this be achieved?

The solution is not merely the division of labour; 'organic solidarity' as Durkheim called it, or the market mechanism as Adam Smith or Mandeville put it. This division of labour or organic solidarity does not generate the strong feelings which is essential to change enlightened self-interest into a striving for wider goals and the social good.

What is needed is a multitude of 'artificial' groupings to make joint activity possible, as with a games' team or orchestra. As Tocqueville pointed out, the need to get things done meant that the English – and even more so their offshoot the Americans, joined together. 'That being so, the need to club together is more generally felt, because the urge to get things is more general and stronger'.[1] As Pierre Maitland observed, 'the French think in terms of family and the nation, the English tend to think in terms of the individual and society'.[2] In other words, the constituent element was the individual, not the group, yet the individuals formed a society or 'Civil Society' through numerous associations.

THE ENGLISH PROPENSITY to form into clubs and associations has been noted by many. Just as the English gave the world team games, so they gave the world many of its associations – Cubs, Brownies, Girl Guides, Boy Scouts, Salvation Army, Oxfam, Samaritans, Amnesty International, Rotarians, Independent Order of Oddfellows and many others. To this we might add many other institutions – the political clubs, the Royal Society and British Academy, the Trades Unions and the BBC. All are associational entities within this associational culture

Just in relation to the delimited field of nature and travel, Veliz notes how the English have invented 'a numerous and vigorous progeny of mountaineering clubs, geographic societies, yachting associations, hang gliding federations, botanical gardens, zoological societies, societies royal for the prevention of cruelty to animals, wilderness societies, gardening subcommittees, conservations societies, green parties, angling clubs, landscape painting societies, animal liberation zealots, bird-watching clubs, bush-tucker clubs, four-wheel-drive associations, Antarctic societies, and international associations for the protection of the kangaroo.'[3]

Sometimes the 'clubs' were informal – a group of like-minded friends. 'The English always conduct their business round a dinner-table; it is there that they are happiest and most liberal.'[4] Sometimes it was an instituted club like the political, social, scientific, academic and other clubs which have for long multiplied across England. These clubs did not take over the individual. A member, like a games player or member of an orchestra, retained some of his or her own autonomy as a member – but also collaborated with others.

Tocqueville noted this preservation of individual liberty combined with membership. 'On reflection I incline to the view that the spirit of individuality is the basis of the English character. Association is a means suggested by sense and necessity for getting things unattainable by isolated effort. But the spirit of individuality comes in on every side; it recurs in every aspect of things'. This need to join into associations to attain certain ends Tocqueville found very different in England from the situation in France; the spirit 'prompts people to pool their efforts to attain ends which in France we would never think of approaching in this way. There are associations to further science, politics, pleasure, business...'[5]

Tocqueville also observed the paradox that such clubs both merged people's personalities to a certain extent, but did this by excluding others. 'Example a club; what better example of association than the union of individuals who form the club? What more exclusive than the corporate personality represented by the club? The same applies to almost all civil and political associations, the corporations.'[6]

Uncharacteristically, this puzzled him. 'I cannot completely understand how "the spirit of association" and "the spirit of exclusion" both came to be so highly developed in the same people, and often to be so intimately combined'.[7] Yet it seems fairly obvious that identity and mutual solidarity is largely created by setting up symbolic boundaries in opposition to others.

Usually the 'we' and the 'they' are kinship or caste groups. In England it is football supporters, members of a College, members of a particular darts team, or members of a particular business or social club. What had been a central principle in England where there were also other ways of unifying people – an old country with class, regional and other unifiers – became even more important where unifying institutions were stripped away in the new, individualistic and egalitarian country of America. 'The English often perform great things singly, whereas the Americans form associations for the smallest undertakings. It is evident that the former people consider association as a powerful means of action, but the latter seem to regard it as the only means they have of acting'.[8]

A century earlier, Rochefoucauld had observed the importance of associations. 'In every county, every town, and every country place in England there are clubs. This is perhaps one of the soundest institutions and one which is evidence of the confidence in the general probity which prevails – quite apart from the benefit it confers upon country districts.'[9] Amongst others, he noted the presence of mutual assurance funds which would later become the Building Societies.

> It is an admirable thing for the peasants, uncultivated people who have to earn their living by manual toil, that they should have sufficient trust in the honesty of a society to put a portion of their money into the common fund and to be certain that they will get real help from it when occasion arises. This trust is general – one hears nothing of any instances in which it has been betrayed, either by requests from men not really ill or by a failure to distribute benefits on the part of those responsible for the administration of the funds.[10]

Here is a list of some of the basic features of the clubs and associations which now form the bedrock of British social structure.

- They are based on achievement rather than ascription.

- They are based on contract (voluntary, revocable, exchange of benefits) rather than status (involuntary, irrevocable, innate qualities).

- They are of limited purpose/ends – with a particular goal or set of goals – not generalized but specific.

- They are selective – only certain people are members of any particular one – though they may be replicated by competing clubs.

- There may often be an implied or explicit competition with others of the same kind – as in games, music and education.

- They have a bureaucratic organization to run them – chairman, secretary, bursar, and committees.

- They often own assets – courts, buildings, and meeting rooms.

- They often have symbols – crests, badges, ties, and mottoes.

- Present members select new members by voting for or against proposed candidates.

- They are not formally associated or controlled by the State.

- There may be specific criteria which a person has to have to be elected – wealth, gender or skill.

- They collect membership fees and subscriptions to pay for their activities.

- They have a name and a history.

- They are usually face-to-face – the members know each other (as opposed to the 'imagined communities' of nations).

- They limit themselves and do not interfere in other aspects of their member's lives.

- They have an explicit set of rules of behaviour.

- They can and do expel members who break these rules.

- A strong character (for example Baden-Powell – the Scouts, or John Wesley – the Methodists) often invents them.

- They can border on any kind of activity, including crime but are usually legal.

- They tend to endure for some years, and sometimes for centuries.

My own life illustrates the importance of these associational groupings.[11] Since childhood, my life has been a constant experience and training in joining and performing in clubs and groups – teams, dormitories, houses, colleges, departments.

♦

WE MAY WONDER how this unusual associational world grew up on this island. Here we will turn to a more technical history of the origin and effects of these groupings. In the thirteenth century, arising from earlier roots, a legal accident occurred in England that was to change the world we live in.[12] Lawyers were, as ever, trying to find a way round a tax regime. When a wealthy man died, his landed property, held in the strict feudal system directly of the King, was forfeited back to the Crown. In order for his heirs to re-claim it, they had to pay a heavy death duty on the estates. Naturally the rich and powerful did not like this. Their legal advisors saw that the problem could be avoided if they made the man at his death no longer the owner of the property. If he did not hold the property at death, the Crown could not seize it and insist on a tax before it passed on to his heirs.

So the lawyers invented the device of the Trust. A group of friends of the property holder were chosen and the estate was legally conveyed to them. They held it 'in trust for the use of another'. It was legally theirs to do with what they liked, but the owner trusted them to pass it on at his death to his heirs and to carry out his wishes in whatever way he had privately told them.

The Trust created a strange and anomalous thing. Trustees were appointed to work together to hold and administer property and to take collective decisions. The Trust had a name, a separate existence, a body that existed through time. So it was technically a 'corporation', a 'body'. Yet it had not been set up by the State, it had not been 'incorporated' or licensed by the

State with a formal document. It had been set up by a group of private citizens, yet it was recognized by national law.

Such entities were threatening to the State if they became powerful since trustees could make their own rules. It also allowed citizens to work together and create alternative loyalties. Consequently trusts were banned during the French, Russian and Chinese revolutionary periods, and by Mussolini and Hitler. In England, Henry VIII tried to destroy them but it was too late. Abolished for a few years, the Trusts were restored by lawyers, who claimed that the late King must have misunderstood the effects of what he had done.

There were diverse effects of this revolutionary innovation of the new legal device. One was in contributing to political freedom. One benefit of the trust was to help keep the judiciary independent. Lawyers were trained, and found their social and moral life sustained, by the Inns of Court. If these had been appropriated by the Crown through incorporation, for example, the great struggle between the Common Lawyers and the Crown in the seventeenth century might have turned out differently. More generally, the constraints which the law put on the tendency for power to grow were dependent on the independence of the judiciary, as Montesquieu and Tocqueville had noted.

ANOTHER IMPORTANT AREA was in the right to political associations. There were the various political clubs, essential to the balance of British politics. There were also numerous other political associations set up for particular purposes. Maitland mentioned in passing 'those political societies which spring up in England whenever there is agitation: a "Tariff Reform Association" or a "Free Food League" or the like'. On several occasions he mentions Trade Unions as one of the fruits of the right of free association arising from the idea of the trust.[13] The idea of a legal, unincorporated, association of free people pursuing political ends was essential to democracy.

Another effect Maitland noted was on the de–centralization of power and the autonomy of local and regional bodies. He believed that the 'English county' was one example of an unincorporated, yet existing, body.[14] It was this which prevented it becoming merely a servant of the central government.

All power tends to corrupt, but it does so far less if the power is not looked on as the personal property of the powerful, but rather as a temporary force held 'in trust' for others. This, Maitland, suggests, is what the idea of the Trust and the trust it entailed performed: 'In the course of the eighteenth century it became a parliamentary commonplace that "all political power is a trust"; and this is now so common a commonplace that we seldom think over it. But it was useful.'[15]

Above all it permeated the delicate relationship between the King and the people, enabling a new kind of constitutional monarchy to emerge. 'Possibly the Crown and the Public are reciprocally trustees for each other; possibly there is not much difference now–a–days between the Public, the State, and the Crown, for we have not appraised the full work of the Trust until we are quitting the province of jurisprudence to enter that of political or constitutional theory.'[16] This was an established fact by the later nineteenth century and Maitland briefly suggests how the application of the concept of trust had spread and influenced events in the aftermath to the confrontations between king and people of the seventeenth century.

Having established a concept of trust between monarchy and people by the eighteenth century, the idea found a further extension and application as a metaphor to hold together the largest Empire the world has ever known. A political example of how this worked was in relation to India. Maitland shows how the East India Company, which in practice ruled India, was replaced by the British Crown which held India as a Trust. The transition was made much easier by the Trust concept.

This was just part of that wider concept that all power was held in trust. The whole of the British Empire came to be seen as held 'in trust' for the peoples themselves, until they were ready to take over.

> Open an English newspaper, and you will be unlucky if you do not see the word "trustee" applied to "the Crown" or to some high and mighty body. I have just made the experiment, and my lesson for today is, that as the Transvaal has not yet received a representative constitution, the Imperial parliament is "a trustee for the colony." There is metaphor here.

Maitland noted government ministers of his and earlier times saying that Victoria's government 'is a trustee for "the whole empire"'.[17] Perhaps this is part of the explanation for Tocqueville's question as to how such a small country as England could hold such a large Empire. The mechanism of the trust both gave the metropolitan government confidence and an easy conscience and allowed elastic forms of delegation of power without posing a direct clash between the centre and the periphery.

Equally important, as Maitland realized, were the effects of the possibility of having 'non–incorporated bodies' in the field of religion. He shows how the trust became a key defence of religious nonconformity and the sects. Any religious organization needs to form itself into some kind of permanent group. For instance, it needs a place of worship. Since such buildings had to be funded and maintained, how was this to happen? The State, associated with a Catholic or Anglican settlement was hardly likely to give them corporate status. What the Methodists, Baptists, Quakers and others did was to set up trusts. Groups of trustees ran their affairs and were recognized by the law. As Maitland pointed out, it is likely that without this legal loop–hole, the whole of nonconformity would have been crushed. Religious liberty and the trust were closely linked. It is intriguing that the Catholic Church in England is still a registered trust. For example, the Catholic diocese of Plymouth is registered as charity number 213227 by the Charity Commission.

That England – and later America – were lands of toleration and sectarianism, exhibiting that mysterious relation between private and public which puzzled Tocqueville, but which he saw as a central feature of America, is partly explained by the device of the Trust. The presence of the Trust explained why, if one searched through the voluminous records of Common Law, 'in the hope of discovering the organization of our churches and sects (other than the established church) you will find only a few widely scattered hints.'[18] It was equity and the trust that provided the infrastructure for the distinctive Protestant sectarianism of England and America.

LINKED TO RELIGIOUS freedom was economic liberty. In terms of economic development, a device was needed which would allow people to come together to co–operate in some venture of a new kind. This was the era when new insurance facilities were needed. It was a time when traders and manufacturers needed to form themselves into joint–stock arrangements and to issue shares. The law of trusts made all this possible allowing joint–stock arrangements and limited liability.[19] In all these cases the entity was recognized by the law, yet did not draw its strength directly from the Crown. It was a free association of individuals who had bound themselves together.

Maitland describes two examples in some detail. He traces the history of the development of a late seventeenth century coffee house owned by Edward Lloyd, embodied in the mid–eighteenth century in a small trust fund and later, in 1811, in a trust deed with eleven hundred signatures. Thus was developed the great insurance firm of Lloyds. His second example was the London Stock Exchange. He describes how, in the eighteenth century, it grew from people meeting in a coffee house into a group of trustees. By the later nineteenth century it was vast and wealthy. In 1877 some people recommended that after all these years as a trust it should be incorporated. 'And so the Stock Exchange was incorporated? Certainly not. In England you cannot incorporate people who do not want incorporation, and the members of the Stock Exchange did not want it.'[20]

One of the advantages of the fact that many of the pivotal economic institutions in England from the sixteenth century developed as trusts would have been appreciated by Adam Smith. New economic enterprises – for example, long distance trade, or marine insurance, or making a new product – are risky. The individual needs protection, some limitation of liability and mutual assurance. Yet if the protection is given by the government, it very often takes the form of a monopoly. As Smith pointed out, this could easily turn over time into something that would inhibit creative development. Yet it was of the essence of trusts that they were not state monopolies. If someone else wanted to set up a marine insurance company or a building society the trustees could not prevent them. It provided a protection for the members without inhibiting newcomers. It was thus the ideal situation for competition with protection, for uniting individuals in a way that did not inhibit other individuals. It is difficult to see how the wealth of industrial England could have been created without the trust concept.

A third area which Maitland touched on was in relation to social and intellectual liberties. He noted that a foreigner thinking of England would have noted 'you have been great makers of clubs.' Many were of pivotal importance in political, legal and social life. For instance, 'every judge on the bench is a member of at least one club'. Maitland took as an example the Jockey Club. 'I believe that in the eyes of a large number of my fellow–countrymen the most important and august tribunal in England is not the House of Lords but the Jockey Club; and in this case we might see "jurisdiction" – they would use that word – exercised by the *Verein* [club] over those who stand outside it. I must not aspire to tell this story. But the beginning of it seems to be that some gentlemen form a club, buy a race–course, the famous Newmarket Heath, which is conveyed to trustees for them, and then they can say who shall and who shall not be admitted to it.' Newmarket Heath had been purchased by the Jockey Club 'without asking the King's or the State's permission. He also referred to 'your clubs and those luxurious club–houses which we see in Pall Mall.'[21] But there were numerous others.

Clubs were also closely related to intellectual activities – for example, the Royal Society, the British Academy, and numerous working men's clubs were of enormous importance in furthering science and learning. Maitland noted that 'many learned societies', including the one he had founded, the Selden Society, were run by trustees, as were key institutions such as the London Library.[22]

A FINAL AREA which Maitland sees as important is what he calls 'social experimentation' and which we might roughly term 'innovation'.

> First and last the trust has been a most powerful instrument of social experimentation. To name some well–known instances: it (in effect) enabled the landowner to devise [leave] his land by will until at length the legislature had to give way, though not until a rebellion had been caused and crushed. It (in effect) enabled a married woman to have property that was all her own until at length the legislature had to give way. It (in effect) enabled men to form joint–stock companies with limited liability, until at length the legislature had to give way. Thus the device of the trust affected not only individuals, but categories – married women, the poor (through boards of guardians, Poor Law funds and charity), the young.

The way it raised the status of married women by protecting their property particularly impressed Maitland. In general it allowed a flexibility and vagueness which allowed change: 'let us observe that Englishmen in one generation after another have had open to them a field of social experimentation such as could not possibly have been theirs, had not the trustee met the law's imperious demand for a definite owner.'[23]

◆

SUMMARIZING MAITLAND'S ILLUMINATING insight into the solution to Tocqueville's puzzle concerning the origins of associations, we can say that in England from about the thirteenth century there began to develop a society which had various essential constituents. It had a powerful Crown and a ruling group in parliament. The centre was strong – but it was limited in its power by two other levels. In the middle was a crowd of unincorporated bodies, to a certain extent 'nobodies', in Maitland's phrase, but nobodies which are the essence of what would now be called 'Civil Society'. The secret, anti–State, organizations (mafia, triads) which have been the bane of most governments were not necessary. The rights of association, so important later for the trades union and the labour movement, allowed people to form into groups. They were encouraged to put their energies into open activity.

Thus through the widening development of the concept of the Trust, there also, indirectly, developed a world of trust and openness, which is the basis not only of capitalism but also for modern science.[24] Maitland points out that this is such a large feature of the development of English civilization that it has become invisible. 'Now we in England have lived for a long while in an atmosphere of "trust," and the effects that it has had upon us have become so much part of ourselves that we ourselves are not likely to detect them. The trustee...is well known to all of us, and he becomes a centre from which analogies radiate.'[25]

The whole system is based on trust, both presuming a widespread level of trustability and, by that assumption, creating it.

'If I convey land to you as a trustee for me, or as a trustee for my wife and children, there is not merely what our law calls a trust, there really is trust placed by me in you; I do trust you, I do place confidence, faith, reliance in you.' In many civilizations such trust in unrelated individuals would not be easy. Nor would it be easy to find people who were prepared, for no obvious reward, to carry out such duties, for 'a very high degree not only of honesty but of diligence has been required of trustees'.[26] The whole wide concept of public and disinterested service for others and for the community is related to the development of the trust.

♦

THE EFFECTS OF trust were combined with the image of the gentleman and the culture of pubs and clubs described in earlier chapters. When all these were joined together they provided a social context which made modern science and technology possible, as we shall see when we come to investigate 'Knowledge'. They also made the development of a modern capitalist economy possible. Much could be said about this, but I shall confine myself to some recent comments by Joel Mokyr.

Mokyr writes, 'The emergence of a plethora of networks, clubs, friendly societies, academies, and associations created a civil society, in which the private provision of public goods became a reality and created what might be called a *civil economy*... Roads, harbors, bridges, lighthouses, river navigation improvements, drainage works, and canals were initiated through private subscriptions... Voluntary associations founded hospitals, schools, orphanages, prosecution societies, and charitable relief committees, as well as turnpike and canal trusts. Amateurs provided local administration and justice.'[27]

The universal problem which societies face in trying to create public trust and philanthropy was solved to an unique extent by this development of civil society.

What made this trust possible were social networks such as permanent members of taverns, coffee-houses, and inns, friendly societies, religious communities, Masonic lodges, and similar organizations in which businessmen and craftsmen got together and exchanged information and gossip. In eighteenth-century Britain, to be a gentleman one had to be sociable, to be part of a community.... Informal institutions, in other words, allowed society to operate far more efficiently than it would if every player had ... displayed selfish and uncooperative behaviour. The British entrepreneur, far from being a ruthless egotist, was very much part of a shared value system... The typical entrepreneur did his best to come across as trustworthy. Gentlemen, ideally, were men without occupation and presumably generous and not driven by greed.'[28]

In brief, it is impossible to understand the emergence and continuation of the modern world on the small island of Britain without considering the role of civil society. Without the trust and co-operation which brought together this individualistic and mobile peoples, the developments in political integration through parliamentary democracy, the uniquely plural and tolerant religious settlement, the innovative technologies and superb scientific achievements, let alone the sports, games, literature and arts would have been impossible to achieve.

CHAPTER NOTES

1. Tocqueville, *Journeys*, 75.

2. Quoted by Barker, *Character*, 39.

3. Veliz, *Gothic*, 105.

4. Rochefoucauld, *Frenchman*, 245.

5. Tocqueville, *Journeys*, 74-5.

6. Tocqueville, *Journeys*, 74-5.

7. Tocqueville, *Journeys*, 74.

8. Tocqueville, *Democracy* (abridged), 199.

9. Rochefoucauld, *Frenchman*, 242.

10. Rochefoucauld, *Frenchman*, 246.

11. See my 'Understanding Life Backward', *The Fortnightly Review*, March 2012.

12. This summary is taken from Macfarlane, *Letters*, Letter 16; for a detailed account, Macfarlane, *Making*, chapter seven.

13. Maitland, *Collected*, III, 387; III, 400.

14. Maitland, *Collected*, III, 400.

15. Maitland, *Political*, xxxvi.

16. Maitland, *Political*, xxxvi.

17. Maitland, *Collected*, III, 403; *Political*, xxxvi, note 3.

18. Maitland, *Collected*, III, 369.

19. Maitland, *Collected*, III, 389–92.

20. Maitland, *Collected*, III, 372, 374.

21. Maitland, *Political*, xxxiii; *Collected*, III, 378, 376, 385, 377.

22. Maitland, *Collected*, III, 388.

23. Maitland, *Collected*, III, 356, 283.

24. For the necessity of trust in economic development, see Fukuyama, *Trust*; for science, Shapin, *Social*.

25. Maitland, *Collected*, III, 402.

26. Maitland, *Equity*, 44; *Collected*, III, 352.

27. Mokyr, *Enlightened*, 381.

28. Mokyr, *Enlightened*, 387.

CHAPTER 10

POWER AND BUREAUCRACY

IT IS GENERALLY agreed that although full democracy, in the sense of a system where all qualifying adults have a vote to elect their rulers, is less than a hundred years old, the modern idea of democratic government was developed over the centuries first in England. It was associated with the idea of a balance of power between the State and the citizen and a feeling of liberty of thought, word and association which we call modern freedom.

I shall be using 'Democracy' here not so much in relation to a form of voting, but as suggesting a general freedom to discuss, act and participate in running one's own life. In the thirteenth century Encyclopedia *On the Properties of Things*, it had been suggested that freedom was widespread. England in mid-thirteenth century was seen as uniquely free, 'men oft times able to mirth and game, free men of heart and with tongue, but the hand is more better and more free than the tongue...'[1]

In the middle of the nineteenth century Taine noted 'British citizens enjoying full freedom of speech and association'. Yet he realized how difficult this was. He wrote that 'almost the whole of Europe has tried or actually adopted the English system ... and look at the outcome – in Greece, grotesque; in Spain, lamentable; in France, fragile; in Austria and Italy, uncertain; inadequate in Prussia and Germany; successful only in Holland, Belgium and the Scandinavian countries.' The reason for this was that 'the Constitution of a nation is an organic phenomenon, like that of a living body. Consequently that Constitution is peculiar to the state in question, no other state can assimilate it, and all it can do is to copy its appearance. For beneath these, beneath the institutions, the bills of rights and the official almanacs, there are the ideas, the habits and customs and character of the people and classes; there are the respective positions of the classes, their reciprocal feelings – in short, a complex of deep and branching invisible roots beneath the visible trunk and foliage. It is these roots that sustain and nourish the tree, and if you plant the tree without the roots it will wilt and fall to the first storm of wind. We admire the stability of British government; but this stability is the final product, the fine flower at the extremity of an infinite number of living fibres firmly planted in the soil of the entire country'.[2]

Here I shall try to describe a few more of the living fibres or deeper roots of democracy, the contested story of power threads its way through English history. Let me just note a few instances. In *The Discourse of the Common Weal* of 1585 the terms used were 'common wealth' or 'common weal', not of an absolute monarchy. The book suggested that 'the English had always been, and at present were, a free people, such as in few or no other realms were to be found the like.'[3]

WHEN FRENCHMEN CAME to the country in the seventeenth and eighteenth centuries they noticed this unusual feature: 'The English can boast of having a great advantage over other nations: in England everyone is master of his own property and can spend his life without suffering at the hands of the great and, if he so desires, without knowing them.'[4] As Voltaire wrote:

'The English are the only people upon earth who have been able to prescribe limits to the power of Kings by resisting them; and who, by a series of struggles, have at last establish'd that wise Government, where the Prince is all powerful to do good, and at the same time is restrain'd from committing evil; where the Nobles are great without insolence, tho' there are no Vassals; and where the People share in the government without confusion.'[5]

Montesquieu was well aware of the power of French absolutism and saw the laws and customs of England as very different from the rest of Europe. In England, 'Their laws not being made for one individual more than another, each considers himself a monarch; and indeed, the men of this nation are rather confederates than fellow-subjects'. He continued that in England, 'as no subject fears another, the whole nation is proud, for the pride of Kings is founded only in their independence.'[6]

Karl Jaspers, who had been imprisoned as a Jew during the Second World War, summarized the long struggle. 'In the West, certain fundamental determinants of the idea of political freedom have been evolved (originally, above all, in England and America, from whence they were taken over by France and other States after the French Revolution; they were elaborated philosophically during the period of the Enlightenment, for instance by Kant).' Later, he adds:

If we look at the course of world history, we see that the political liberty of men is rare, indeed an exception. The majority of men and the greater part of history are destitute of political liberty. Athens, republican Rome, and Iceland were exceptions of this kind. And the greatest, most effectual and most powerful exception of all is England together with America. This was the birthplace of the influence that set free the States of the continent, but only in part and without the vigours of the daily, deliberate assertion of liberty.

He dates this liberty from at least the twelfth century: 'The classical development of political freedom, which gives at least an orientation to all and is for many exemplary, occurred not more than seven hundred years ago in England. On this spiritual-political fundament, liberty was created afresh in America.'[7]

ONE OF THE central themes of Tocqueville is the paradox or conflict between centralization and de-centralization. He noted the combination of both in England and America: 'There are two great drawbacks to avoid in organising a country. Either the whole strength of social organisation is centred on one point, or it is spread over the country. Either alternative has its advantages and its drawbacks. If all is tied into one bundle, and the bundle gets undone, everything falls apart and there is no nation left. Where power is dispersed, action is clearly hindered, but there is strength everywhere'.[8]

He realized that centralization of power and justice is essential in a modern country. 'In England, the centralization of the government is carried to great perfection; the state has the compact vigour of one man, and its will puts immense masses in motion, and turns its whole power where it pleases. But England, which has done so great things for the last fifty years, has never centralized its administration'.[9] The legal system has to be centralized. 'The English are the first people who ever thought of centralising the administration of justice. This innovation, which dates from the Norman period, should be reckoned one of the reasons for the quicker progress which this nation has made in civilisation and liberty'. On the other hand, administration should be local: ''England is the country of decentralisation. We have got a government, but we have not got a central administration. Each county, each town, each parish looks after its own interests'.[10]

The decentralization avoids the danger of the inflation of the bureaucracy which had undermined France; '...a taste for holding office and a desire to live on the public money is not with us a disease restricted to either party, but the great, chronic ailment of the whole nation; the result of the democratic constitution of our society and of the excessive centralisation of our Government; the secret malady which has undermined all former governments, and which will undermine all governments to come'.[11] On the other hand in England the balance of centralization and de-centralization led to the remarkable strength, liberty and wealth which emerged there.

The English were prepared to take their conflicts to central courts, but they liked to rule themselves. 'Finally, the Englishman's great objection to allowing the government to do his business even well, is simply his wish to do it himself. This passion for being master at home, even to act foolishly, essentially characterises the British race. "I had rather plough badly for myself than give up the stilts into the hands of the government".' We ourselves have some of this feeling in private life. The English carry it to the greatest extent in municipal life'.[12]

Tocqueville saw that a unique political system had emerged on this island and spread to America. The elections to parliament were only one aspect. The system of local government made each parish an almost self-governing community. Tocqueville's companion Beaumont had urged Tocqueville to go to a meeting of the church vestry. 'One must go to the meetings of a Vestry to judge what extraordinary liberty can be joined to inequality. One can see with what independence of language the most obscure English citizen expresses himself against the lord before whom he will bow presently. He is not his equal, of course, but within the limits of his rights he is as free, and he is fully aware of it. His right is that of discussing the interests of the parish and this right he exercises not only freely but with a propriety and, sometimes, an ability which is surprising in an orator whose blackened hands and coarse clothes declare him to be an artisan or a man of the lowest class. The ensemble of English institutions is doubtless an aristocratic government, but there is not a parish in England which does not constitute a free republic.'[13]

As Drescher puts it, 'The parish, then, was the fundamental unit of public participation, the center of a multitude of interests vital to everyone in the community. For Tocqueville it was a complete democracy at the base of the social edifice.'[14] We are told that in his notes, Tocqueville wrote that if he were a friend to despotism, he would allow 'the deputies of the country [to deliberate] freely about peace and war, about the nation's finances, about its prosperity, its industries, its life. But I would avoid agreeing, at any price, that the representatives of a village had the right to assemble peacefully to discuss among themselves repairs for their church and the plan for their parsonage.'[15]

This was not a new outcome. It was not the result of the English revolution of 1688, for example. Tocqueville noted the great difference between the Continent and the Anglo-American system in 1650.[16] And indeed he believed, like Montesquieu, that the contrast went back to a difference which had been growing since medieval times.

♦

IN ORDER TO pursue the theme back into the earlier centuries, let us look through the eyes of someone who has examined the legal and constitutional history of England through primary sources, namely Maitland. Maitland noticed that from the Anglo-Saxon period, but particularly from the legal reforms of the twelfth to thirteenth centuries, England, was both the most centralized, yet also de-centralized, polity in Europe. All justice flows from the Crown and is centralized – though it can be sub-delegated to lower courts, such as the quarter sessions and manorial courts. In military matters, unlike the Continent, all subjects owe prime allegiance to the Crown and not to their lords. 'Military service is due to none but the King; this it is which makes English feudalism a very different thing from French feudalism'.[17]

In terms of property law, the military and taxation, England, a small, sea-surrounded country, was the most centralized and feudalized in Europe – yet in other respects it was the least feudalized. There was the curiosity of English land law – 'insofar as feudalism is mere property law, England is of all countries the most perfectly feudalized... ' but it was also the least feudalised in the sense that all subjects owed their primary allegiance to the Crown and not to their overlords.[18] So England had a 'highly centralized feudalism'– it was very different from French feudalism.[19] 'If now we speak of the feudal system, it should be with a full understanding that the feudalism of France differs radically from the feudalism of England... The phrase has thus become for us so large and vague that it is quite possible to maintain that of all countries England was the most, or for the matter of that the least, feudalized; that William the Conqueror introduced, or for the matter of that suppressed, the feudal system.'[20]

♦

THE MIXTURE OF centralization and devolved power which was worked out in England in the five hundred years up to the sixteenth century was then expanded. This is the system of indirect rule, using local forces to rule rather than intervening directly, delegating power to trusted 'leaders'. Such a system is the one which held together the vast British Empire for a couple of centuries with a very thin veneer of bureaucrats and relatively few troops. They were given delegated powers – to tax, punish and settle disputes. They were supported by the centre in London and reported to it.

Much of the system was based on an 'imagination' that there was somehow democracy. Of course, for ninety percent of its history, the system excluded most of the population – all women, all those who were not forty-shilling freeholders or whatever the financial bar was. The politics was often corrupt and the voters soon found that they often lived in what Tocqueville called 'elective dictatorship', where they were presented with a wide set of policies, some of which they might disagree with yet have to cast a vote in favour in general, and then were at the mercy of those they had voted for who could change their minds or go to war without consulting them.

Yet the British system, whether practiced in imperial India or at home in Britain, tended to encourage participation in local issues, some sort of 'ownership', as the current phrase has it, of the issues which affect a person on a daily basis. To a considerable degree for some centuries this worked and still works in Britain today.

♦

ONE CENTRAL ODDNESS which increasingly differentiated England from continental countries was the nature of royal power. In the contest between the King, lords, towns and Church during the eighth to thirteenth centuries on the continent, the Crown finally emerged triumphant. Supported by an absolutist Roman Law, the ruler became the source and fount of power – Divine and absolute. Though some English rulers would have liked to follow suit, and some, such as King John, Charles I and James II made some attempts to do so, they did not succeed.

The constitutional position, re-enforced by Magna Carta in 1215, is stated firmly by Maitland. 'The King can do wrong; he can break the law; he is below the law, though he is below no man and below no court of law. It is quite conceivable that he should be below a court of law.' In the same way as there is no legal distinction between social classes; 'The rights of the King are conceived as differing from the rights of other men rather in degree than in kind.' Magna Carta was not inventing this, but re-affirming it, as were the lawyers who supported the overthrow of Charles I and James II. For Magna Carta, 'in brief it means this, that the King is and shall be below the law'.[21]

The heart of the English system was the idea of a political contract between the people and their rulers. Feudalism is a contractual system, the lord does certain things, his followers do certain things. If either side breaks the terms of the implicit agreement, the contract is over. In the middle of the fifteenth century, the Lord Chief Justice Sir John Fortescue instructed the young King Henry VI in the central political difference between France, where they were both temporarily exiled, and England. France was an absolute monarchy, where all law emanated from the King and the people were subjects. England was a limited monarchy, based on the voluntary acquiescence of the people, and where the King himself was bound by the same laws as his countrymen. England was an association of free men held together by mutual contracts. Fortescue explained that 'I do most evidently see that no nation did ever of their own voluntary mind incorporate themselves into a kingdom for any other intent, but only to the end that thereby they might with more safety than before maintain themselves and enjoy their goods from such misfortunes and losses as they stood in fear of ...'[22] This is the essence of democracy and the system which John Locke set out, which was elaborated by Montesquieu and became the foundation for democracy in America.

The final result of all this impressed Voltaire and other visitors to England in the eighteenth century. One of the most enthusiastic was De Saussure and he caught a number of the features. He noted the general satisfaction with the liberty which many enjoyed. 'England undoubtedly is, in my opinion, the most happily governed country in the world'. He believed that the lively literary scene 'is cultivated by the liberty which the government afford, and in which Englishmen take great pride, for they value this gift more than all the joys of life, and would sacrifice everything to retain it'.[23]

Saussure noted the limited and circumscribed nature of power. 'She is governed by a King whose power is limited by wise and prudent laws, and by Parliament, this being composed of lords spiritual and temporal in one house and of the people's deputies in the other. The King cannot levy any new taxes, neither can he abolish privileges or make new laws without the consent of Parliament'.[24] And he caught the essence of power which was that, like a game of football,bough it did not work unless there was a contest. There had to be sides, arguments, and divisions.

As I remember from school, if our team became too weak and was being overwhelmed, a good player would cross over to give us strength. 'Numbers of prudent politicians, who are not blinded by foolish prejudices or by their own particular interests, are convinced that this form of government is the happiest in the world, and they sometimes side purposely with the weakest party, so as to preserve to the country a wholesome equilibrium'. So it was the very divisions and separations, not just as been discussed between politics and other spheres, but within the political field, that provided space and liberty. 'Though many people look on these different parties which divide England as a misfortune, others, on the contrary, think that they contribute to the maintenance of the liberties and privileges of the people'.[25]

It was a contest and people had the right to disagree and fight for what they believed was fair. No single group should prevail – there should be a constant struggle. Old elements were allowed to survive, new elements co-existed with them. The conqueror has to tolerate the conquered, the state has to accept rivals. James Stephen, a political theorist in the later nineteenth century, captures the spirit of this never-ending contest. 'Every event of our lives, from schoolboy games up to the most important struggles of public life, even, as was shown in the seventeenth century, if they go the length of civil war, is a struggle in which it is considered a duty to do your best to win, to treat your opponents fairly, and to abide by the result in good faith when you lose, without resigning the hope of better luck next time. War there must be, life would be insupportable without it, but we can fight according to our national practice like men of honour and people who are friends at bottom, and without attaching an exaggerated value to the subject matter of our contention.'[26]

◆

IN ALMOST ALL peasant civilizations taxation is arbitrary and ruthless. The rulers will extract anything that they feel the people can just about bear. Any wealth they detect is threatened. Taxes and forced gifts are ubiquitous. Brutal, arbitrary, exaction regimes are widely documented in almost all agrarian civilizations.

In 1559, for example, John Aylmer, later Bishop of London, described what he had seen during his ten-year stay in France. 'The husbandman in France, all that he hath gotten in his whole life, loseth it upon one day. For when so ever they have war (as they are never without it) the kings soldiers enter into the poor man's house, eateth and drinketh up all that ever he hath … the poor man never goeth to the market, to sell anything: but he payeth a toll, almost the half of that he selleth: he eateth neither pig, goose, capon, nor hen: but he must pay as much for the tribute of it there, as it might be bought for here: O unhappy and miserable men that live under this yoke…' The English audience, whom he was addressing were more fortunate. 'Thou are twice or thrice in the lifetime called upon to help thy country, with a subsidy or contribution: and they daily pay and never cease.'[27]

Sir John Fortescue who had also been in France for some years a century earlier, noted the same oppression of the rural population by government troops; 'so that there is not the least village there free from this miserable calamity, but that it is once or twice every year beggared by this kind of pilling (pillage).' This and other exactions, such as the salt tax, led to the great poverty of the rural inhabitants which Fortescue observed around him. In England, on the other hand, the position of rural inhabitants was different. The absence of heavy taxation, of billeted soldiers, and of internal taxes, meant that 'every inhabiter of that realm useth and enjoyeth at his pleasure all the fruits that his land or cattle beareth, with all the profits and commodities which by his own travail, or by the labour of others he gaineth by land or by water.'[28]

Adam Smith believed that one of the three necessities for the growth of wealth is 'easy taxes'.[29] Some have interpreted this as meaning light taxation, but that is not what Smith meant. He would have been well aware that the English were the most heavily taxed country in the West and that the affluent English usually produced much higher taxation than almost all other countries. Recently, Mokyr writes, 'Despite the uniqueness of their political system or perhaps because of it, the British did not enjoy low taxes but rather the reverse: during the eighteenth century they were taxed at rates far higher than anyone else in the world save the Dutch. Yet the tax burden never led to really major political crises.' By 1715 the government collected about 10 per cent of national income in taxes, by 1810 it was over 18 per cent.[30]

What Smith meant by 'easy' is something different and foreshadows the principles of modern systems. The first principle of taxation was equality. 'The subjects of every state ought to contribute towards the support of the government, as nearly as possible, in proportion to their respective abilities; that is, in proportion to the revenue which they respectively enjoy under the protection of the state.' This was achieved to an unusual extent in England, for though the rich benefited from an annual land and income tax (though there was the equivalent of death duties), they did not escape taxes altogether, and the very poor were protected to a certain extent.

Mokyr shows how taxes tended to fall most heavily on the large English 'middling sort', rather than on the very rich or

the very poor. 'For most of the eighteenth century, customs revenues and excise taxes accounted for about two-thirds of the
state's revenues. Such taxes are highly regressive, so that the
rich and powerful represented in Parliament paid a proportion-
ally low amount whereas many of them were clearly beneficia-
ries of the expenditures. Yet, unlike the nobility in France and
Spain, they were not exempt from these taxes; they just paid less
than what seems to us their fair share.'[31]

The burden on the middle classes grew over time and found
a new form in the growth of the 'national debt', where many
citizens trusted their government and lent it money – a pretty
unusual state of affairs. 'By the middle of the eighteenth century, the national debt was owned by perhaps 50,000 individuals,
many of them located in London, a powerful group that guarded
its interests well. Taxes in Britain were paid disproportionately
by the middle class – neither gentry nor paupers, which was already large in 1700, and kept growing throughout the eighteenth
century. This class was large enough to pay for the extravagantly expensive wars that others decided to fight. It did so, not so
much by being taxed to pay for the war as much as by being
taxed to service the debt that paid for the war.'[32]

Secondly, Smith argued, that taxation must be certain – that
is to say predictable and not arbitrary. 'The time of payment, the
manner of payment, the quantity to be paid, ought all to be clear
and plain to the contributor, and to every other person.' This
seems to have been achieved in England.

Thirdly, Smith wrote that 'Every tax ought to be levied at the
time, or in the manner, in which it is most likely to be convenient for the contributor to pay it.' Smith might have expanded
this to state that it should be paid on items which were not of
such vital necessity that the very poor were crippled by taxation
in hard times. Mokyr points out that 'There are good explanations of the British state's ability to tax its citizens so heavily
without leading to a tax revolt or even to massive non-compli-

ance... Parliament avoided taxing the basic necessity of life, namely bread.'[33]

The situation is explained by Laing. 'We have no direct taxes in England affecting the labouring class, or reaching so low as the class-tax or poll-tax, or the trade-tax of the Continental states. House-tax, window-tax, income-tax, property-tax, or assessed tax of any description, never come down to the labouring man with us, not even to the tradesman, artisan, or master or journeyman workman in good circumstances, and belonging rather to the lower ranks of the middle than to the lower class. His contributions to the public revenue, are taken from him altogether in heavy indirect taxes on what he consumes. His tea, tobacco, ale, spirits, and every article of luxury he uses, is taxed more or less exorbitantly ... a man escapes them just in proportion to his frugal, economical, sober habits.'[34]

Finally, it should be economically collected, as little as possible being siphoned off in the collection. This was achieved by the development of perhaps the first modern and efficient taxation system in Europe. 'What is equally interesting is that the British tax collection system was efficient by the standards of the time, as taxes were collected by a professional administration and no longer farmed out to private entrepreneurs, a source of endless chagrin elsewhere in Europe.'[35]

Furthermore, a large part of what was levied was returned in the form of services to the individual – in communications, education, naval defence and imperial protection. So a largely 'modern' and capitalistic taxation regime was in place in this civilization many centuries ago. Furthermore the taxes were to be agreed on by those who paid the bulk of them, that is the upper and middling ranks represented in parliament. The cry of 'no taxation without representation' of the American settlers was based on comparing their condition to that in the homeland.

Finally, it is worth noting that a good deal of the taxation – for local services such as helping the poor, local highways and bridges, was administered at a local level by the middle classes, the gentry, yeomanry and ordinary citizens who lived in the localities and who collected and disbursed what was needed in a way analogous to modern council taxation.

So what Smith was holding up as an ideal was realized to a considerable extent. Without much objection or blatant tax evasion or avoidance, the system raised enormous sums for the British state and for local community amenities, and hence played a crucial part in the development of a modern social and economic world. It had its roots in medieval England, but was unlike anything anywhere in the world, with the possible exception of Holland. Taxation is a good index of many other aspects of a society – the prevalence of trust or its obverse, corruption, the nature of power relations, the size and wealth of the various classes. The unusual tax system is both a sign of, and a vital part of the form of civil society and democracy that emerged in England.

♦

THERE IS A widespread tendency for the family to become the ultimate unit of political power. This operates at all levels. Within the family the head often has patriarchal, that is almost total, power over other members of the family – over women, children, younger brothers and so on. Family members are not citizens of a commonwealth, but subjects of a king (the father). Parallels tend to be drawn between the absolute monarchy and the family.

Each family becomes a political unit in opposition to other families, a tendency described, for instance, for Mediterranean countries as 'amoral familism'. Loyalties are enormously strong within the family, but weak outside. The loyalty to kin far exceeds that to non–kin, including the political authorities. This is a world of feuds, factions and familistic and dynastic quarrels, famously displayed in Romeo and Juliet, the novels of Walter Scott and much literature.

At a higher level, the nobility or chiefs (for example in a Scottish clan system) have enormous power – the world of the over mighty subject. Political power is decentralized and flows through blood ties. This is a world of over–mighty subjects, of mafia, of outlaws and bandits of nepotism, of patronage and fictive kinship ties being used to give and receive favours.

If we turn to the documents for England during the period from the thirteenth century onwards, how far does it seem that political power is coincidental with family ties? Within the family, power is not patriarchal; women and children and servants are, as Locke pointed out, in a contractual relationship towards the head of the household. He is a limited monarch, subject to the law. He has never had the power of sale, of life and death, unlimited chastisement, rights over personal possessions, which is to be found in the *patria potestas* of Roman Law.

At the next level up, we find that village politics is not based on family ties. There are no family feuding groups, no mafia, no strong divisions along family lines. Patronage of kin is weakly developed – even between father and son, let alone more distant kin. Political obligations are to the State directly, not to one's close kin. Military recruitment and recruitment to national politics, elections and political posts are usually on the basis of non–kinship ties. Succession to local offices of power, Justices of the Peace, constableships and so on, are not on the basis of kinship.

Godparenthood, which is often used as a quasi–kinship mechanism of recruiting a following or obtaining favours, is undeveloped. On the other hand, there is a developed concept of the political individual, who has rights in and of himself, independent of his family. In fact, the source of political power is in the end, economic. Any male with enough property has a right to vote. But law hedges about all political power.

In conclusion, one might say that power flowed chiefly from wealth and that political power was independent of kinship. One's allies were not mainly kin, but those with whom one exchanged and collaborated. One found one's way through the patronage of non–kinsmen, through a master of some kind, whether in apprenticeship or education. This represents one of the very few known cases of a large society where the basis of politics is not the family. The curiously institutionalized and separated political sphere, with its absence of familism, is a crucial feature at the root of modern democracy, which treats each individual as having equal political rights, whatever his family connections.

◆

ANOTHER SIDE EFFECT of the political system of devolution of power, combined with affluence and a particular capitalistic and individualistic system, was the development of the first national poor relief system. In a number of European and other nations, religious charities or individual philanthropists helped the poor. The English poor laws however were unique; nowhere else in the world did one have a well-organized and compulsory system of poor relief like the English one. 'If there was any striking and unique feature in the British eighteenth-century polity, it was the Poor Law. .... Britain's Poor Law was far more inclusive and generous than that of any other country. Until 1834, there was considerable redistribution from the well-to-do and the powerful to the poorest citizens. It differed from other eighteenth-century European relief systems in that it was not financed by voluntary donations but by a local tax, the poor rate. The Poor Law was in part motivated by a genuine concern for the poor, especially those whose destitution was patently not their fault, such as orphans, invalids, and the aged.' In the late eighteenth and early nineteenth century it covered between ten and fourteen per cent of the population.[36]

The effects amazed visitors. In the early eighteenth century the Abbé Prévost wrote: 'In all the towns and villages of England you find hospitals for the sick, almshouses and asylums for the poor and aged of either sex, schools for the education of children, in short a thousand monuments of piety and zeal for religion and their country.'[37] The system required the presence of thousands of volunteers who would give time and money in their villages and towns to organize this early welfare state. Simond wrote that 'One of the marvels of English liberty is the multitude of men who give their time to public works in every town and country and whose mind and character are formed by the occupations and duties of a citizen.'[38]

Rochefoucauld noted that once a person had a right of settlement in a parish – in other words, had been living there for a year – then 'This right entitles him to be treated if he falls sick for any length of time and is unable to pay; to be taken care of if he falls into poverty; and to receive assistance in his old age – assistance which in England is so excessive that, once given, the recipients have no further need to work and from poverty they pass to ease and idleness.'[39] The provision for the poor led to a paradox, as Kames noted at the same time. 'England in particular overflows with beggars, though in no other country are the indigent so amply provided for'.[40] There was a system already operating at the parish level in the medieval period, but this was unified and institutionalized, with systematic taxation and buildings, under Queen Elizabeth in the sixteenth century.

It is not difficult to see how this system fitted with the family structure. As many are discovering today, with high social and geographical mobility, where the family is no longer a fundamental unit of production and consumption, there is a large question as to who will look after the old, the sick or the out-of-work. A state provision of welfare and a solid pension system has to be built up. It is one of the fundamental institutions of modernity. Such a system was in embryo present in England many hundreds of years ago – well before any other country.

It might be thought that such a national safety net would dry up private charity, yet it was not so. In America and in England private charity flourished. Saussure wrote. 'Here are some traits of charity. No rich person dies without leaving large legacies. Most parishes in London and in the country have hospitals for the sick, the poor, and the aged; also charity schools were poor children are fed, taught, and clothed'.[41] Furthermore, those who tried to unite to better the position of the workers were not regarded as enemies to be destroyed, as often was the case in absolutist countries, but as people to be engaged with. 'For the British employer, a union may have been an adversary, a strike vexing and costly, the effort of labour to raise wages chimerical. He did not like these things, but he was prepared to face up to them. For the continental employer, however, a union was a conspiracy against public order and morals; a strike, an act of ingratitude; the effort of labour to raise wages, the indiscipline of an impatient son. All of this was evil. And there is no negotiating with evil.'[42]

♦

As Maitland shows, the English political system is continuous and early established. Maitland could end his two-volume history of English law in 1307 because by then the English legal, administrative and political framework was established. It would remain intrinsically the same from then on.

The absence of a radical break can be seen in the absence of political revolutions in English history. The one supposed 'Revolution', according to certain historians, was the English Civil War. Yet at the time it was not regarded as a revolution, but more, as Clarendon called it, a Great Rebellion. In other words it changed the players (for a time) but not the rules.

Tocqueville, looking from post-revolutionary France, stressed that the English 'revolution' was entirely different. The ruling class was not swept away. 'Your biographies show the truth of your remark, that no two things can be more unlike than your Revolution of 1640 and ours of 1789. No two things, in fact, can be more unlike than the state of your society and of ours at those two periods'. The ruling groups were 'divided; they were opposed to one another, and they fought; but never, for a single day, did they abdicate'. It was relatively mild – not a class war. 'The consequences were, less boldness of intention, less violence of action, and a regularity, a mildness, even a courtesy, admirably described by you, which showed itself even in the employment of physical force'.[43] Writing about his own time, Tocqueville wrote 'if one understands by a revolution a violent and sudden change, then England does not seem ripe for such an event, and I see many reasons for thinking that it will never be so'.[44]

Burckhardt, from Germany, says the same. 'In the Civil War in England, quite particularly, we find nothing of the kind. It has no place in the present discussion because it did not for one moment attack the principles of civic life, never stirred up the supreme powers of the nation'.[45] And the 'Glorious Revolution' of 1688 was no revolution, but a restoration of an earlier tradition, resisting the revolution of the kind James II intended. So the development is of a gradual, continuous, evolutionary development - the 'changing same'. It was nothing like the French, Russian or Chinese revolutions which at their start swept everything away.

◆

THE SCOTTISH PHILOSOPHER and historian John Millar outlined the advantages of being an island. He noted that 'the fate of the English government was different from that of most of the other feudal governments upon the continent.' Furthermore, 'The fortunate situation of Great Britain, after the accession of James I, gave her little to fear from any foreign invasion, and superseded the necessity of maintaining a standing army, when the service of the feudal militia had gone into disuse'. Or, as he also comments, 'During the highest exaltation of the feudal monarchy in modern Europe, the safety which England derived from its insular situation, and its remote connection with the disputes and quarrels upon the continent, gave the sovereign ... few opportunities of acting as the general of the national forces'.[46]

The safety and strength was increased in 1603 'When King James of Scotland became King James of England, the country obtained the benefit of being an island, protected by the sea. There was no longer a hostile and warlike neighbour, compelling military preparation and the concentration of power, which made foreign governments absolute. An English officer once congratulated Moltke on the splendid army which he had created and led. The marshal shook his head, and replied that the German army was a terrible burden on the country, but that the long Russian frontier made it a necessity.'[47]

Continuing liberty depends on the wealth and strength of a country. Millar was well aware that many attempts to create liberal societies had been crushed by their neighbours – the Italian republics were an obvious example. Yet England was large enough and wealthy enough to protect itself – just – against Spaniards and later French attempts to conquer it.

Its growing wealth was also due to its geographical position. 'When the people of Europe had become qualified for extensive naval undertakings, the distance of Britain from the continent, and her situation as an island, afforded her a superiority to most other countries in the number of such harbours as have a free communication with all parts of the globe'. Likewise, 'Her insular situation was, at the same time, no less advantageous with respect to inland trade, from the numerous bays and rivers, which, by intersecting the country in different places, extended the benefit of water-carriage to the greater part of the inhabitants'.[48]

The fact that England was an island also fed into the unusual social structure – the odd aristocratic – gentry – yeomanry shape which I have discussed. This meant, as Taine noted, the 'English government is stable because the English have a supply of natural representatives'.[49] At the local level, where democracy flourished through the magistracy and the jury system, there was no need for a professional government bureaucracy. The upper middle classes ran the country and were tough and opposed to absolutism. They were wealthy, literate and ubiquitous. A powerful ruler could not just gain the support of the aristocracy, he had to win the towns and the gentry. As Charles and James found these could not easily be bullied or bribed. So England grew in its peculiar devolved yet centralized shape – and after half a millenium of such a system it was only natural that it applied the same system to the ruling of its Empire.

The advantages continued into the period of industrialization as Hobson pointed out. He noted that 'In many branches of the textile arts, especially in silk spinning and in dyeing, in pottery, printing, and other manufactures, more inventive genius and more skill were shown on the Continent, and there seemed *a priori* no reason why England should outstrip so signally her competitors.' He believed one of the explanations for why it did so was 'The insular character of Great Britain, her natural facilities for procuring raw materials of manufacture and supplies of foreign food to enable her population to specialise in manufacture, the number and variety of easily accessible markets for her manufacturers, gave her an immense advantage.' Above all England was free from the devastating warfare suffered by continental nations. Hobson argues that 'the most important factor determining the priority of England was the political condition of continental Europe at the very period when the new machinery and motor-power were beginning to establish confidence in the new industrial order. When Crompton's mule, Cartwright's power-loom, Watt's engines were transforming the industry of England, her continental rivals had all their energies absorbed in wars and political revolutions.'[50]

CHAPTER NOTES

1. *Property of Things*, II, 734.

2. Taine, *Notes*, 161-2.

3. Barker, *Character*, 33.

4. Muralt in Wilson, *Strange,* 54.

5. Voltaire, *Letters*, 41-2.

6. Montesquieu, *Spirit*, I, 307ff, 314, 315.

7. Jaspers, *Goal,* 160, 170, 203.

8. Tocqueville, *Journeys*, 4.

9. Tocqueville, *Democracy* (abridged), 64.

10. Tocqueville, *Journeys*, 75, 45.

11. Tocqueville, *Recollections*, 33.

12. Tocqueville, *Memoir*, 1 378.

13. Quoted in Drescher, *Tocqueville*, 91.

14. Drescher, *Tocqueville*, 92.

15. Boesche, Tocqueville, 246.

16. Tocqueville, *Democracy* (abridged), 47.

17. Maitland, *Constitutional*, 32.

18. Maitland, *History*, I, 235.

19. Maitland, *History*, II, 265.

20. Maitland, *Constitutional,* 143.

21. Maitland, *History*, II, 515-6, 512, 173.

22. Fortescue, *Governance*, fol.33v.

23. Saussure, *Foreign*, 336, 179.

24. Saussure, *Foreign*, 336.

25. Saussure, *Foreign*, 351.

26. Stephen, *Liberty*; I owe this reference to Michael Lotus.

27. In Orwell, *Pamphleteers*, 29-33.

28. Fortescue, *Governance*, fols 80, 84v-85.

29. Smith, *Wealth*, II, 350-351 – where the following quotations from Smith are to be found.

30. Mokyr, *Enlightened*, 427, 429.

31. Mokyr, *Enlightened*, 427-8.

32. Mokyr, *Enlightened*, 431.

33. Mokyr, *Enlightened*, 431.

34. Laing, *Observations*, 303.

35. Mokyr, *Enlightened*, 432.

36. Mokyr, *Enlightened*, 440.

37. Quoted in Wilson, *Strange*, 87.

38. Wilson, *Strange*, 162.

39. Rochefoucauld, *Frenchman*, 27.

40. Kames, *Sketches*,III, 49.

41. Saussure, *Foreign*, 185-6.

42. Landes, *Prometheus*, 192.

43. Tocqueville, *Memoir*, 2 377-8.

44. Tocqueville, *Journeys*, 51.

45. Burckhardt, *Reflections*, 146.

46. Millar, *Historical*, III, 123-4.

47. Acton, *Modern*, 195.

48. Millar, *Historical*, II, 387-8.

49. Taine, *Notes*, 162.

50. Hobson, *Evolution*, 94, 96.

CHAPTER 11

LAW AND VIOLENCE

THIS IS, IN many ways, the most important peculiarity of England, both expressing and causing its different trajectory. It is really significant because the law and legal process is like the oil which allows the parts of a civilization to work together. If the essence of modernity is the separation and tension between the contrary demands of politics, religion, economy and society, it is the legal system which holds them in balance – and which underpins them all. It is difficult to conceive of a game of football or cricket without rules, referee or umpire.

In relation to the economy, for example, Adam Smith placed 'a due administration of justice', alongside peace and easy taxes, as one of the three requisites for wealth. The other half of *The Wealth of Nations* are his recently discovered *Lectures on Jurisprudence*, first published in 1978. Smith wrote about how English law seemed in its certainty, its complexity and its concern with property to be ideally suited to be a foundation for commercial capitalism. He noted for that 'there is no country in Europe, Holland itself non-excepted, of which the law is, upon the whole more favourable in this sort of industry.'[1] He also writes of 'that equal and impartial administration of justice which renders the rights of the meanest British subject respectable to the greatest, and which, by securing to every man the fruits of his own industry, gives the greatest and most effectual encouragement to ever sort of industry…'[2]

Almost all legal systems in history, including Roman Law, are based on the assumption that people are born unequal and remain so. Nobles and commoners, men and women, parents and children, free and slaves, all are permanently unequal. It is one of the central features of modern legal systems that this premise of legal inequality is rejected. Many believe that the premise of equal rights and duties was a product of the American or French revolutions. It is quite clear, however, that the idea of legal equality was fully established in England by the thirteenth century and that it was taken first to America, then to France and Europe. It has now come to dominate much of the world.

The idea that everyone is equal in the eyes of the law, that women, children, lower castes, all have rights of their own, was both a premise of English law and also, for example during the extension of British law in India, a deeply shocking concept. It cut across birth status and subverted the power relations of the castes and the family. In the middle of the nineteenth century, Maine noted that many complained that 'life in India had become intolerable since the English criminal laws had begun to treat women and children as if they were men.'[3]

Maitland shows that equality was found in England from very early. We have seen that the social classes had no particular legal status – aristocracy, gentry, yeomen and others were not legal, but culturally ascribed statuses. A duke was subject to the same law and had no privileges by birth even in comparison to a labourer. If the Queen breaks a speed limit or commits a crime she will be tried in the normal courts in England today.

This absence of birth-given status differences applies to everything. An uncle could not expect superior treatment to his nephew, a father to a son, a man to a woman, a King to his subject. The law regarded them all as individuals with rights to be adjudicated. 'The world into which Maitland's real actions fit is essentially a flat world, inhabited by equal neighbours.'[4]

The great shift which Maine thought of as the hallmark of modernity had happened in feudalism. 'The master who taught us that "the movement of the progressive societies has hitherto been a movement from Status to Contract," was quick to add that feudal society was governed by the law of contract. There is no paradox here.'[5] This was widespread in the tenth and eleventh centuries. Yet all over Europe contract turned back into status so that by the eighteenth century, most continental countries had legal and social systems based on blood and birth status differences, or in Tocqueville's well-chosen analogy a 'caste' society. Yet this never happened in England – the modern, egalitarian legal framework continued.

Of course, this does not mean that there was no inequality in practice. In the legal game you started with equal rights, but, as in any game, clever, and, in this case, well-funded players often had a great advantage. Money could buy better legal services, though, to a surprising degree, money could not buy the decisions. The jury system made it more difficult to buy and browbeat twelve other people, and high pay and prestige helped English judges avoid serious corruption. So that while money could be applied to making a better case, the outcome could only partially be determined through wealth and connections. Even the Crown could not buy itself out of its contractual obligations and when found at fault was also subject to a remorseless law. 'The distinction between high and low justice always remained foreign to the English system'.[6]

♦

THIS UNIFORMITY AND equality was implicit in Anglo-Saxon law, but was given its permanent stamp mainly in the eleventh to thirteenth centuries. Looking back from the present, it all seems very early. As Maitland wrote, 'If we could look at western Europe in the year 1272, perhaps the characteristic of English law which would earn the most prominence would be its precocity.' And it was modern; by 1272 'English law is modern in its uniformity, its simplicity and its certainty...'[7]

This was its attraction. Sir Edward Coke in the early seventeenth century wrote,

> There is no jewel in the world comparable to learning; no learning so excellent both for prince and subject, as knowledge of laws; and no knowledge of any laws (I speak of human) so necessary for all estates and for all causes, concerning goods, lands, or life, as the common laws of England. If the beauty of other countries be faded and wasted with bloody wars, thank God for the admirable peace, wherein this realm hath long flourished under the due administration of these laws: if thou readest of the tyranny of other nations, wherein powerful will and pleasure stands for law and reason, and where, upon conceit of mislike, men are suddenly poisoned, or otherwise murdered, and never called to answer; praise God for the justice of thy gracious Sovereign, who (to the world's admiration) governeth her people by god's goodness, in peace and prosperity by these laws, and punisheth not the greatest offender, no, though his offence be *crimen laesae Majestatis*, treason against her sacred person, but by the just and equal proceedings of law.[8]

How and why England remained what John Baker calls 'an island of law' is a large subject. Baker himself gives one of the most succinct accounts of how England resisted status-based Roman Law which swept across the rest of Europe from the fifteenth to eighteenth centuries.[9] Tocqueville gives an even more concise account. 'Aided by Roman law and by its interpreters, the kings of the fourteenth and fifteenth centuries succeeded in founding absolute monarchy on the ruins of the free institutions of the middle ages. The English alone refused to adopt it, and they alone have preserved their independence'.[10]

♦

ONE ASPECT WHICH made the English legal system feel 'modern' was that it was, from a very early period, universal in its geographical coverage. The Anglo-Saxons in unifying England had brought it into one unified legal system and the Angevins finalized this. As Tocqueville noted, 'That is what happened in France, where the barons went so far as to abolish the right of appeal to the king's courts. That is what did not happen in England. William, master of all, gave lavishly but kept still more'.[11] Bloch later wrote,

> Thus it might be said that the kings reassembled France rather than unified it. Observe the contrasts between France and England. In England there was the Great Charter; in France, in 1314-5, the Charters granted to the Normans, to the people of Languedoc, to the Bretons, the Burgundians, to the Picards, to the people of Champagne, of Auvergne, of the *Basses Marches* of the West, of Berry, and of Nevers. In England there was Parliament; in France, the provincial Estates, always much more frequently convoked and on the whole more active than the States-General. In England there was the common law, almost untouched by regional exceptions; in France the vast medley of regional "customs".[12]

Maitland outlines the process. The custom of the King's court becomes the custom of England, the Common Law. The process was one where 'Slowly but surely justice done in the King's name by men who are the King's servants becomes the most important kind of justice, reaches into the remotest corners of the land, grasps the small affairs of small folk as well as the great affairs of earls and barons.'[13] 'Our system is a single system and

revolves round Westminster Hall'.[14] This was strongly related
to the small island effect: 'England is small: it can be governed
by uniform law: it seems to invite general legislation. Also
we should notice that the kingship of England, when once it
exists, preserves its unity: it is not partitioned among brothers
and cousins.'[15] By the end of Maitland's history of English Law
(1307), and indeed before, all of England was governed by a
centralized, yet delegated, unified and tough Common Law.

One striking feature throughout its history is that despite
the voluminous records of cases, the law was ultimately based
on oral traditions and on remembered precedents rather than a
fixed written code. An oral, precedent based, system has only
been found in two of the fourteen legal traditions surveyed by
Wigmore, namely England and Japan.[16] So there was an inbuilt
flexibility and subjectivity. Orality allows constant small change
and adjustment; 'the memory of man' is fairly flexible. It is
constantly made and re-made by judges.

In the thirteenth century compendium which formed the basis of English law, Bracton's *On the Laws and Customs of England*, a distinction was made between law and custom. This
has always been central to English civilization. Law is the language, custom is the dialect. Laws are the underlying rules of
the game – thou shalt not kill, thou shalt not rob, thou shalt not
pick up the ball in football unless you are the goalkeeper, thou
shalt not hit below the belt. The customs are variable, cultural
and local – you can eat, dress, believe as you like within the
laws and according to your customs. The law requires an heir
if property has not been disposed of before death – but whether
it is one heir or a group, the youngest or the oldest, a man or a
woman, that is up to local custom as found, for example, in the
various customs of each English manor. The law requires that a
man leaves property to his widow. but what part should be left
is often determined by custom. The Statutes of the University of
Cambridge determine the general rules. But the customs of each
Cambridge College are different.

This distinction between English Common Law and local custom, which started on one island, became a flexible device to provide the underpinning of a world Empire. There were the British laws, but local magistrates and rulers could also keep the customs of their own peoples.

Another parallel system of increasing importance was the development of Equity courts, which dealt with equity or fairness, rather than strict law. Laws, however detailed, can never produce real justice, for there are many situations where something is clearly wrong, but not strictly provable to be so by law. So 'equity', which grew up in England under the protection of the powerful Lord Chancellor from the fourteenth century, filled a large gap. It was particularly important in relation to property, with which no systematic legal system can properly deal on the basis of written laws and documents. Thus the Court of Chancery, for example, dealt with cases concerned with unwritten promises, good faith, trust, lost documents, the rights of disadvantaged groups including women, children and the poor. It was particularly important in dealing with the ambiguities and complexities created by the growth of a capitalistic world system where rigid laws could often not be applied.[17]

Finally there was a parallel system of the law of the Church, canon law, which dealt with morality, sin and strictly church matters which lie outside Common law. The Church was under the Law, and the secular courts never condemned people to prison or death on the basis of trials in the Church courts, as happened in Catholic countries with the Inquisition. Yet much of the popular control of morality could be left to the Church Courts until the later seventeenth century when they died away.

♦

ONE CENTRAL MANIFESTATION of these differences was in legal process, particularly in criminal cases where the subject and the Crown clashed. In the Roman law system of the examining magistrate, a State appointed official is both the interrogator and the judge. He could in the past use torture, he could use informers, he could threaten and lie, he could use all and any means to try to extract 'the truth' and when he was satisfied of guilt, he must force a confession – again under torture if necessary. After the confession, in serious cases the person who confessed was burnt, hung drawn and quartered, broken on the wheel or whatever the often extremely harsh punishment was.

In England it was different. A formal accusation in the form of an indictment, stating precisely what, where and when the offence took place, had to be entered. This was first examined by the Grand Jury – a group of local gentry unafraid of the Crown or of the accused and his friends. If they thought the case needed to be answered it was entered as an indictment to proceed to trial.

The trial was in open court, which the public could attend. There was a jury made of the peers of the accused. Even this jury was subject to some approval by the accused. 'Six-and-thirty persons are chosen as jurymen. The accused is allowed to refuse twelve of the number without giving any reason, and twelve others, but giving his reasons, and the twelve remaining men will constitute the jury.'[18]

The judge was an umpire, there to see fair play between the prosecutors and the defence. The jury were there to state who had won. It was like a boxing match or dancing competition. Only if the prosecution could prove 'beyond reasonable doubt', and on the basis that a person was 'innocent until proven guilty', was the accused pronounced guilty. 'Englishmen say that it is better that twelve culprits should escape human justice rather than that one innocent man should perish'.[19]

No torture or threat of torture was permissible. Barbaro, a Venetian ambassador in the sixteenth century reported the non-use of torture as an interesting fact in England.[20] In the early eighteenth century Saussure wrote that 'In this country torture is not resorted to make a man confess a crime; it is thought that many an innocent person might be sacrificed were this barbarous custom adopted'.[21] The major exception was that a person must plead guilty or not guilty (ie recognize that the court had the right to hear him or her). If they refused, physical pressure could be applied – in earlier periods squashing with heavy weights until they pleaded one way or the other. There was no need for a forced confession. If found guilty by their peers, those accused could maintain their innocence – but were guilty in the eyes of the law. They were then fined, imprisoned or executed by hanging.

♦

IN DICKENS' *BLEAK House*, the Chancery lawyer answers Mr Jarndyce's complaint about the judicial systemby saying, 'we are a prosperous community, Mr Jarndyce, a very prosperous community, Mr. Jarndyce, a very great country. This is a great system, Mr Jarndyce, and would you wish a great country to have a little system?' He was right.

If we look at the business of the various courts of England, or if we look at the great legal treatises explaining the laws and customs of England, from Bracton through Coke to Blackstone, we see that about ninety percent of the cases and the discussion is about property law. The English obsession with wealth is reflected in the most complex, sophisticated and inscrutable set of clashing and contested sets of rules about making money in the world. The types of property, the complex bundles of rights which could be distinguished, the ability to share, sub-let, protect and pass around these rights leads into a bewildering maze of property law. As David Sugarman, director of Lancaster University's Centre for Law and Society, noted, 'A King's Counsel informed the Royal Property Commissioners in 1829 that there were no more than six persons who understood the laws of real property'.[22]

Max Weber was faced with a problem here, for the English case, the first capitalist country, seemed to go against his idea that rationalization is the central background feature of capitalism. 'On the one hand, England seemed to lack the calculable, logically formal, legal system that he frequently identified as necessary for initial capitalist development. On the other hand, capitalism once it became established in England, had little, if any, appreciable effect on the rationalisation of English law...'[23]

A number of features provided the essential tools for capitalist growth. I have already touched on the absolute support for individual property, which cannot be violated by naked power. A person was safeguarded against the Crown or his fellows. If property – that is, rights of many different kinds – were formally attacked, there were a host of lawyers and courts to whom the attacker could be taken. As Maitland observes, by the thirteenth century, and drawing on earlier centuries, there had emerged 'that wonderful calculus of estates which, even in our own day, is perhaps the most distinctive feature of English private law.'[24] As Emerson was also to write,

> With this power of creation, and this passion for independence, property has reached an ideal perfection. It is felt and treated as the national life-blood. The laws are framed to give property the securest possible basis, and the provisions to lock and transmit it have exercised the cunningest heads in a profession which never admits a fool. The rights of property nothing but felony and treason can override. The house a castle which the king cannot enter. The Bank is a strong-box to which the king has no key.'[25]

There were many ingenious fictions and devices developed which have become the bedrocks of modern global capitalism. For example the idea of patents. 'Here Britain led the Continent by a large margin. British patent law dates from 1624, whereas France did not have a similar law until 1791 and most other European countries established patent laws only in the early nineteenth century.'[26]

♦

THE ENGLISH CREATED hybrids which are impossible in the more centralized and principled Roman Law. Maitland showed in his work on trusts how the English developed artificial communities, non-incorporated corporations, which merged the law of persons and of things and which appalled European lawyers. The English could do this partly, as M.G. Smith notes, because the fundamental starting point is different in Roman and Common Law. 'British law permits equally flexible accommodation. Per contra, French law which most perfectly expresses the dominant rational Western theory of law, assumes a primary sovereign corporation, the state, and accordingly denies the legality of prior or independent units unless the latter are expressly recognized by the state'.[27] So in England the Crown, as Adam Smith advocated, is the umpire, the referee, the arbitrator, but ultimately a spectator in the capitalist game.

Of course it was all largely a game or fiction. Emerson noted, 'Their law is a network of fictions. Their property, a scrip of certificate of right to interest on money that no man ever saw.'[28] There were fictions which have made the City of London, the Stock Exchange, the Bank of England, the heart of English wealth throughout the imperial and post-imperial period. It was higgledy-piggledy because it has to deal with compromises, to overcome contradictions. As Taine wrote, in England 'there is no code of laws as with us, based on implied philosophical principles, but a mass of statutes and precedents more or less disparate and sometimes contradictory'.[29]

This is the innate nature of a system where there is constant tension between the separated spheres – economic, political, social, and economic. From the vantage point of systematizers, it is a mess, yet ' the creation of a completely original legal system' in England was an achievement.[30] English law adjudicates between the powerful contesting forces and thereby keeps the productive balance and tension to stop the Crown, the Church, the Nobility and the Merchants from becoming dominant. It turns anger into process – drawing it out, breaking it into small bits, and channeling it like a complex game. Law is the essential underpinning for self-confidence and sustained development.

The end of all this is a paradox. On the one hand, English behaviour is minutely regulated by a combination of law, customs and social etiquette. On the other hand, people feel free. Huizinga had found that 'Life in England had seemed less earnest, the air less heavy and the people, puritanical as their law-makers might be, more light-hearted.' This seems to be because they choose between the rival pulls of their political, social, economic and religious obligations, none of which dominates their life to the exclusion of the rest. This combination of constraint and freedom is described by Pierre Maillaud, approvingly quoted by Huizinga:

> There are more restrictions in England on the exercise of the daily freedoms than elsewhere, yet there is at the same time an almost unrivalled sense of personal independence because the plain human relationship between people is uncommonly flexible, because acquaintanceship, friendship or even kinship places neither burdens nor fetters on the individual nor do they trespass on his privacy... Attraction, love, companionship are all less binding, less exacting ... The foreign visitor feels an uncanny elasticity...he senses, without fathoming it, what Clive Bell describes as the "frivolity" of the English, a disinclination to overstress, to strain things, activities, pastimes or human beings to the utmost."[31]

♦

AS FOR THE policing which led to the maintenance of order and the avoiding of offences against the Crown, this again was unusual and an example of distributed and consensual system.[32] The basic system in medieval England onwards combined two law-enforcement and detection systems. One was that people were divided into small units or 'tithings', required mutually to police their group and to be communally responsible. As well, each householder took it in turn to be a parish constable.

The duties of such an officer listed in the sixteenth century are described by Mildred Campbell:

In his oath the constable swore to arrest all rioters or persons breaking the king's peace; to apprehend all felons and barrators [people contentious in law], or pursue them with hue and cry if they tried to escape to another parish; to apprehend all rogues, vagabonds, nightwalkers, and other suspects; to keep an eye on the people who managed alehouses, ordinaries and inns, for the curbing of unlawful games and inordinate drinking; and to present all offenders to the proper court, according to the nature of their misdemeanor.' Furthermore, they should arrest all those who were supporters of the pope, failed to attend church regularly, maintain archery, help to find labourers to save crops at harvest time, see that the surveyors of the highways were chosen, test the quality of malt, execute all warrants given to them by J.P.'s. They were frequently given other duties, including levying money for the repair of bridges or to supplement the poor stock. 'And often a multitude of smaller details, from the mending of the village stocks to assisting unfortunates who came through the parish with a permit to beg, fell within the range of their duties.'[33]

Just as the gentry class provided the magistracy, so it was the 'middling sort' – the yeomen and husband and large numbers of artisans and small shopkeepers – who acted as constables. They were not armed, they were part of the community, and they took it in turn. If they failed in their duties or colluded in crime, those just above them, the Justices of the Peace, could discipline them.

In other words there was no professional police force; 'the feeling that professional police on the French model would be the death of traditional English liberties was deeply rooted in the political culture'.[34] There was no use of the army. 'The English form of government does not admit of the maintenance of any standing troops, even in small numbers, for the arrest of malefactors, such as would correspond to our constabulary.'[35]

The absence of armed police reflected an unarmed populace. People might have had small knives, but guns or large weapons were strictly controlled and only the gentry tended to have them. For example, a study of an English parish quite near to the Scottish border between 1500 and 1720 showed, from inventories taken at death, that over nine-tenths of the population seem not to have had even hunting weapons.[36]

It was a country where there was real support for the police. 'My friend added that here, when an arrested man starts to struggle, the people on the spot ask what it's all about and if they consider the policeman within his rights, lend him a hand. In the same way, whenever there are disturbances all classes provide volunteer constables. On the whole, whereas we *suffer* our government, the English *support* theirs.'[37] The police were usually not seen as oppressive, armed, agents of the state as they almost always are, but local, 'one of us', yet with responsibilities to maintain the peace.

It seems to have worked in creating a safe countryside. As Sir Thomas Overbuy put it, a milkmaid 'dares go alone and unfold sheep in the night, and fears no manners of ill because she means none'.[38] Much earlier, a churchwarden in the reign of William I wrote that 'everyone may travel through England with his belt full of gold without danger…'[39] Another form of safety was that people felt secure from arbitrary arrest. As Rochefoucauld wrote, 'The right of not being arrested save for felony is peculiar to England. If you happen to be unjustly arrested you may always proceed against the magistrate who has made an unjust use of his power, and the considerable fine which he will incur will make him hesitate to make the mistake a second time.'[40] Orwell singled this out: '… everyone takes it for granted that the law, such as it is, will be respected, and feels a sense of outrage when it is not. Remarks like "They can't run me in, I haven't done anything wrong", or "They can't do that; it's against the law", are part of the atmosphere of England'.[41]

There were some highwaymen near London in the early eighteenth century. Yet there were no lawless regions – water margins, forests, and mountain fastnesses, legal no-go areas which we find in most peasant civilizations where bandits live. Even Robin Hood was probably a myth. My study of the borders of England and Scotland, the likely area for banditry showed crime, but capitalist crime and not banditry.

The outcome is well captured by George Orwell. He had not been impressed by arrogant English imperialism in Burma and was not fond of the ruling class. Yet he also wrote, 'Here one comes upon an all-important English trait: the respect for constitutionalism and legality, the belief in "the law" as something above the State and above the individual, something which is cruel and stupid, of course, but at any rate *incorruptible*'. In a famous passage he wrote: 'The gentleness of the English civilization is perhaps its most marked characteristic. You notice it the instant you set foot on English soil. It is a land where the bus conductors are good-tempered and the policemen carry no revolvers.'[42]

◆

THAT PEACEABLENESS HAS other expressions and correlates. One was the absence of feuding. The feud – a perpetual oscillating blood competition, usually between kinship groups, but also sometimes village communities or even castes – is almost ubiquitous elsewhere. It is found particularly in pastoral societies such as Scotland, Albania and Montenegro, in the Middle East and North Africa, China, and elsewhere through much of history. Its absence in England is therefore remarkable. There was some element of feuding in late Anglo-Saxon England and the payments were carefully specified. Yet in England, from at least the Norman period, there is no evidence of institutionalized feuding. Feuding in England, we are told, was eradicated 'with marvellous suddenness' by the thirteenth century.[43] In England after the Conquest, 'the disappearance of any legal right to vengeance was one of the aspects of the royal "tyranny"'.[44]

Royal justice set itself against all private vengeance – anyone who took the law into his or her own hands was fiercely punished by the State. 'Vengeance is mine, I will repay' was the view of the State and this remains true until today. There are still laws which prevent a householder from going beyond reasonable self-defence – keeping an unlicensed gun, pursuing and shooting an intruder and lynching are all often severely punished.

The general tranquillity of the countryside can also be seen in the absence of defensive fortifications over the last six hundred years. In most countries it was essential to defend the village and the house. Pastor Moritz contrasted English towns with Prussian: 'No walls, no gates, no sentries, no garrisons. You pass through town and village as freely and unhindered as through wide-open nature'.[45] Laing wrote of 'our open unwalled towns' and Emerson wrote, 'They have no revolutions; no horse-guards dictating to the crown; no Parisian *poissardes* and barricades; no mob; but drowsy habitude, daily dress-dinners, wine, and ale, and beer, and gin, and sleep.'[46]

All of this, 'due administration of justice' and generalized 'peace' constituted two out of three of Adam Smith's *desiderata* for the 'natural progress' of wealth. To be able to assume peace and order, to trust that the general populace will abide by, and even esteem, the law, is an important foundation for modern capitalism – another aspect of trust and the ability to calculate rationally on costs. The absence of the 'friction of violence', which normally raises transaction costs (as we can currently see, for example, in piracy off the Somali coast), the assumption of good will and good order, is unusual in history and worked in incalculable ways to improve the positive feedback of wealth into further order and then to further wealth. Just one example, from historian David S. Landes, is worth quoting: '

> Generally speaking, Britain took social order for granted. The industrialist had no illusions about the hostility of the working class or the possibility of violence; but he never doubted that the law would prevail…His French counterpart…was never sure when labour unrest or unemployment would turn into political revolution.[47]

This 'island of law' spread from England to North America in the seventeenth century and then, in the eighteenth century, to India. It has now influenced many of the legal systems around the world. Its opposite, which covered all of Continental Europe with the revival of late Roman Law from the fourteenth century, is worth noting. It is the system which, with varieties, is to be found in most agrarian civilizations – centralized, rule generating, attempting to find a solution to every problem before it occurs, giving the State immense powers and the citizen or subject, little protection.

CHAPTER NOTES

1. Smith, *Wealth*, I, 442.

2. Quoted in Wrigley, 'Modernization', 238.

3. Maine, *Communities*, 116.

4. Milsom in Maitland, *History*, I, xlvii.

5. Maitland, *History*, II, 232-3

6. Bloch, *Feudal*, II, 370.

7. Maitland, *History*, I, 224, 225.

8. Coke, *Reports*, II, preface.

9. Baker, *History*, 11ff

10. Tocqueville, *Memoir*, I 428.

11. Tocqueville, *Journeys*, 4.

12. Bloch, *Feudal*, II, 425-6.

13. Maitland, *English Law*, I, 84.

14. Maitland 'Why', 483.

15. Maitland, *History*, I, 21.

16. Wigmore, *Panorama*

17. See Maitland, *Equity*.

18. Saussure, *Foreign*, 118.

19. Saussure, *Foreign*, 119.

20. Sumner, *Folkways*, 256.

21. Saussure, *Foreign*, 119.

22. Sugarman, 'Law', 17.

23. Trubek, quoted in Sugarman, 'Law', 10.

24. Maitland, *History*, II, 11.

25. Emerson, *English*, 127.

26. Mokyr, *Lever*, 247.

27. Smith, *Corporations*, 131.

28. Emerson, *English*, 77.

29. Taine, *Notes*, 210.

30. Bloch, *Feudal*, I 274.

31. Huizinga, *Confessions*, 68.

32. For a longer account, Macfarlane, *Culture*, chapter 3.

33. Campbell, *Yeoman*, 320-1.

34. McLynn, *Crime*, 17

35. Rochefoucauld, *Frenchman*, 118.

36. Macfarlane, *Culture*, 66.

37. Taine, *Notes*, 179

38. In Morley *Seventeenth*, 70.

39. Bloch, *Feudal*, II 412.

40. Rochefoucauld, *Frenchman*, 117.

41. Orwell, *Lion*, 45.

42. Orwell, *Lion*, 44, 41

43. Wormald, 'Feud', 55, citing Maitland.

44. Bloch, *Feudal*, 1 128.

45. Porter, *Eighteenth*, 254.

46. Laing, *Observations*, 166; Emerson, *English*, 127.

47. Landes, *Prometheus*, 191.

CHAPTER 12

EDUCATION, LANGUAGE AND ART

IN THE PAST, education in England was a path to social mobility – as it still is. With no legal statuses and the many parallel ladders, it was the way to move up, or to move one's children up. One view of what education was about in the late Imperial phase is as follows:

The mere accumulation of knowledge stunts rather than educates the mind…[England] still holds a leadership, almost unchallenged except by other English speaking countries, in that education of character which is obtained from individual activities, rather than from instruction whether verbal or in print. The playground had a notable share in the "real" education of her youth…[1]

Taine describes how the boarding school prepares boys for the future in an individualistic, capitalistic, competitive, yet orderly and co-operative society.

> On the whole, then, human nature is treated here with more respect and is less interfered with. Under the influence of an English education boys are like the trees in an English garden; under that of our own, like the pleached and pollarded trees of Versailles. Here, for instance, schoolboys are almost as free as undergraduates... Initiative and responsibility: it is curious to see babies of twelve raised to the dignities of manhood.[2]

Taine examines team games and sports:

> Here then, thus early, are the seeds of the spirit of association, an apprenticeship in both obedience and command, since every cricket team accepts a discipline and appoints a leader. But this principle is applied very much more widely; boys and youths together form an organised body, a sort of small, distinct State with it own chiefs and its own laws. The chiefs are the pupils in the highest class ('sixth form'), more especially the fifteen highest pupils in the school ('monitors') and, in each house, the highest pupil. They maintain order, see that the rules are obeyed and, in general, do the same work as our ushers. They prevent the strong from bullying the weak, are arbitrators in all disputes, take a hand when a small boy gets into some kind of trouble with a villager or a shop-keeper, and punish delinquents. In short, pupils in England are governed by pupils, and each one, having first been subject to authority, comes in due course to wield it. During his final year each is enrolled on the side of the rules, the law, and it becomes his business to see that it is respected; he learns its value, and adopts it of his own free will, instead of kicking against it, which is what a French schoolboy would not fail to do.

Taine noticed the result of this system:

> Consequently when they leave school and began their adult lives they are less inclined to consider the rules absurd and authority ridiculous. They reconcile liberty and subordination, are nearer to an understanding of the conditions in which a society can exist and the rights and duties of a citizen.[3]

Children were independent legal, social, moral persons in relation to their parents and became 'adult' very quickly. 'The English children come very early to be rational, conversable beings'.[4]

Schools (and for others servanthood and apprenticeship) took you out of the home – they separated economy and society, and placed you on the ladders of market and social mobility. As separated individuals you were fully right-and-duty bearing in the law, and your social networks, religious and political beliefs, were not shaped by your parents but by friends, teachers and employers. You learnt to be alone, to draw on your own resources, to be independent and tough. Among other things, this would prepare you for extreme hardship: 'as the businessman Roger Cooper explained on leaving Iran in 1991, anyone who had been through his experiences at Clifton College in Bristol could have survived the time he spent in Tehran's notorious Evin prison after a conviction for spying. It was not just the bad food and general hardship, but the fact the education allowed the individual to live at arm's length from the physical reality around them, whether it be in Bristol or in darkest Sudan.'[5]

The system of grammar and public schools and the university education in England is unusual. To a considerable extent, the system was designed to teach people to think – to remember, to argue, to disagree, to try out new ideas, to invent new solutions, to persuade others. Many educational systems are designed to teach people to think, but in rather narrow and focused ways along the current political or religiously acceptable lines; mon-asteries, madrasas or Confucian education are examples.

Secondly it was a powerful process because education out-side the home started very early in life. As we have seen, from eight or nine, the poor became servants or labourers for others, the slightly richer were apprentices, the middle classes went to grammar or public schools, the very richest were taken in as pages in upper class houses. In this way a tradition developed which led to one of England's most famous institutions. By 1820 there were some 20,000 preparatory schools in the coun-try and many famous public schools such as Eton, Winchester, Rugby, Westminster and Charterhouse.

Here the character of children was formed, a character based on success in non-family relations and struggle with a wider world rather than the familistic education of most civilizations. In the boarding schools, in particular, the boys were channeled through a series of institutions, the Preparatory School, Public School and then University, and supposedly made into tough and supposedly self-confident and resourceful adults. Alongside the tools of the mind they were taught the skills which would make them effective whether in the East India Company, the Civil Service in India or the City or Law in London. The spirit of collaboration and courage in games, the prefect system which was designed to teach responsibility and the art of ruling, the inner strength against outside threats, a set of skills were meant to be taught. They were skills for public life rather than family life. This system, like the Confucian one which held China to-gether in the past, is central to understanding the invention of our modern world.

◆

THIS SYSTEM FED directly into the imagined Empire which grew in England from the later sixteenth century. It also underpinned the governmental system – the ruling gentry had been through the same sorts of schools, had networks of contacts at Eton, Cambridge and the Inns of Court, and then went on to run an integrated politico-legal-economic system. The education system was a bastion of privilege, yet to some degree open. It was a particularly important part of English life. As Cammaerts noticed, English schools and colleges 'have played a far larger part in English life than any prominent educational institution has done in the life of other countries... they have succeeded in preserving and developing a certain type of character and a certain ideal of service, without which England would never have become what she is today'.[6]

In most European Empires the imperialists tended to 'go native'. That is to say the children were sent to missionary or other schools in the overseas territories, in Indo-China, Latin America or Africa. After a couple of generations of such local schooling, frequent inter-marrying with the indigenous peoples and absence from the homeland gave them a strong sense of difference. The same happened to a certain extent with the white part of the British Empire – there were good schools and universities such as Harvard and Yale. After two or three generations they felt distanced from the homeland – and in America they decided to separate from the homeland.

Yet in the three quarters of the British Empire which was not basically a white settler sphere, that is the West Indies, India, Burma and Africa, the system that developed was like the one in Britain, but stretched out all over the globe. Parents in India or Africa sent their children off to boarding schools, but not in another county, but across the seas to 'home' in Britain.

Many of my own family over many generations went through the same process. We were 'sent home' – in my case from India – when we were aged between six and eight and were placed on the lowest rung of the boarding school ladder. There we 'became' British. We learnt the games, the slang, the irony, the class system, the myths and rituals of the tribe. After ten years of boarding, topped up perhaps with three years at University or military college, we were fully 'British' from tip to toe. We were then ready to start the process again by joining the Indian Civil Service or going out to a tea plantation. As we sat in remote parts of the world there was no doubt in our minds that Britain was 'home', that we were just sojourners in a foreign land, and if we had children we would send them back to get onto the same ladder.

In other words, we learnt to play the game of being British. We became part of 'the Breed'. It is famously expressed in Andrew Newbolt's poem based on his life at Clifton College, and how lessons learned there are carried wherever in the world one might be. This is a poetic expression of the belief that the Battle of Waterloo was won on the playing fields of Eton.

There's a breathless hush in the Close to-night –
Ten to make and the match to win –
A bumping pitch and a blinding light,
An hour to play and the last man in.
And it's not for the sake of a ribboned coat,
Or the selfish hope of a season's fame,
But his Captain's hand on his shoulder smote –
'Play up! Play up! And play the game!'

The sand of the desert is sodden red, -
Red with the wreck of a square that broke; -
The Gatling's jammed and the Colonel dead,
And the regiment blind with dust and smoke.
The river of death has brimmed his banks,
And England's far, and Honour a name,
The voice of the schoolboy rallies the ranks:
'Play up! Play up! And play the game!

This is the word that year by year,
While in her place the School is set,
Every one of her sons must hear,

And none that hears it dare forget.
This they all with a joyful mind
Bear through life like a torch in flame,
And falling fling to the host behind –
"Play up! Play up! And play the game!"[7]

♦

THERE HAS BEEN much discussion about whether literacy
rates or formal education are correlated with industrialization.
Mokyr is probably right that 'In sum, there is little evidence to
suggest that education played a central role in England's Industrial Revolution, suggesting in turn that it has been possible for
economies to compensate for poorly educated work forces with
other offsetting advantages.'[8] Japan, for example, had higher literacy rates than England in the early modern period and this did
not lead to industrialization.

It may be that the equation was the other way round, as implied by Laing, namely that industrialization led to a growing
interest amongst urban workers in reading and writing. 'If a
stranger to Europe – an educated American, for instance – were
to travel over England and Germany, he would pronounce England to be the more educated and more reading country of the
two, from the indications of printing, stationery, books, pamphlets, newspapers, handbills, advertisements, notices, placards,
all showing that reading and writing are necessaries of life, not
merely amusements, among our lowest classes, and enter into
their daily business in every station.'[9]

The way in which the English education system inter-linked
with the class, and economic and legal system, and thus formed
part of the background package where the first industrial revolution occurred is however more complicated. It is not a simple
matter of the statistics of literacy. The important factor lies in
the severing of the family, the generic training in independent
activities away from home. The particular skills of numeracy

and literacy may be useful, but were not essential for the general workforce, though the odd system of grammar and boarding schools were an essential part of the formation of a gentry ruling class and Imperial diaspora.

It is also worth noting that while literacy rates may not have been as high as in some countries, the peculiar English social structure gave literacy a wider distribution than in most societies. Usually in *ancien regime* societies, the top five percent, at the most, would be highly literate, the peasants totally illiterate. In England, the half of the population from the 'middling sort' upwards was at least partially literate. For example, up to the sixteenth century, the yeomanry were amongst the largest class sending their children to University. The yeomanry were the backbone of literate groups, as Latimer said in a sermon to King Henry VIII, 'for if ye bring it to pass that the yeomanry be not able to put their sons to school…(you) ultimately destroy the realm'.[10] Widespread literacy was probably a necessary, but certainly not a sufficient, cause of economic growth.

The Englishness of English Language.

ONE CENTRAL FEATURE, fitting with the social structure and absence of legal statuses, is the egalitarian nature of the English language. 'In Germany, there is one speech for the learned, and another for the masses, to that extent, that, it is said, no sentiment or phrase from the works of any great German writer is ever heard among the lower classes. But in England, the language of the noble is the language of the poor. In Parliament, in pulpits, in theatres, when the speakers rise to thought and passion, the language becomes idiomatic; the people in the street best understand the best words. And their language seems drawn from the Bible, Milton, Pope, Young, Cowper, Burns, and Scot.'[11] This shows that it is more than the well-known fact that all Romance languages are filled with status markers – 'vous', 'tu'. Something happened to the English language which kept it way from honorific and status distinctions, and those few which remained were challenged, for example in the case of the Quakers who objected to the use of 'thee' and 'thou'.

Bloch thought England exceptional in its language in Anglo-Saxon times for it was not split between a vernacular and courtly – English was spoken and written by all. All over Europe the language of the elite became latin. But in the West 'one society long remained an exception. This was Anglo-Saxon Britain. Not that Latin was not written there and written very well, but it was by no means the only language written. The old English tongue was elevated at an early date to the dignity of a literary and legal language. It was King Alfred's wish that young people should learn it in the schools before the more gifted passed on to Latin. The poets employed it in their songs, which were set down in writing as well as recited. It was also used by the kings in their laws; by the chanceries in the legal documents … This was something unique in that age, a culture that was able to keep in touch on its highest levels with the medium of expression employed by the mass of population.[12] The situation was partly overlain for a couple of centuries after the Norman invasion when French was used by some of the ruling class – but this distinction fades and by the fourteenth century the national language was English, though Latin remained a scribal language, important in religion and certain branches of law.

Elsewhere in Europe the languages split. 'In a great part of Europe, the common languages, which were connected with the Germanic group, belonged to quite another family from the language of the educated… Thus the linguistic separation was reduced, in the long run, to the division between two human groups. On the one hand there was the immense majority of uneducated people, each one imprisoned in his regional dialect, limited, so far as literary culture was concerned, to a few secular poems transmitted almost exclusively by word of mouth…'[13]

So in its grammar and vocabulary we find a national, non-class, language. Yet because of the importance of minor differences of wealth and education, the game of language as social differentiation was played in another way. This was partly by accent. Any Englishman can tell in a few seconds another's social class by the accent. Yet accent is something that can be learnt – this is the theme of Shaw's *Pygmalion* (re-made as the film 'My Fair Lady') and was one of the central roles of expensive boarding schools and universities.

The other is the complexity of the linguistic codes used. The middle and upper classes use complex codes, the lower groups more restricted ones. Yet this can be changed and people can switch codes. As those of us who have children or grandchildren at school will know, how schoolchildren talk amongst their friends and at home may differ widely. So in England, as in games, the rules were universal and based on equality, but different social groups, in different regions of the country or professions played the game in different ways. Yet, overall, English is a rather surprisingly democratic, active and direct language. Shakespeare's Prince Hal did not talk significantly differently to his father or to Falstaff, nor did Lear to the Fool or to his daughters. The language of the very diverse characters in Chaucer is rather uniform.

Another absence was gender differentiation – again so much stressed in Romance and other languages. The anthropologist Alfred Kroeber wrote that 'sex gender is an old part of Indo-European structure. In English, by the way, it has wholly disappeared, so far as formal expression goes, from noun, adjective, and demonstrative and interrogative pronoun. It lingers only in the personal pronoun of the third person singular – he, she, it. A grammar of living English that was genuinely practical and unbound by tradition would never mention gender except in discussing these three little words.'[14] Females do not, as in most societies, have to address males in a special deferential language; the entire world is not, as in France, gendered with male and female nouns. English language is uniformly neutral, at least from the thirteenth century onwards. It may partly account for the attraction of English around the world as the position of women improves, and the way that English-medium schools seem to help the self-confidence of girls.

Finally, it was a national language. Although there have been very considerable dialect differences, the people south of the border on the small island of Britain spoke one language (apart from parts of Wales), as it practiced one law. This is a very great difference from all parts of continental Europe until the later nineteenth century.

◆

THE SHARED PREMISES of conversation feed into the emphasis on under-statement. 'An Englishman understates, avoids the superlative, checks himself in compliments, alleging, that in the French language, one cannot speak without lying.'[15] Or as Maurois observed, 'If you are a world tennis-champion, say "Yes, I don't play too badly." If you have crossed the Atlantic alone in a small boat, say, "I do a little sailing."[16] The middle class in particular depreciates hyperbole, flattery, an over-elaborate use of language.

A second manifestation is irony, and its stronger form, satire. Many of the greatest English writers from Chaucer, through Shakespeare, Pope and Swift, to Austen, Wilde and Sullivan are masters of this. Paxman describes how in Alan Bennett's *The Old Country*, a spy who has defected muses about England. 'We're conceived in irony. We float in it from the womb. It's the amniotic fluid. It's the silver sea. It's the waters at their priest-like task, washing away guilt and purpose and responsibility. Joking but not joking. Caring but not caring. Serious but not serious.'[17]

I am amazed at how much of my schooling was devoted to learning how to master the rhetorical and literary skills of irony and satire. Playing this game, saying the opposite of what you mean, and conveying to the other the hidden message is central to much of English humour. The anthropologist Kate Fox found ironic humour to be central to English life today. 'We are accustomed to not saying what we mean: irony, self-deprecation, understatement, obliqueness, ambiguity and polite pretence are all deeply ingrained, part of being English. This peculiar mindset is inculcated at an early age, and by the time our children go to primary school, they have usually already mastered the art of the indirect boast, and can do their own self-deprecatory trumpet-blowing.'[18]

For irony to work, the audience must be able to read below the surface, in other words share the hidden and oblique side of an utterance. That there is so much shared in the way of values and themes of conversation in the culture of England allows irony and satire to spread widely.

The second background is a mixture of fluctuating inequality of power. The obvious examples are political. The great age of English irony and satire, of Dryden, Pope and the *Beggar's Opera* was the eighteenth century. Much the same happened in Eastern Europe in the last decades of communism, when the political system was in control and could not be overtly criticized, yet there was much to criticise. Again, Victorian hypocrisy and the gap between word and deed left society open to the irony of a Wilde or Shaw. One had to make oblique attacks against political foes and also against the socially powerful.

Much irony and satire plays with the comedies of manners. Of course this is not just an English device. France with Molière, Racine or Voltaire was full of irony – but somehow French satire has a different flavour, at times more obsessed with the court, more bitter and vitriolic. In England it can be malicious, but often it is not. As with Jane Austen, it is more feline and stroking. It is best when the concealed meaning suddenly strikes the listener or reader, and even then they are never quite certain whether the bomb is there or imagined.

Irony is particularly important within a wider context, namely the fact that humour is probably the most important cultural feature of the English. Here I will not elaborate this, but just quote from a long documentation of the subject by the anthropologist Kate Fox: 'the English do not have any sort of global monopoly on humour, but what is distinctive is the sheer pervasiveness and supreme importance of humour in English everyday life and culture... Virtually all English conversations and social interactions involve at least some degree of banter, teasing, irony, wit, mockery, wordplay, satire, understatement, humorous self-deprecation, sarcasm, pomposity-pricking or just silliness... when in doubt, joke.'[19]

◆

THE ENGLISH LANGUAGE is old and little influenced in its roots by Latin. Like English law it is continuous. Though it takes getting used to, Anglo-Saxon and medieval literature feels familiar and Chaucer largely comprehensible. Many of the writers, such as Blake, Wordsworth, Cobbett, Dickens, Kipling and Orwell are simple and direct.

English is subtle, multi-layered, suitable for irony and satire and different nuances. It is a language for shop-keepers and lawyers and administrators, but also for scientists and artists. It is individualistic, with its stress on the personal pronouns; like the kinship terminology it is ego-centred. Yet it also envisages the other – collaboration, friendship and co-operation. It has a great emphasis on time and movement, with many complexities to the verb forms.

The language is also musical, rhythmical, allusional so that in the hands of a Milton, Keats or Hopkins it can say the profoundest truths in a melodious and direct way. 'English is a poet's language. It is ideally suited for description or for the expression of emotion. It is flexible, it is varied, it has an enormous vocabulary; able to convey every subtle diverse shade, to make vivid before the mental eye any picture it wishes to conjure up. Moreover its very richness helps it to evoke those indefinite moods, those visionary flights of fancy of which so much of the material of poetry is composed. There is no better language in the world for touching the heart and setting the imagination aflame.'[20]

As David Cecil also writes, 'Every great nation has expressed its spirit in art: generally in some particular form of art. The Italians are famous for their painting, the Germans for their music, the Russians for their novels. England is distinguished by her poets… The greatness of English poetry has been astonishingly continuous. German music and Italian painting flourished, at most, for two hundred years. England has gone on producing great poets from the fourteenth century to to-today: there is nothing like it in the history of the arts.'[21] And the poetry was not confined to what we consider poems. Perhaps its greatest expression was when the Bible was translated into English in the *Standard Authorized Version* at the start of the seventeenth century. It became a great treasure of poetry and literature that still moves many of us today.

The Englishness of English art.

AS A HIGHLY intelligent and knowledgeable mid-European Jewish immigrant working under the shadow of the Second World War and absorbed into English culture, Nikolaus Pevsner is particularly perceptive about some characteristics of English art. In his Reith Lectures, expanded into the book *The Englishness of English Art* (1956), he noted a number of features, a few of which I shall cite here.

One is the point often made about English character – that it is filled with so many contraries and oppositions, that the only way to understand it is through the dynamic interplay of different unresolved tensions. Thus he writes that the 'history of styles as well as the cultural geography of nations can only be successful – that is approach truth – if it is conducted in terms of polarities, that is in pairs of apparently contradictory qualities.'[22] He cites approvingly Blake's remark – 'Without Contraries is no progression. Attraction and Repulsion. Reason and Energy, Love and Hate, are necessary to Human existence.'[23] He then gives an example. '… Perpendicular is downright and direct. Decorated is perverse, capricious, wilful, illogical, and unpredictable. It is unreasonable, where Perpendicular is reasonable.'[24] His search is for a deeper logic which connects these apparent contradictions.

One device the English use to make the never resolvable contradictions tolerable is through what Pevsner calls at different times hypocrisy or cant. Rather than speak of hypocrisy, Pevsner thinks we should speak of 'compromise'. For example, 'Reynolds's official portraits in any case are a blatant example of compromise.'[25] He gives another example with William Morris, and then links this feature to the wider feature of tolerance, treating each case on its own merits, a distaste for fanatical uniformity and consistency. The memories of what had happened under Hitler, Mussolini, Stalin and Franco may have been in the back of his mind.

So Pevsner gives the example of William Morris, who preached socialism while making amazing expensive artefacts for the very rich. This and many examples are illogical and inconsistent. 'Or perhaps is illogicality another national characteristic? That is no doubt the case, and fascinating illogicalities in English architecture of diverse ages will be considered later. For the time being it is enough to remember how close to each other dwell illogicality, compromise, and cant in the English heart, and to realize – which is the next step – that "Every case on its own merit" is only a fourth facet of this same quality… "Every case on its own merit" is one of the greatest blessings of English civilization… So detachment is the corollary of "Every case on its own merit"'.[26]

There is, however, a cost to this lack of unifying, passionate, consistent vision, Pevsner believes, namely that the English did not produce the very greatest artists either in music or in painting or in architecture (though he does not balance this in literature and science, where Shakespeare, Milton, Newton, Darwin and others are not inconsiderable in their grand designs). 'There is no Bach, no Beethoven, no Brahms. There is no Michelangelo, no Titian, no Rembrandt.... What the amateur painter must be lacking in, in order to remain an amateur, is a violent compulsion towards a single-minded self-expression to which a lifetime must be devoted.' In the final conclusion to the book Pevsner repeats the list of great figures of whom the English have no equivalents and gives the same reason. The absence of towering geniuses, 'in my opinion is due to the growing importance in the national character of practical sense, of reason, and also of tolerance. What English character gained of tolerance and fair play, she lost of that fanaticisms or at lest that intensity which alone can bring forth the very greatest in art.'[27]

♦

PEVSNER CONSIDERS A particular architectural style to be the most specifically English part of English art, namely English perpendicular architecture of the thirteenth to sixteenth centuries. This is particularly interesting for the argument of this book for several reasons. The style is early, before the Reformation of the sixteenth century and it is something unique to England. It lasts right across the period from the fourteenth to sixteenth centuries with hardly any change, making us wonder whether the whole ideology of the society was changing from a medieval pre-capitalist world.

Furthermore the style is a statement in architecture of the essence of the early separation of the spheres of life. What is most distinct about English medieval art, Pevsner believes, is that it separates parts of the church into rectangular boxes, which are not unified into one dominant space. Only finally in an afterthought, as it were, does it unify the space – as is done so gloriously in King's College Chapel at Cambridge.

I shall let Pevsner explain this, but as he implies it is part of the non-totalitarian system of art, the tensions and separations are not suppressed. It is a pragmatic, ad hoc art. And Pevsner constantly links this to other features of England – the pragmatic philosophy, legal system, individuality and liberty.

The style, obviously drawing its elements from many traditions, is in another sense purely English. 'There is little that is in every respect so completely and so profoundly English as are the big English parish churches of the Late Middle Ages, the age of Henry V, Henry VI, Henry VII.'[28] Secondly, it is very conservative, showing a desire to keep something that works and a rejection of the new styles on the continent which emerged with resurgent Roman influences. ' Conservatism also shows itself in the fact, so surprising to foreigners, that once the Perpendicular style had been created – that most English of architectural styles – it remained virtually unchanged for over a hundred years' (between 1350-1450).[29] The Englishness and continuity are re-stated: 'But it is very much of England all the same, so much so that the Perpendicular style has in its details not even a remote parallel abroad, and so much so that it lasted unchanged for nearly two hundred years. This has been adduced as a sign of conservatism, but it is really also a sign of Englishness.'[30]

What then is the essence of the perpendicular style? Pevsner describes it in a way which shows that it is the absence of centralization, of a total and encompassing and unified conception. 'Almost without exception English churches of the later Middle Ages have timber roofs instead of stone vaults. These roofs are just as complex as the most elaborate stone vaults, and they are just as angular. They are a triumph of the joiner... they also prove negatively a peculiarly English neglect of space-moulding, one might even say of pulling a building together. Where there is a stone vault, the substance and character of the walls is continued without a break until it achieves itself in the crown of the vault above our heads. The vault rounds off the space, and connects all parts. In England on the other hand what one experiences is one wall, another wall, and beams across. Parts are left as parts, separated from each other.'[31]

He then itemizes the features. 'Angularity must be taken first. The flat chancel ends of the Perpendicular church has its immediate parallel in the flat-topped tower of the Perpendicular church – something extremely rare on the Continent... the square-topped tower remains England at its most English, also in its absence of demonstrated aspiration, its compromise between vertical and horizontal, and even a certain matter-of-factness.' Another feature is the chancel. 'The English unrelieved rectangularity comes out equally convincingly in the plans of churches. There the most telling example is the history of the square-ended chancel.'[32]

The contrast with what was happening on the continent at the same time makes his point about the peculiarity. 'Indeed ... English Gothic cathedrals remain far more isolated than those of France.... The French innovation more closely moulded, unified volume and space is not accepted. That may be called conservatism but it is also a sign of a specifically English dislike of subordination. Parts, to say it once more, remain co-ordinated, added to one another, and in addition box-shaped rather than rounded.'[33]

The English system is inconsistent, illogical, pragmatic, ad hoc, unprincipled, all those things which Ruskin had noted. Pevsner gives the example of Lincoln cathedral. 'The "crazy vaults" of Lincoln... Their illogicality is staggering...' Pevsner continues that 'Illogicality must certainly be listed as an English quality... The distaste of the English for carrying a thought or a systems of thought to its logical extreme is too familiar to need comment.'[34]

Another way of putting the contrast is between pragmatic reasonableness, and passionate intensity. 'It will surely not be denied that rationalism and often, to use a more homely term, reasonableness lies behind Palladian as well as Perpendicular architecture... If one compares Lincoln with Chartes, begun within five years or less of one another, there is, to reiterate, nothing more striking than the contrast between French verticalism and English balance of directions – or indecision, or compromise... What by such means Lincoln lacks in enthusiasm... it gains in mellow humanity, in sheer happiness.'[35]

As to what caused these differences, Pevsner is no social or economic historian. His favourite explanation of the particular character of English art, particularly painting, seems to be climate. It is a little difficult to see how this could explain the perpendicular style, except through a long chain of argument leading to the widespread presence of oak trees for the roofs. What does seem a promising speculation, in is a set of comments which link the art to the early spread of middle-class monetary values and pragmatism.

Early in his book he had noted in relation to his detailed study of Hogarth, how middle class he and other painters were. Hogarth 'did not only belong to the middle class, he did so demonstratively. His sisters sold frocks and haberdashery.... The majority of artists through his and the preceding century came, one can safely state, from such a class... it will be demonstrated later than Englishness had taken peculiarly middle-class features in at least one of its most English periods of history before.'[36]

That earlier period was the most distinctively English perpendicular period. Illustrating his case with examples, Pevsner argues that 'rationalism, or in everyday language, sensible behaviour, is decidedly a middle-class ideal. Hence it is not surprising to find it in command in the Late Middle Ages. There is nothing new in viewing the later fourteenth and the fifteenth centuries in terms of a predominance of the merchant.'[37]

CHAPTER NOTES

1. Marshall quoted in Mokyr, *Industrial*, 300

2. Taine, *Notes*, 102

3. Taine, *Notes*, 104. Taine noted that 'learning and cultivation of the mind come last, character, heart, courage, strength and physical address are in the first rank'. (Taine, quoted in Paxman, *English*, 190.)

4. Boswell, *London*, 66

5. Paxman, *English*, 182-3

6. Cammaerts, *English*, 133

7. Quoted in Paxman, *English*, 197-8

8. Mokyr, *Industrial*, 303

9. Laing, *Observations*, 314-5

10. Peacock, *English*, 171

11. Emerson, *English*, 79

12. Bloch, *Feudal*, I, 75

13. Bloch, *Feudal*, I, 77

14. Kroeber, *Anthropology*, 238

15. Emerson, *English*, 93

16. In Wilson, *Strange*, 260

17. Paxman, *English*, 18

18. Fox, *Watching*, 364

19. Fox, *Watching*, 402

20. Cecil, *English*, 61

21. Cecil, *English*, 61

22. Pevsner, *Englishness*, 24

23. Pevsner, *Englishness*, 128

24. Pevsner, *Englishness*, 129

25. Pevsner, *Englishness*, 60

26. Pevsner, *Englishness*, 67

27. Pevsner, *Englishness*, 80, 206

28. Pevsner, *Englishness*, 90

29. Pevsner, *Englishness*, 84

30. Pevsner, *Englishness*, 94

31. Pevsner, *Englishness*, 93-4

32. Pevsner, *Englishness*, 94-5

33. Pevsner, *Englishness*, 98

34. Pevsner, *Englishness*, 101-3

35. Pevsner, *Englishness*, 122

36. Pevsner, *Englishness*, 54-5

37. Pevsner, *Englishness*, 123

CHAPTER 13

KNOWLEDGE

THE UNIVERSITY IS basically a west European invention – though madrasas, Buddhist monasteries and other institutions overlap a good deal with the idea. For example, in his comparison of the growth of science in Europe, Islam and China, Huff writes of Islam that 'Islamic law does not recognize corporate personalities, which is why cities and universities and other legally autonomous entities did not evolve there.' In so far as there were centres of learning in China, '…the Chinese educational system was both rigidly controlled and focused on literary and moral learning, while the European universities were both autonomous and self–controlled as well as centred on a core curriculum that was essentially scientific.'[1]

The importance of some kind of institutionalization was noted long ago by Bernal. 'The foundation of the early scientific societies had another and more permanent effect: it made science into an institution, an institution with the insignia, the solemnity, and … pedantry of the older institutions of law and medicine.'[2] Likewise Cohen points out that 'The first uniquely Western feature from which a somewhat more solid social basis for science sprouted than had been available elsewhere was the rise of the mediaeval university.'[3]

Universities are both a cause and consequence of 'modernity'. They have been centres of the discovery of new theories and inventions and, more importantly, because they were arenas of relative freedom of thought. Of course the pressures from political, religious, economic and social forces are always there, but they are muted.

The idea of a University as a place for education and discovery is old and was widespread in Europe by the end of the fourteenth century when many universities were present. Yet it appears that between then and the end of the eighteenth century the older idea of free, collegiate, universities died out all over Europe – except in England. There the universities of Oxford and Cambridge had survived as a form of semi-autonomous institution to encourage thought and educate the ruling class.

TO TAKE THE case of the University of Cambridge, it is doubtful whether many poets (from Spenser to Wordsworth) or scientists (from Gilbert to Newton) would have made their contributions if they had not been to this University. Thus much of the contribution of the English to the arts, humanities and sciences would have been missing. Of course a great deal happened outside the Universities. But without the work on electricity, on optics, on the circulation of the blood, on gravity, it seems unlikely a number of inventions, whether in navigation or the application of steam power, would have been made.[4]

More important than specific inventions or events were other less direct features. One was that the universities, along with the Inns of Court, preserved a tradition of enquiry by contest, by confrontation, by argument and disputation, by putting forward a hypothesis and testing it. Francis Bacon summarized this in what we call the 'experimental method'. It sped up the evolution of ideas in the same way as selective breeding of animals sped up stock improvement. And both changed the world.

The first scientific society in the world was the Royal Society of London founded in 1660. It is an institutionalization of the experimental method and the subsequent history of great science flows from it. The formal method of enquiry is what distinguishes science from the high-level investigations which had long been going on in Islamic civilizations and China. Yet the 'open' world of experimental science was present several centuries before this, in the work of scholars all over Europe, including that of Robert Grosseteste, Roger Bacon and William of Ockham in England from the thirteenth onwards.

♦

THE SURVIVAL AND flourishing of science in England from the thirteenth to nineteenth centuries is both a sign and consequence of the central theme of this work. By separating religion, politics, economy and society, space was left for specialist institutions to flourish: the 'technique of creating a neutral world of fact as distinguished from the raw data of immediate experience was the great general contribution of modern analytic science. This contribution was possibly second only to the development of our original language concepts... The concept of a neutral world, untouched by man's efforts, indifferent to his activities, obdurate to his wish and supplication, is one of the great triumphs of man's imagination, and in itself it represents a fresh human value.'[5]

All over the Continent, as had happened much earlier in China and the Islamic world, those with power were jealous of the wealth and independence of institutions and afraid of their free enquiries. 'Knowledge is power', as Francis Bacon wrote, and power could not be allowed to be situated away from the absolutist political centre. So free universities did not survive. But in England, which passed the same idea to the free universities of America, knowledge was largely autonomous and not seen as a threat – but a benefit. The modern world of universities was preserved against the odds.

In relation to this open world, Robin Horton, Karl Popper and others have put the autonomy of thought in a rather different way.[6] In *ancien régime* thought systems, the answers were given at the start – the founder of the philosophy revealed all, thought was closed, the sayings of the Prophet, of Confucius, of Christ or Aristotle had given us all the answers. To enquire for too much new knowledge is subversive. The quintessence of the open rationality of modernity is the premise of an expanding universe of knowledge, that all present knowledge is provisional and imperfect, that there are always going to be new things under the sun.

Such a premise is clearly present over much of Western Europe and the Middle East from the eighth to fourteenth centuries in Islamic knowledge and the revival of Greek thought. But it is a difficult and uncomfortable to maintain. As humans, we seek for certainty. The probabilistic, 'it is only true until it has been disproved', 'conjectures and experiments' world described by Karl Popper seldom survives for long. Any political or religious authority with complete power will want to close it off – as we saw with Soviet or Nazi science.

What is amazing is that with scarcely an interruption, this idea of the open, questioning, challenging, 'finding new things' approach outlined by Francis Bacon, seems to have been present as a thread through English thought from the thirteenth century onwards. The English were not just content to explore the physical world as they later did with their enormous Empire, but constructed an 'Empire of the Mind'. 'The English think deeply; in that their mind is one with their character; delving deeply into things, and rich   in experience they extend far and wide the empire of the sciences.'[7]

♦

ONE WAY TO approach the question of what happened in terms of the modernization of thought is through the speculation of the philosopher and anthropologist Ernest Gellner concerning the growth of rationality or 'disenchantment of the world'. He argues that there is a 'radical discontinuity' which exists 'between primitive and modern mentality'.[8] This is the 'transition to effective knowledge', which he describes many times.

There is 'the great transition between the old, as it were non–epistemic worlds, in which the principles of cognition are subject to the pervasive constitutive principles of a given vision, and thus have little to fear, and a world in which this is not longer possible', a 'fundamental transition indeed'. While overlapping with Popper and Kuhn, Gellner's stress is on the fact that the attainment of a scientific world is very difficult indeed. The 'attainment of a rational, non-magical, non-enchanted world is a much more fundamental achievement than the jump from one scientific vision to another. Popper underestimates the difficulty of establishing an Open Society, for he seems to suppose that an open society was always within our reach'.[9]

Gellner's work incorporates some of Weber's thought on the growth of rationality. The modern world of rationality has two central features; coherence or consistency, and efficiency. Coherence means 'that there are no special, privileged, insulated facts or realms'. Efficiency means 'the cold rational selection of the best available means to given, clearly formulated and isolated ends.' This is 'the separation of all separables...the breaking up of all complexes into their constituent parts...'; it creates 'a common measure of fact, a universal conceptual currency... all facts are located within a single continuing logical space ... one single language describes the world...'[10]

Put in another way, 'rationality' here means that spheres have become sufficiently disentangled for the mind to move without constantly bumping into wider obstacles created by impenetrable barriers whether of religion, kinship or politics. Within the new world 'there also is and can be no room either for magic or for the sacred'.[11] What has happened is that thought, has been set free from its usual masters – politics, religion or kinship. We are open to all thought and to all doubt. God is irrelevant, the father is irrelevant, the King is irrelevant. We are our own masters, to think what we please. The barriers are down and everything is leveled onto one plane in the intellectual sphere.

Normally in a world where religion, politics, economy and society are fused together, by a curious paradox, there are separate mental spheres. The thinker who tries to cross the boundaries into religion or politics, to apply logic to the King or the Pope's edicts, will quickly be abused or disabused. But modernity is premised on the exploration of a common space. David Hume applied rational logic to religion, Locke to politics, Charles Darwin to the origins of life. They could do so with some confidence, even if there were some pressures to desist. In most civilizations they would quickly have been stopped, or discouraged by family, friends and their own good sense from even starting.

What became accepted was a value-free exploration in a measurable world. People were not trying to carry a ruling imperial message, but to seek out new worlds and find valuable and curious things. And part of the approach was not to start with *a priori* or fixed sets of principles, as in pure mathematics or physics, but with hypotheses, guesses, tested and refined by observations. In order to control and improve our lives we need to map, to measure, and not to accept anything until proven by the senses.

This cast of mind, which feels so 'modern' in its expression from Grosseteste in the first half of the thirteenth century to Rutherford some seven hundred years later, was at the heart of all aspects of life, from agriculture to law, from shipbuilding to sports. It is, of course, found in a subdued form in all societies and with everyone. People observe and change their behaviour. In England it became almost a practical religion which was oddly combined, as we have seen, with a large amount of useless play and recreation. It is a paradoxical and contradictory subject.

♦

THE EMPIRICISM OF English philosophy and investigation of the world overlaps with another feature, namely its pragmatism and interest in practical results. People who came to England particularly noted two aspects of this. Emerson in the nineteenth century commented: 'For they have a supreme eye to facts, and theirs is a logic that brings salt to soup, hammer to nail, oar to boat, the logic of cooks, carpenters, and chemists, following the sequence of nature, and one on which words make no impression.' 'The bias of the nation is a passion for utility. They love the lever, the screw, and pulley, the Flanders draught-horse, the waterfall, wind-mills, tide-mills; the sea and the wind to bear their freight-ships.' Or again: 'A strong common-sense, which it is not easy to unseat or disturb, marks the English mind for a thousand years'. 'For, the Englishman has accurate perceptions; takes hold of things by the right end, and there is no slipperiness in his grasp. He loves the axe, the spade, the oar, the gun, the steam-pipe; he has built the engine he uses. He is materialist, economical, mercantile.'[12]

Taine explained how travel, involvement in business and widespread interests meant that 'positive information flows into the English brain as into a reservoir.' Yet he believed that 'the availability of all these sources does not wholly explain the fullness of that reservoir: there is something more, a slope, as it were, which determines the flow of waters, the innate bent of the race, to wit their taste for facts and their fondness for experimental demonstration, the instinct for inductive reasoning and their need for certainty. Whoever has studied their literature and philosophy, from Shakespeare and Bacon down to the present day knows that this inclination is hereditary in the English, that it belongs to the very shape of their minds, that it is part of their way of understanding truth. By the English way of looking at things, a tree must be known by its fruits, and theory judged by practice. A truth has no value unless it leads to useful applications in practice. Beyond such practically applicable truths lie nothing but vain chimaeras.'[13]

This pragmatism or empiricism is the central theme of Anglo-Scottish American philosophy, from Bacon through Hume to Pierce and James. 'Pragmatism has been described as America's national philosophy and as the theoretical expression of the spirit of modern industrial capitalism, with its alleged emphasis on the practical and on the utility of thinking', and it was Britain which was the 'classic land' of the materialistic and pragmatic mode.[14] In summarizing the British philosophical tradition, Kenneth Matthews wrote: 'The native characteristics of British philosophy are these: common sense, dislike of complication, a strong preference for the concrete over the abstract and a certain awkward honesty of method in which an occasional pearl of poetry is embedded. It is as easy to perceive a common parentage in the philosophies of John Locke and Bertrand Russell as in the seamanship of Francis Drake and Horatio Nelson...The British philosophers, at least the most typical of them, stand with both feet on the ground...'[15] One branch of this, Utilitarianism, a cost-benefit analysis of pleasure and pain, is another example and Bentham a very English philosopher.

It would not be difficult to show that the tradition of linking philosophy to a supposed world of observable facts, and to useful outcomes, is old. For example Veliz argues that the individualism and positivism of the English goes back to William of Ockham and English scholastic philosophy.[16] The difference between English and Continental philosophy by the eighteenth to nineteenth centuries was marked. 'Even in the field of science it seems possible to discern a similar difference of approach between Continental and English thinkers. The most important Europeans tended to emphasize mathematics within a context of philosophical speculation, whereas the English scientists focused on the empirical method'.[17]

Taine in the nineteenth century noted the views of an Englishman he met: 'He claims that this need for facts is the basis of the English character; let the machine run uncoupled to work and it wrecks itself.'[18] Taine notes in English philosophy a taste for facts and their fondness for experimental demonstration, the instinct for inductive reasoning and their need for certainty; 'it is part of their very way of understanding truth'.[19] As Orwell put it, 'In England such concepts as justice, liberty and objective truth are still believed in. They may be illusions, but they are very powerful illusions. The belief in them influences conduct, national life is different because of them.'[20]

Many nowadays take it as self-evident that science is based on 'facts', that empirical methods and experiment are central to it, and that a major purpose of science is to improve our lives. Yet if we place ourselves in most civilizations two or three hundred years ago, this view is decidedly odd. It was not to be found strongly in Islamic, Chinese, Japanese or even most European civilizations. To begin with there were no stable 'facts' to be investigated – the world was subject to magical, mystical forces and miraculous events, filled with illusion, with no ultimate reality or set of firm principles. There was little point in searching for stable facts or deeper certainties.

Secondly, the high prizes of the small circle of privileged people who dedicated their lives to thought went to those who were the most abstract, the most pure. To soil your hands with grossly material things, to grind your own lenses or test theories with physical objects was demeaning, that was the sort of things that craftsmen, or shopkeepers, might do.

That the English were a nation ruled by shopkeepers in their science as well as in their Empire was rather shocking. We need to understand both the stability of the world of facts and its autonomy. We also need to investigate the high status accorded to experiments and those people like Robert Boyle, Earl of Cork, who alongside or instead of hunting, shooting and fishing, dabbled in chemistry. We have to see all this in the context of other features. Especially we have to consider the peace, stability and wealth of the country, the firm but fairly predictable nature of power and religion, and the particular social structure with its markedly unusual absence of that scorn of practical activity on the part of the rich and literate which would be found as a strong force in most civilizations. If we are trying to discover the reasons for the development of science in England over the last half millennium we need to understand it in a much wider social, economic, political, legal and religious context.

In brief, for example, it could be suggested that the system of logical argument and competition encouraged by the unique institution of Common Law, which lay behind Francis Bacon's experimental method, and his advice to 'put nature to the test' has something to do with science. The separation of religious organization and political power and thought, which enabled the peaceful exploration of nature without fear of the Catholic Inquisition, is another factor. The fact that the middle-class had become the wealthiest in Europe on the back of the productive and artifact based developments described elsewhere is important. The growth of London as a great centre of thought and exploration, balanced by the ancient universities and the Inns of Court is worth considering. The associational mechanism which Maitland shows lay behind many types of organization, including debating groups, the Royal Society and libraries, is important.

The absence of the usual confrontational divisions between a small literate elite and a large illiterate peasantry, which allowed many of the great scientists like Newton or Faraday to emerge from relatively humble backgrounds is significant. The curiously positivistic bent of the English, perhaps again related to the legal system with its obsession with fact, its assumption of 'the truth', its trial by peer (jury) review, is another element. The development of that trust which is essential for science. The development of that gaming and sporting instinct which became a passion is another feature.

♦

DURING THE LATE nineteenth and first half of the twentieth centuries it seemed self-evident that the first industrial revolution and the first scientific revolution both occurred in England. It was also obvious that increased knowledge fed into innovations and inventions. Then, from the middle of the twentieth century there was a reaction and it was suggested that theoretical science had little effect on technology until the middle of the nineteenth century, well after the industrial revolution had been achieved. More recently, as historians have looked more deeply at the ways in which science fed into discoveries and innovations of a practical kind, this revised view has been challenged again.

Many now argue that England was the first country to develop a kind of practical modern scientific culture, from the late sixteenth century, which in turn was an essential basis for the first industrial revolution. In both respects it became increasingly different from anywhere else in the world, including Holland, France and Italy. The support for this argument is now widespread.[21] Let me just take one authoritative recent account by Margaret Jacob. I shall explain her ideas in detail since her recent book, a revised version of an earlier work, lays out well the differences between English and continental science and takes account of recent research on the impact of science on technology.

Let us start with the fact that scientific knowledge was essential for the industrial revolution. Jacob writes that 'Industrial development occurred first in Britain for reasons that had to do with science and culture, not simply or exclusively with raw materials, capital development, cheap labor, or technological innovation.' In other words the 'elements of the natural world encoded in science were not peripheral to industrialization and Western hegemony; rather they were central to it.' In fact, she argues strongly, 'The industrial application of scientific knowledge constitutes historically the single most important use to which Western science has ever been put ...' This momentous event 'occurred first in England in the second half of the eighteenth century.'[22]

Jacob's work is mainly concerned with case studies of how this worked in practice, for example the effects of the work of Boyle and the vacuum on James Watt. I shall not repeat her detailed evidence, but just mention two cases she summarizes. 'The steam engine cannot be severed from the diffusion of the English Enlightenment, from the science that lay at the heart of that cultural transformation.' She writes that 'A variety of projects, long regarded as central to the historical process of British industrialization, in particular canal building and the use of steam power, illustrate how scientific knowledge could affect profit and productivity.' So she concludes the book by writing that 'The open, public science commonplace in eighteenth-century Britain may not be highly original science – although that is by no means foreclosed – but it can be innovative in application, widely adaptable to profit seeking.'[23]

It is quite clear to Jacob, who has made an extensive survey of science and technology across Europe, that Britain was different. Her central questions is 'What made the British absorb and use science – invent a culture of practical science – that was different from what can be seen in France?' She puts this also in a rhetorical question. 'Did the new science integrate differently in the British social and cultural landscape from what happened in western Europe during the eighteenth century? The answer is yes.' This difference, she believes, goes back to the seventeenth century. 'I shall be arguing that, from at least as early as the mid-seventeenth century, British science came wrapped in an ideology that encouraged material prosperity.' Her goal is to explore 'the marked differences between the scientific cultures found in Britain in comparison to France or the Netherlands, by trying 'to recreate the different universes wherein entrepreneurs actually lived.' The puzzle is that 'The remaining records ... suggest that in widespread scientific education of a mechanical sort, the British were at least a generation ahead of their European counterparts.' Or to put it in a more colourful way, 'it was possible to learn more about applied mechanics at a London coffee house lecture series than it was in any French *collège de plein exercise* prior to the late 1740s.'[24]

Jacob's main task is to explain this difference. Her basic assumption is that science is a cultural, political and social phenomenon, not just an intellectual one. Therefore in order to understand the reasons why British science and technology developed in a different way we have to look in these spheres. This assumption of inter-connectedness and context is stated a number of times.

She suggests that 'What is missing in the story of early industrialization to date is any convincing cultural paradigm – a set of recognizable values, experiences, and knowledge patterns possessed among key social actors – that offers insight into the formation of the industrial mentality of the late eighteenth century.' Therefore it is necessary to look at culture very widely if we are to understand the differences. 'Thus when we invoke a cultural setting in eighteenth-century Europe we must include the symbols of birth and authority – the political culture and value system of the *ancien regime* – just as we need to understand knowledge systems made available in formal and informal institutions of learning.' The last sentence in her book re-enforces this. 'The framing of nature cannot be divorced from other experience. In that sense, the language and practices of science are also socially anchored, and true creativity, relevant to its time and place, is rooted in social experience as transformed by ingenuity.'[25]

The factors which she suggests inhibited the growth of practical science on the Continent are described in various case studies. One factor was religion. Almost all over Europe, the counter-Reformation was dampening down enquiry and weakening the universities. 'By the late seventeenth century rigid censorship was already an established fact of life in much of Catholic Europe, as was clerical control over the universities.' This could undermine new knowledge, for '.... If clergymen more concerned with orthodoxy than with material progress control the schools and universities, then theory may dominate over application, or science in general will receive less attention.'[26]

Italy is a particularly well known case. The homeland of Galileo became largely sterile by the end of Galileo's century. 'In the late seventeenth century the intellectual crisis that afflicted much of Western Europe, was also felt in Italy, and out of it came the linkage between science and hetereodoxy. The search for philosophical liberty among scientifically minded Italian intellectuals in turn galvanized the Inquisition "against mathematics and physico-mathematics" because they were seen as pernicious "to the sincerity of religion."'[27]

In reverse the toleration and relatively weak political power of the Anglican Church in England was an important background to what was allowed to happen. For example, Jacob shows the strong link between the Unitarian church, a very non-dogmatic branch of deistical Christianity, and the new science and technology in England.

Holland is a particularly interesting case. The Calvinists were less tolerant than the Lutherans in England, for, as Jacob writes, 'the power of Calvinist orthodoxy produced widespread public opposition to aspects of the new science, for example, smallpox inoculation', nevertheless there was no Inquisition.[28] Furthermore, Holland in the early seventeenth century was one of the most advanced countries in its scientific knowledge. Jacob explains the curious petering out of Dutch science in the eighteenth century largely in terms of the negative effects of commercial economy that developed there.

'Now we might ask, what happened? After this extraordinary head start, Dutch science seemed to stall. By mid-century the Republic evinced no widespread program of popular scientific education aimed at adolescents, merchants or elite audiences, nothing comparable to efforts visible in Britain at precisely the same time.' She argues that 'Many groups with vested interests in the *status quo* thwarted the development of a vibrant scientific culture. The traditional elite made its money from international trade and commerce and their wealth was such that little else interested them.' One of Jacob's final conclusions to the book is that 'If oligarchs grown rich through commerce control local education and sponsor academies, as was the case in the Dutch Republic, then innovators with industrial ambitions may have no place to implant their values, or, as happened in the eighteenth century, to foster mechanics.'[29]

Potentially the greatest rival to England was the more powerful, populous and, in many ways, intellectually distinguished France. For a long time the religious orders, especially the Jesuits, clung to the Cartesian system and held out against the much more effective Newtonian science. Furthermore 'France did have many active scientific academies.... Yet aristocratic domination in the provincial societies and academies hardly permitted the kind of gentlemanly zeal for practical science that we see in late eighteenth-century Derbyshire or Birmingham.' Furthermore, the relations with government were different. 'In any survey of the social relations of eighteenth-century European science two patterns seem most prominent: the French, where scientists in the first instance serve the state, and the British, where they service the needs of entrepreneurs.' The divisions between groups in France were much greater. 'On the whole prior to 1789 French entrepreneurs and engineers occupied separate universes, did not possess a common technical vocabulary, and the details of public works were a matter solely for the engineers.'[30]

Turning to the unique English case, what does Jacob think lay behind the development of practical science? She lists many causal factors. 'British scientific culture further rested on relative freedom of the press, the property rights and expectations of landed and commercial people, and the vibrancy of civil society in the form of voluntary associations for self-education and improvement. In early eighteenth-century Britain these structural transformations worked for the interests of practical-minded scientists and merchants with industrial interests.'[31]

The roots of all this were deep, certainly back into the early seventeenth century:

By 1800 so pervasive was the new scientific learning that it fuelled the imagination of British entrepreneurs ... The Royal Society of London as early as the 1680s discussed the labor-saving value of machines.' And the culture spread across all of the large middle class who shared a common language and set of expectations. 'The public culture of British science created, perhaps also required, a distinctive social ambiance among engineers and their employers. Collecting, experimenting at philosophical gatherings, as well as reading and discussions of literature, even the habits of sermon and lecture attending, gave engineers and entrepreneurs a common discipline and vocabulary.[32] Many of the most important figures were amateurs ('devotees'). 'Of the hundred or more leading British scientists from 1700 to 1800, for example, nearly half would have to be classified as "devotees"...and of that hundred, 45 percent made their living as doctors, technicians, or churchmen.' These people were able to join in the process largely because of the flour-

ishing associational culture, what we call civil society. Jacob
writes:

> Having a common cultural legacy – a common technical
> but utilitarian language – provided by applied scientific
> education, formal and informal, buttressed by a volun-
> tarism found more in civil society, in associations, societ-
> ies, and clubs than in the individual singularly conceived
> – or than in the formal state institutions of an aristocratic
> or rigidly oligarchic regime – may go part of the way to-
> ward explaining the particular unleashing of industrially
> focused talent that occurred in eighteenth-century Brit-
> ain.[33]

The curious social and political context also fed into the process in another way – through the role of politics. Parliament
which the prime source of legislation and was increasingly filled
with people who were in favour of the new science and technologies, and understood it. This was crucial. 'Such mechanically
minded men also went to Parliament to represent their towns
and shires; first and foremost they represented the interests of
people like themselves. Having them in Parliament provide crit-
ically important as key moments in the process of mechanizing
occurred. In 1775 the House Commons set up a committee to
investigate Watt's claim that his engine was markedly different
from all competitors.'[34]

So Jacob concludes that 'a multitude of factors went into
successful industrial and commercial decision making: the ability to comprehend increasingly complex technical knowledge
through a mastery of basic mechanics, the presence of entrepreneurs willing and able to push a particular project through
Parliament, MPs learned enough to understand the technical
details, sufficient surplus capital from large and small investors
to be invested in shareholding companies, and never least, the
ability of laborers to dig the canal or feed the furnaces.' Without

this political context, the industrial revolution would not have occurred.[35]

This account is particularly interesting for it shows how the scientific and technological break-through which ushered in our modern world happened on one island and was only possible because of a whole set of inter-connected causes came together. It shows that Italian, Dutch, German and even French science and technology were stalled. Without the English case, it is difficult to see that the revolution in knowledge, practical and theoretical, could have occurred. And it shows that in order for it to happen there needed to be the civil society of clubs and associations, the large middle class, tolerant Anglicanism and a strong parliament.

CHAPTER NOTES

1. Huff, *Science*, 276

2. Bernal, *Science*, 318

3. Cohen, *Scientific*, 368

4. For an extended treatment, see Macfarlane, *Cambridge*

5. Mumford, *Technics*, 361

6. Popper, *Open*; Horton, 'Open'

7. La Fontaine quoted in Hazard, *European*, 64, note 1

8. Gellner, *Plough*, 42

9. Gellner, *Legitimation*, 182

10. Gellner, *Nations*, 21,20,22,21

11. Gellner, *Plough*, 66

12. Emerson, *English*, 65, 67, 176, 177

13. Taine, *Notes*, 248; for a thorough recent treatment of this, see Mokyr, *Enlightened*

14. Morris, *West*, 275, 15

15. Matthews, *English*, 271

16. Veliz, *Gothic*, 93ff

17. Fox, *Emergence*, 25

18. Taine, *Notes*, 59

19. Taine, *Notes*, 248

20. Orwell, *Lion*, 45

21. A recent, immensely detailed account supporting the linkage is Mokyr, *Enlightened.*

22. Jacob, *Scientific*, 2, 3, 202, 202

23. Jacob, *Scientific*, 95, 188, 207

24. Jacob, *Scientific*, 3, 4, 4, 105, 133, 136

25. Jacob, *Scientific*, 105, 141, 207

26. Jacob, *Scientific*, 76, 207

27. Jacob, *Scientific*, 162-3

28. Jacob, *Scientific*, 145

29. Jacob, *Scientific*, 143, 145, 307

30. Jacob, *Scientific*, 136, 139, 184

31. Jacob, *Scientific*, 107

32. Jacob, *Scientific*, 113, 114

33. Jacob, *Scientific*, 133, 185

34. Jacob, *Scientific*, 190

35. Jacob, *Scientific*, 201, 204

CHAPTER 14

MYTHS OF UNITY

BY THE LATE Anglo-Saxon period, England was not only a State but also a Nation. By then, a common language, law, currency and government largely unified the country. This sense of unity and pride in the English nation can then be found throughout the rest of English history, but it was taught indirectly.

The Scotsman Lord Kames was disappointed that the rulers of Britain were not taught patriotism at their boarding schools. 'It is deplorable that, in English public schools, patriotism makes no branch of education: young men, on the contrary, are trained up to selfishness.'[1] The same was true at my preparatory and public school. But the reason seems clear. There was no need to teach patriotism overtly – it was assumed that as we learnt about the glorious history, literature and inventions of our nation in numerous lessons and on playgrounds with our friends, we would pick up a deep sense of loyalty and patriotic warmth. We did not need to be taught. Unlike other larger European countries like Italy or Germany which remained States but not Nations until the nineteenth century, England felt itself to be united from very early on. The famous speech before the Battle of Agincourt in Shakespeare's play Henry V is but a late echo of this.

When trying to understand the central core of his adopted England, Huizinga believed that it was an ancient and powerful myth of unity, of 'We the English', or 'We the British', which covered over the reality that it was a nation composed of people of diverse origins. He believed that 'the one and only distinctive quality of the British was their exceptionally strong love of country, patriotism, nationalism, civic sense, tribal instinct or whatever one liked to call it...' As to what caused this, Huizinga admitted, 'I have no idea ... nor ever would have. Not having been born among them nor brought up in their patriotic faith nor having fought with them, I could obviously never hope to "get religion" and thus be vouchsafed the revelation myself.'[2] I was brought up in this nationalist religion and may be able to provide a few further clues as to what causes it.

Even if he did not understand its origins it is intriguing that Huizinga, from the famously independent and nationalist Holland, should feel that 'in so far as one can speak of a distinctive national character at all, religious, mystical patriotism more than love of freedom was its central feature... an intense, overriding patriotism was indeed the quality that more than anything else distinguished the English from other peoples.' Of course, the unity is mythical, or, in the modern jargon, the English had 'imagined' their community in the face of all its divisions. Huizinga recognized this: '... every political entity, however closely knit, was essentially a myth and only able to manifest itself as reality by virtue of the believers' willingness to live up to – and, if need be, die for – their myth. The strength of their belief, and not whether they had chosen to inscribe it on tablets of stone or merely to carry it in their hearts, was what really mattered.'[3]

◆

WHAT IS MORE, such was the strength of this sentiment, and the peculiar practice of sending children home from the Empire that England was later carried everywhere. The sentiment of Sir Thomas Brown was prevalent. 'All places, all airs make unto me one country; I am in England, everywhere, and under any meridian'.[4]

The English made their Empire in their image and carried 'the home country' in their hearts. Of course nearly all countries carry their own culture with them – overseas French, Italians, Chinese, Indians. What is special is the artificial way in which by sending their children back to the motherland for ten or more years of intensive indoctrination in 'Englishness', this was refreshed and the children, on the whole, did not 'go native'. I experienced this in my life. I was trained to be 'English', learning the history and culture which define me.

What we were learning during our days at school was to recognize the powerful symbols of our imperial identity. It is these shared symbols that make a community hold together – the flag, the mottoes, the music, the art, the processions and the pomp hold together far flung people. People become 'we' when they share symbols, feel them in the blood, distinguish themselves from others who have their own different system.

So we were learning the pomp and majesty, the 'habits of the heart' of being united – though we might be spread six thousand miles apart. Through sports triumphs, through the symbols of common religious heritage, Christmas as a family feast, Easter Eggs, Goodwood and the Boat Race, we 'felt' linked together even if there was no Internet or television. All this came together when a new monarch was crowned. I was a little boy of twelve at school, watching it on television, but sensed something of what Huizinga witnessed the at the Coronation of Queen Elizabeth II in 1953. What struck him 'as much as anything in this superb spectacle was the primitive, tribal aspect of the ritual.' Later he notes that the 'ceremony had been unique also in its mingling of fantasy and reality, past and present, superb charade and solemn constitutional act, Christian dedication and tribal sacrifice, hymn and martial trumpets.'[5]

Anthropologists distinguish between ritual and ceremonial or secular rituals. Puritan England is not over-fond of ritual (in the sense of actions which automatically have spiritual effects, such as the Catholic mass), but as I have seen in England, we are a ceremonial people. We put on big shows, whether our own such as the Coronation, or those of our ex-colonial peoples, such as Carnival. We put large emphasis on the processes of symbolic unity, though we are also suspicious of submerging ourselves in the crowd. These British mass ceremonials were also important in various parts of the overseas Empire, as in the Indian durbars.

These ceremonials had a strange feeling about them. Maillaud described two Coronations he had witnessed in England which 'have left on my mind a single impression: a feeling of "out-of-timeness", by which I mean something very different from archaism. the sensation was not that the clock had been put back some hundreds of years because the rites performed, the scenes enacted and garments worn had not changed for centuries; it was that what I saw and heard did exist irrespective of time and present circumstances, and that both were transcended. Here was a national symbol of permanence beyond the reach of contingency.'[6]

The pleasure of these large ceremonials is to have a well ordered, concerted, unified and dignified process. And we were trained at school how to behave and react during them. We learnt, for example, how important our house and school colours, crests, mottoes, flags and songs were. We were deeply affected as we processed onto the stage after the grueling ten-mile run and sang the school song.

The point about symbols is that they are multi-stranded and can be read by many different peoples in different ways, yet they unite. The inner feelings of thousands watching the Remembrance Day laying of wreaths at the Cenotaph or the Christmas lights in Piccadilly are all different – but each is united to the others by the focus on the symbol.

♦

THE BRITISH, LIKE all peoples in civilizations with writing, have a vast range of stories about their history and attributes. These tell us a great deal about what they think themselves to be. They have also contributed powerfully to our current world through the spread of British culture, often by way of America. British poetry, drama, novels and children's stories are a notable contribution to the stock of the world's great literatures, alongside the great traditions of India, China, Japan and Russia.

Let me start with the literature. Here several features stand out. One is the continuity and continuing intellectual and emotional resonance of the works. Beowulf, Gawain, Chaucer, Shakespeare, Milton, the Romantics, the great eighteenth and nineteenth novelists, all seem alive today. It is seamless. There are great differences between Chaucer and Dickens, or between Shakespeare and Oscar Wilde, but there are also continuities.

At a deeper level, it would seem that much of the great literature in Britain has been about certain themes or contradictions which, as Levi-Strauss argues, is the essence of myth, trying to express some of the most intractable contradictions of our divided and uncertain modern world. There is predestination and free-will (Shakespeare, Milton, Hardy); love and duty (Shakespeare and Jane Austen); mortality and immortality, social class and social conformity (Swift, Pope, Austen, Wilde, Shaw).

I think that the reason why we find this corpus is still alive, that Shakespeare and Wyatt and Spenser still amuse and amaze us, and even Chaucer feels relevant, is that they are all 'modern' in the sense which I have defined. We recognized the conflicting emotions, the contradictions of head and heart, the divided oppositions, the profit motives, the individualism and conformity, the class and gender oppositions, the loneliness and the fun. Yet when Shakespeare's 'King Lear' was taken to a very different setting as in the Japanese filmmaker Kurosawa's *Ran*, it has to be totally changed in its inner dynamic to fit with another emotional world.

So the literature provides the introspective playing with irresolvable oppositions which continues through the great children's story traditions. The folk traditions of the Grimm Brothers, Perault or Hans Anderson are not to be matched in England – though there is something of them in Celtic folklore. Instead the world of *Alice in Wonderland*, *The Wind in the Willows* and the stories Beatrix Potter up to the *Lord of the Rings* and Harry Potter and Narnia is something special – modern in its characterization and concepts.

There is something special about this literature which I have found well expressed by French observers. It is partly to do with fantasy and imagination. As Maillaud wrote, one word which captures the essence of a part of Englishness is 'fancy'. 'It conveys to my mind a combination of qualities which have been traditionally characteristic of the English: not only fantasy of which it is the contraction, but nimble freedom of will, dislike of rational obligations, whim and imaginative moodiness. The word has, so to speak, a propulsive suggestion; yet, like all others, it also has its brakes: reserve, a touch of shyness, some elusiveness, and an instinctive reluctance to follow any pursuit, cultivate any taste, or carry any belief to the point of mental strain.'[7]

Or, to put it in another way, there is a kind of escape from the heavy weight of too much rationality and this-worldliness. Cammaerts writes of this when he draws attention to the strong tradition of nonsense verse in England, which again links to children's stories:

> Of all the surprises I experienced in the course of my study of English literature, the most striking was the discovery of the poetry of nonsense. (Lear, Carroll, Belloc, Kipling *et al*) ... How was I to explain the care lavished by some of the best modern English poets on a world of topsy-turvy-dom and freakishness?' He thought that 'There seems little doubt that, like many excellent things, the poetry of nonsense was born in the / nursery, and that the attraction it still has for adult writers and readers is due to the hold that the nursery retains on them. The child possesses a powerful imagination, yet he moves in a narrow world. His only means of satisfying this imagination is either by "slipping through the crack" into a new world of dream and wonder, or by upsetting completely the conventional relation of the objects with which he comes into contact... In other words, the child-poet may either fly to the moon or compel the cow to jump over it.[8]

◆

IT IS A noticeably 'modern' literature that I learnt at school. My reading at secondary school was Chaucer (in depth over two years) Shakespeare (seven plays over four years)), Milton's 'Paradise Lost' (books 1 and 2), and the Metaphysicals, then Dryden, Wordsworth, Keats, Coleridge, Shelley and Gerard Manley Hopkins. We also studied Samuel Johnson, Hazlitt's *Spirit of the Age* and Jane Austen's *Pride and Prejudice* and the Brontes. We were learning a literary landscape which would mean that later in our lives, as we travelled round the country, it resonated with associations, weaving together my past and present with ties that fed my patriotism: 'the landscape of England is the landscape of its imaginative inheritance. The Chilterns are Bunyan's Delectable Mountains, Langland's Field of Folk lies beneath the Herefordshire Beacon, Dorset belongs to Hardy, Sussex to Kipling, George Herbert claims Wiltshire as power-fully as Wordsworth the Lake District, Jane Austen Hampshire or Emily Brontë the moors of west Yorkshire.'[9]

I was soaked in all this so that, as I pined in foreign parts – as an eighteen year old lonely, homesick, seasick – on a Norwe-gian cargo ship, I wrote to my parents for a copy of the famous speech of Bolingbroke when he was exiled from England in Shakespeare's Richard II. It still spoke to me and soothed me. The British Empire was held together by the shared tradition of 'Once More into the Breach ...', 'To Be or Not to Be', 'My heart aches and ...', 'Silent, upon a peak in Darien'. We were British middle class because our hearts were filled with the na-tionalistic, joyful, yet moving 'slow sad music of humanity', through our poetry and literature which bound us to our 'emer-ald isle' and to each other, just as other countries are united by the *Bagavad Ghita* or *The Dream of the Red Chamber* or *The Tale of Genji*.

Our romantic ruralism was partly a product of our far-flung Empire. As Raymond Williams wrote of England, 'Its green peace contrasted with the tropical or arid places of actual work; its sense of belonging, of community, idealized by contrast with the tensions of colonial rule and the isolated alien settlement. The birds and trees and rivers of England; the natives speak-ing, more or less, one's own language: these were the terms of many imagined and actual settlements. The country, now, was a place to retire to.'[10] Abroad was a temporary posting, the heart was always in England. Here the English were different from many imperial races, as Elspeth Huxley observed of East Africa, 'Africa ... is seldom home. He[the white official] is a man of divided loyalties, looking back and looking forward to the first and the last periods of his life spent in another continent, and with other ties. This is where he differs most from the settler, the

European who has come to Africa to make his home, as a white African to live and die.'[11]

♦

WE WERE ALSO held together by a distinctive representation of history. Our historical tradition began early and it is significant that the first great work, completed in about 731 A.D. by Bede was entitled the *Ecclesiastical History of the English People*, (or Nation – *Gentis Anglorum*). England was conceived of by Bede, a century and a half before the final political unification by Alfred the Great, as one people, one nation.

The history was written and re-written over the centuries. For example, Sir John Fortescue in his *Governance* did not believe that the rich and free land he was describing in the middle of the fifteenth century was new. His explanation for its existence to his royal pupil Henry VI was a combination of natural fertility, limited monarchy and Common Law. He wrote that 'The customs of England are of most ancient antiquity,' and traced them back through the Normans, Saxons, Danes, and Romans to the ancient Britons. There had been no basic changes in the customs in the preceding thousand years or more; 'in the times of these several nations and of their kings this realm was still ruled with the self same customs that it is now governed withal.'[12]

One could find similar sentiments in many other works. It is to be found indirectly in books on laws such as Bracton's great treatise on *The Laws and Customs of England* in the early thirteenth century, or Coke's majestic *Institutes of the Laws of England* in the early seventeenth. It culminated in the historical accounts of Macaulay, Froude, Green and Maitland and later Trevelyan and Churchill. On the way the Scottish historians, particularly Hume and Robertson, had enriched it.

Much of the history was implicitly or explicitly within what is called the 'Whig' theory of history, most famously in Macaulay's three volume *History of England*. It was a story of continuous evolution, progress, development, and organic growth from acorn to oak. It spoke of a manifest destiny. It was a suitable origin myth for the greatest Empire in history. It harked back to rougher glories, watched as the Enlightenment added its touch, saw the emergence of reason from the superstitions of the darker past, watched the early stream of the Anglo-Saxons was made broader and stronger by the Vikings, the French, the Huguenots and the Scots. It told how the British never had been slaves, how they still spoke a sturdy language and ate roast beef and good bread.

Shorn of its triumphalism and evolutionary fervour, it reached its highest peak in the works of the late nineteenth century constitutional historians who based themselves on meticulous study of English primary sources. One was William Stubbs, Professor of History at Oxford. In various books he laid out the basis of the system of English government which were complete by the mid-thirteenth century. In fact, it was already old, for the political and social system was already present in Anglo-Saxon England. Stubbs wrote:

> The great characteristic of the English constitutional system … the principle of its growth, the secret of its construction, – is the continuous development of representative institutions from the first elementary stage, in which they are employed for local purposes and in the simplest form, to that in which the national parliament appears as the concentration of all local and provincial machinery, the depository of the collective powers of the three estates of the realm.' It grows out of strong Anglo-Saxon roots and is consolidated by the Normans. In the eleventh and twelfth centuries 'The nation becomes one and realizes its oneness…. It is completed under Henry II and his sons. It finds its first distinct expression in Magna Carta.'[1215][13]

Stubbs was of course aware that there were turmoils ahead and that political and constitutional changes of considerable importance would occur over the next six centuries. Yet he believed that the basic rules changed little. There is no notion of any 'revolution' in Stubbs's work, no hint of a cataclysmic change from a 'medieval' to a 'modern' world. This was not because he was blind to changes when they did occur. He noted that the sixteenth and seventeenth centuries 'witnessed a series of changes in national life, mind, and character, in the relations of the classes, and in the balance of political forces, far greater than the English race had gone through since the Norman Conquest.' These changes he listed as the Reformation, the 'transformation of the baronage of early England into the nobility of later times' and the 'recovered strength of the monarchic principle...'[14] Yet he did not believe that the continuity of English history was ever broken.

Meanwhile F. W. Maitland could end *The History of English Law* in 1307, for the major foundations of modern law, political organization and society had been established by then. His immense work told a story of continuity with change, constant small shifts but not no revolutionare divide. The theme was summarized in his *Constitutional History of England,* originally given as a course of lectures at Cambridge.

It was because English history was so continuous that at school we were encouraged to believe that the present could only be understood by studying the long distant past. Maitland's belief that a lawyer in the late nineteenth century still needed to know a good deal about medieval law was extended over all of our knowledge. To understand democracy, the class system, the Anglican Church, our landscape and art, all required us to go back through the centuries to the Anglo-Saxons. We lived in an old country and to understand our present we must understand our deep past. The past was not a foreign country – or only slightly so.

This was what I learnt at both my schools and also when I studied history at Oxford. The courses started with the Anglo-Saxons and went through until the end of the nineteenth century. It was 'Our Island Story' as Churchill called it, a narrative of a hard drinking, hard fighting, games loving, poetic, rough set of islanders who finally became the rulers of a quarter of the world and created the largest revolution in production of recorded history.

The sense of continuity was reinforced in our historical studies and as we looked around us at our leaders (during my school time Sir Alec Douglas-Home, Sir Anthony Eden, Sir Harold Macmillan and others). We could see that England had always been, and still was, a mixture of aristocracy and democracy. As Huizinga observed, English history and culture 'could be summed up in two interrelated propositions: England was "an aristocratic state, the only one in white civilisation", and the English aristocracy or gentry, which, again in Belloc's words, had "created the whole history of England up to our time" and whose traditional way of life still remained the national ideal, had always had its roots in the countryside.'[15]

The nature of this curious state and its tenacity led to further reflections by the Dutchman Huizinga. He believed on the basis of his many years in the country that 'England was essentially still an aristocratic country "in the sense", as Belloc had said, "that its citizens are ordered, its laws are made and administrated, its customs preserved by a comparatively small governing class and in which such a social structure ... and government by gentlemen is found natural".... I dimly sensed ... the British system of government was not representative government or popular government but something very different, Government by the Right People, Government by Gentlemen.' As he continued to live through a good part of the middle of the twentieth century in England, my original sense of wonder at the discovery in our modern age of the system of government by Gentlemen, or aristo-democracy, has deepened into a sense of marvel at its tenacity, its apparent ability to survive every kind of political, social or economic upheaval.'[16]

♦

THERE IS A paradox in the English attitude to the past. On the one hand, there is a strong sense that people are 'living in an old country'. In this view much of our present world has deep roots in ancient times. There have been no 'revolutions', except perhaps material and technological ones; the laws, language, customs, politics and landscape go back in a continuous line to the Anglo-Saxons. This is tied in with a love of older things – some valuable, some almost rubbish.

In 1930, Cammaerts wrote, 'The present is not, for them, a hard line of demarcation between two opposite worlds, but a gentle mist through which they wander leisurely...They travel through time, as they do indeed through space, dragging behind them a quantity of useless luggage.

> This kind of box-room or lumber-room is not only charac-teristic of the English home but of all English institutions. There is a positive objection in England to anything that looks like "scrapping". Past traditions and titles and cos-tumes are essentially respectable; they may have become useless, but if they do no good they can certainly do no harm, and then – who knows? – there is an attractive el-ement of doubt as their future destiny. The English, for these reasons, preserve their seventeenth-century univer-sity gowns, their Warden of the Cinque Ports, and such obsolete ministerial titles as Chancellor of the Duchy of Lancaster and Lord Privy Seal.... The Beefeaters made a good show on the day of the Opening of Parliament, and the Guy Fawkes carnival enlivens the gloom of our November climate.[17]

The English are filled with nostalgia and memories – though they always believe that this is disappearing. So the museums, the National Trust that was set up to preserve old houses and landscapes, keeping of strange traditions, a desire not to change things, all that is something I have witnessed in the institutions I have moved through.

This does not arise from fear of the future, but respect for the past. 'The English do not wish to preserve for preservation's sake, in order to build up a bulwark against forthcoming changes. It is not because they dread the future that they are fond of the past. Alone among nations, they are equally well-disposed towards the Middle Ages and towards the wildest prophecies concerning the present and the coming centuries. ... The present is not, for them, a hard line of demarcation between two opposite worlds, but a gentle mist through which they wander leisurely, turning sometimes to the right towards a group of Knights galloping out of a Moat House, sometimes to the left towards a number of Robots flying from the tops of sky-scrapers...'[18]

Combined with this nostalgia is the feeling that the old ways are best. 'From this high opinion which the English entertain of their country, and of their nation, it may be explained, why they adhere so much to their old customs, and to certain habits; perhaps, for no other reason, but because they have been told, from their infancy, that nothing is so good and so perfect as Old England.'[19] My own experience is reflected in Emerson's observation of a middle class house. 'Hither he brings all that is rare and costly, and with the national tendency to sit fast in the same spot for many generations, it comes to be, in the course of time, a museum of heirlooms, gifts, and trophies of the adventures and exploits of the family.'[20] As Paxman observes:

> Every traditional English family home has a room, a cupboard, an attic, cellar or garage piled with everything from ancient prams to odd rolls of wallpaper in the patterns of twenty years ago, old light-fittings to the boxes in which long-broken electrical appliances were sold. They are kept because "they might come in useful some day". Really, their pragmatic and sensible owners were just reluctant to part with them.[21]

The paradox arises from the fact that simultaneously there is an acceptance that the past should no longer dictate the present. Here there is something similar to the Japanese belief that past battles are over – 'let the dead bury their dead' – let us forgive and forget the emotions of the past and live into the future. The past is like a finished football game – it was fun to play, we may remember and replay the highlights, but we should not dwell on it too much.

Here the English have exemplified Renan's famous statement that the art of building a nation consists of 'the art of forgetting'. The English half forget so much, both the injustices to themselves, and the horrors they committed. They look on the British Empire with a certain complacency, easily forgetting the abominations in the slave trade, the Opium Wars, the Irish or Bengal famines. They stress the positive, asking that sleeping dogs be let to lie, don't stir up ghosts.

◆

TOCQUEVILLE SUGGESTED THAT egalitarian nations with their disinterest in ancestry cut the web and warp of history. The constant immersion in the pursuit of material goals also altered the whole attitude to time and the momentum of history. Time past was irrelevant. 'Aristocracy naturally leads the mind back to the past and fixes it in the contemplation thereof. But democracy engenders a sort of instinctive distaste for what is old.' Tocqueville saw that political, social and physical time is interrelated, an Einsteinian view of the relativity of concepts of time and social relations. 'Amongst democratic peoples new families are constantly springing up, others are constantly falling away, and all that remain change their condition; the woof of time is ever being broken and the track of generations effaced. Those who went before are soon forgotten; of those who will come after, no one has any idea; the interest of man is confided to shoes in close propinquity to himself.'[22]

The lack of interest in ancestry was something that also struck Fukuzawa in his visit to America in the early 1870s:

> One day, on a sudden thought, I asked a gentleman where the descendants of George Washington might be. He replied, "I think there is a woman who is directly descended from Washington. I don't know where she is now, but I think I have heard she is married." His answer was so very casual that it shocked me. Of course, I knew that America was a republic with a new president every four years, but I could not help feeling that the family of Washington would be revered above all other families. My reasoning was based on the reverence in Japan for the founders of the great lines of rulers – like that for Ieyasu of the Tokugawa family of Shoguns, really deified in the popular mind. So I remember the astonishment I felt at receiving this indifferent answer about the Washington family.[23]

America faced the future and not the past. England is a hybrid case. It reverences and tries to preserve the past and is in some way a vast museum. Yet it also systematically and largely successfully forgets the divisions and conflicts, thus allowing a sense of unity, a combining together at the cenotaph, or the King's College Carols. 'Let bygones be bygones' was a favourite phrase of my mother's parents and many English would agree.

The synthesis between the desire to retain the past and the urge to forget it, to restlessly seek the new while also not wanting to throw aways the old, is described as a characteristic of modern democratic societies by Tocqueville. 'I am not making out that the inhabitants of democracies are by nature stationary; on the contrary, I think that such a society is always on the move and that none of its members knows what rest is; but I think that all bestir themselves within certain limits which they hardly ever pass. Daily they change, alter, and renew things of secondary importance, by they are very careful not to touch fundamentals. They love change, but they are afraid of revolutions.'[24]

With all of this went a sense of the superiority of the English way of life, which could be taken to amusing extremes. Emerson noted in the nineteenth century, 'An English lady on the Rhine hearing a German speaking of her party as foreigners, exclaimed, "No, we are not foreigners; we are English; it is you that are foreigners".[25] It became assumed that the English were the standard, normal, rational – foreigners were odd. I was educated to believe this, and to a certain extent this book is an attempt to reverse this and to stress how peculiar and unusual the world I grew up in was (and still is).

CHAPTER NOTES

1. Kames, *Sketches*, II, 249

2. Huizinga, *Confessions*, 90.

3. Huizinga, *Confessions*, 150, 202

4. In *Quotations* (Oxford), 42

5. Huizinga, *Confessions*, 153, 202

6. Maillaud, *English*, 89.

7. Maillaud, *English*, 58.

8. Cammaerts, *English*, 159-160.

9. Paxman, *English*, 169

10. Quoted in Paxman, *English*, 144-5

11. Huxley, *East*, 231

12. Fortescue, *Governance*, fols, 38, 38v

13. Stubbs, *Constitutional*, I, 544-5

14. Stubbs, *Constitutional*, III, 3.

15. Huizinga, *Confessions*, 61

16. Huizinga, *Confessions*, 96, 101

17. Cammaerts, *English*, 89

18. Cammaerts, *English*, 91

19. Wendeborn in Wilson, *Strange*, 133

20. Emerson, *English*, 85

21. Paxman, *English*, 154

22. Tocqueville, *Democracy*, II, 621; Tocqueville, *Democracy* (abridged), 193-4

23. Fukuzawa, *Autobiography*, 116

24. Tocqueville, *Democracy*, II, 828

25. Emerson, *English*, 116

CHAPTER 15

RELIGION AND ETHICS

THE RELIGIOUS SYSTEM which has evolved over the last thousand years on a small island off north-west Europe shares general features of Christianity. It also has a number of distinctive features. I can only touch on one or two elements, singling out a few of those which seem to be expressions of those distinctions into separate spheres of life which is the theme of this book.

As Max Weber realized, there was a strand within Christianity which was important for the development of capitalism. Briefly, this might be said to be early Christianity's desire to cut out a separate territory for itself and not to enter into alliances with other institutions. In relation to the family, Jesus urged his followers to forsake their fathers and mothers and to follow him. The large monastic organizations are an alternative to the family. In the conflict between family bonds of a wider kind and Christianity, Christ must come first. The de-familization of society was one of its consequences.

Christianity early on was an anti–authoritarian and anti–political religion. Christ may have suggested that his followers render to Caesar that which was Caesar's, but he was crucified because his opponents saw him as a political threat. Through the long years when it was persecuted by the State, Christianity developed a theology which put the calling of God as higher than the duty to the State. Christians called for 'liberty'. This was particularly strongly manifested in Protestantism, where the 'Saints' opposed the ruling powers – whether in Holland, England or Germany.

One of the striking features of English society since well before the Reformation, and certainly after it, has been the systematic elimination of ritual, 'magic' and icons. As Keith Thomas has documented, a magical worldview was eliminated.[1] There was much preaching of ethics and morality, but there were no physical sacrifices, no turning of wine into blood, no 'miracles'. God was in the heart of the believer, but otherwise the world was subject to natural laws. This formed the basis for modern science, and it helped to eliminate obstacles to economic growth.

If religion and ritual pervade all aspects of life and dominate them, one has a magical world in which 'rational', that is means and ends related actions, are impossible. An example is in the debate in the West over usury. Lending money is essential for capitalist enterprise but it has been argued that the Catholic Church's formal ban on lending at interest put a break on growth. Once this religious obstacle was overcome, 'free' and rational activity could take place. Weber saw the 'disenchantment' of the separation of spheres as one of the essential steps in the growth of modern society.

Keith Thomas has indicated that the disenchantment was early; 'since Anglo-Saxon times the Christian Church in England had stood out against the worship of wells and rivers. The pagan divinities of grove, stream and mountain had been expelled, leaving behind them a disenchanted world to be shaped, moulded and dominated'.[2] Although Thomas is right to point out that it is too simple to see this disenchantment as simply equated with Christianity, there is certainly an ascetic stress in Christianity, and particularly in the northern variety, which was hostile to the interfusion of man and nature, to 'magic' and 'symbolic thinking'.

♦

THE FORM OF Protestantism that grew up in England avoided the compact with the State. The Calvinists made the State a Godly project in Scotland and Switzerland, but Lutheranism in England seems to have stressed individual conscience, to have spawned separate sects and sub-groups, and generally to have helped maintain the break between politics and religion which is the foundation of much of the dynamism of England and America.

The freedom of religion and thought was surprising to visitors to England in the eighteenth century. Saussure wrote 'that great liberty of conscience and toleration is enjoyed in England'.[3] Montesquieu a little earlier wrote: 'With regard to religion, as in this state every subject has a free will, and must consequently be either conducted by the light of his own mind or by the caprice of fancy, it necessarily follows that everyone must either look upon all religion with indifference, by which means they are led to embrace the established religion, or they must be zealous for religion in general, by which means the number of sects is increased.'[4] Or again Rochefoucauld reflected that 'All religions are tolerated in England – not by law, but in fact. In my section on London I have already referred to the chapels of the various sects and to the number of them. They are similarly tolerated in other parts of the kingdom. At Bury, for example, there are six different sects, all of which have their tabernacles or chapels and each one of them practises its religion in peace.'[5]

As Caraccioli sardonically put it: 'There are in England sixty different religious sects, but only one sauce'.[6] The result was a surprising freedom to disagree. Saussure suggested that 'This is the reason why so many different sects are to be found in England, and also so great a number of persons with deistical opinions, and who, taking advantage of the leniency of the government, occasionally publish pamphlets against the established religion, that in any other country would, together with their authors, pass through the hands of the executioner'.[7]

Indeed, by the eighteenth and nineteenth centuries, some people were rather scandalized by the way in which religion seemed to be more about life-style, social status and identity, something equivalent to an accent or the style of one's house, than about any real fervent beliefs in the Deity. Prince Puckler-Muskau wrote 'But such is the piety of Englishmen, – it is to them at once a party matter, and an affair of good manners; and as in politics they follow their party implicitly, through thick and thin, reasonable and unreasonable, because it *is* their party; as they submit to a custom for ever, because it *is* a custom; so they regard their religion (without the least tincture of poetry) in exactly the same point of view: they go to church on Sunday, just as regularly as they dress every day for dinner; and regard a man who neglects church, just in the same light as one who eats fish with a knife.' Emerson noted that 'The religion of England is part of good breeding.'

There was some truth in Rochefoucauld's observation that with constant separation into sects, and with each person's opinion their own business, it became difficult to find a common religion. 'The only point on which there is general agreement is that nearly every Englishman holds a different belief; all of them believe in some particular point peculiar to themselves; some of them (and nearly all the women) refuse to accept the Trinity and shut their books when it occurs in the service. From which I conclude that the whole body, which is made up of these individual believers, believes in nothing at all.'[8] Or as Disraeli put it a century later 'Where can we find faith in a nation of sectaries?'[9] Emerson asked 'But the religion of England – is it the Established Church? no, is it the sects? no; they are only perpetuations of some private man's dissent, and are to the Established Church as cabs are to a coach, cheaper and more convenient, but really the same thing. Where dwells the religion? Tell me first where dwells electricity, or motion, or thought, or gesture."[10]

Pevsner gives a delightful illustration. 'If Reynolds exemplifies how a painter can adhere to the Grand Manner without adhering to the Grand Manner, the Church of England demonstrates how one can be catholic without being Catholic, and occasionally protestant almost without being Protestant.' The final outcome was the statement 'made by the Judicial Committee of the Privy Council in the Voysey case of 1871, that clergymen "may follow any interpretations of the Articles, which, by any reasonable allowance for the variety of human opinion, can be reconciled with their language".[11]

Coming from Calvinist Scotland, Hugh Miller noted that the religious separations were linked to the individualistic national character; 'the country of insulated man is the best fitted to be also the country of insulated Churches'; 'the insulating bias of the English character leads to the fanatic of insulated Churches'.[12]

It may be thought that this moral relativism, treating religion as a fashion accessory, was an eighteenth or nineteenth century phenomenon, but we see it well described by John Selden in his *Table Talk* in the middle of the seventeenth century: 'it is like the fashion; one man wears a doublett slashed, another lac'd, a third plaine, but every man has a doublett'.[13]

It would be wrong, however, to infer from this that there had always been open toleration or even apathy. As Rasmussen pointed out. 'Now tolerance and dispassion about religious questions is an English virtue; but in the sixteenth and seventeenth centuries the religious struggles were carried on with great fanaticism in England.'[14]

Religion might be looked at like a serious game – the aim was to lead a good life and to be moderately confident of salvation, if there was indeed a Deity. But the tactics of playing the game was up to each individual. Taine put it in a slightly different way. English religion 'subordinates ritual and dogma to ethics. It preaches "self-government", the authority of conscience, and the cultivation of the will. It leaves a wide margin for personal interpretation and feeling. It is not altogether hostile to the spirit of modern science nor to the tendencies of the modern world. Its priests are married. It founds schools, urges action, and does not advice asceticism. Being thus in close touch and sympathy with the lay community, it has influence over it. The young man starting out in life, the mature man in full career, are, up to a certain point, restrained and guided by a body of traditional, popular and fortifying beliefs which provide them with a rule of conduct and a noble idea of the world.'[15] The forms, the rituals, were conventional and external and indeed Protestantism sets its face against rituals and miracles.

Many in England, within and without the Church, believed that God, Christ and the after-life, all that was secondary – ultimately it was the ethics – the love thy neighbour, the charity, the justice, the forgoing of violence, all of the 'Sermon on the Mount' that is at the heart of Christianity and should be retained.

All this greatly puzzled Huizinga from his Dutch Calvinist background, but he finally felt he had understood what lay behind English religion. 'The first clue I obtained was that the English were not nearly so religious as they looked. They were clearly preoccupied with morals and conduct; their austere and ascetic laws, written as well as unwritten, left no doubt on that score.' Yet 'Their puritanism was not to be equated with a deep religiousness in the sense of other-worldliness...Pierre Maillaud had called the religion of the English "almost wholly unmystical, stressing conduct rather than convictions". Renier had called the English "fundamentally indifferent to religion, indifferent to such a degree that they are prepared to ignore its essence while upholding its externals".[16]

Huizinga himself felt that much of their religion was actually more to do with patriotism than religion as understood by most people. He often felt 'that to the English mind's eye Caesar and God looked much alike, that Britannia and the Deity seemed one and the same – or at any rate so mixed up with one another and their separate identities had become almost indistinguishable. "For this most nationalistic people in the world," Madariaga had said, "Britannia is the highest goddess on their Olympus." "Religious principles," says Pierre Maillaud …. "are often valued here because of the service they perform in the enforcement of social order … Religion in England … strives to maintain or expand social discipline rather than to enhance the sense and quality of worship." Belloc has summed it up in his forceful way, 'The religion of the English,is not Protestantism but patriotism.'[17]

The situation in England today is described by the anthropologist Kate Fox: 'We have no actual objection to God. If pushed, we even accept that He might exist – or that Something might exist, and we might as well call it God, if only for the sake of peace and quiet. God is all very well, in His place, which is the church. When we are in His house – at weddings, and funerals – we make all the right polite noises, as one does in people's houses, although we find the earnestness of it all faintly ridiculous and a bit uncomfortable. Otherwise, He impinges very little in our lives or our thoughts. Other people are very welcome to worship Him if they choose – it's a free country – but this is a private matter, and they should keep it to themselves and not bore or embarrass the rest of us by making an unnecessary *fuss* about it.'[18] Even the Anglican Church seems to accept this humble role. 'In 1991, the then Archbishop of Canterbury, Dr George Carey, said "I see it as an elderly lady, who mutters away to herself in a corner, ignored most of the time".[19] Many might nowadays share the caustic view of Lord Melbourne in the nineteenth century that 'Things have come to a pretty pass when religion is allowed to invade the sphere of private life.'[20]

◆

SOME MIGHT BELIEVE that this heterodoxy was the result of the break with Rome at the Protestant Reformation – yet that seems as much an effect as a cause. As Freeman argued, Protestantism was an epiphenomenon of deep-seated features of English society from the middle ages. 'We did not become free, enterprising or dominant, because we had embraced certain theological dogmas. We rather embraced certain theological dogmas because we instinctively found them to be those which best suited a free, an enterprising, and a dominant nation.' As he also states the English Reformation, 'was only accidentally that the Reformation was theological at all. Henry VIII did little more than succeed in doing what Henry II had failed to do'. 'The Reformation was... a political movement which incidentally became a theological one.' Protestantism – an epiphenomenon of the deep-seated nature of English society from the middle ages. 'Nowhere did Christianity become so thoroughly a national, almost a local faith, as it became in England. Nowhere was the Church so truly the nation in one of its aspects; nowhere was the order and discipline of the Church so easily wrought into the old framework of the national institutions.'.[21]

The fierce battles of Church and State, most pointedly in the struggle between Henry and Becket, placed the Crown above the Church. As Maitland noted, the Church never developed its own separate legal system, just existing on the edges of Common Law. The superior power of the Law and the Crown 'prevented the development of a body of distinctively ecclesiastical law which would stand in contrast with, if not in opposition to, the law of the land.'[22] All were equal under the national law and the Church remained subordinate, like other estates, to Parliament. 'The whole of this religion is founded upon the principle of political equality. The only superior authority is Parliament. Everyone else is on an equal footing.'[23]

Church and State did not form the kind of alliance which led to the Inquisition. The wealth and independence of the Church was always treated with suspicion, most obviously by the Lollards, but elsewhere. Then when the Counter-Reformation swept Europe, as Burckhardt pointed out, the Caesaro-Papist alliance was avoided. 'In the great Western countries, with the exception of England, the Counter-Reformation sealed the "Covenant between the Throne and the Altar" – that is, the Church, to maintain itself, once more made use of the secular arm in the widest sense of the word'.[24]

This does not mean that 'religion' is unimportant in England. There are grounds for thinking that the special variety of religion in England was central to all of English life. The Bishop of Chichester was not exaggerating when he wrote during the Second World War that 'The Church of England is both the most venerable and the most influential of all the factors which have gone to the making of English history and English character. Broadly and deeply planted in the land, mixed up with all our manners and customs, one of the main guarantees of our local government, and therefore one of the prime securities of our common liberties, the Church of England, in Disraeli's words, is part of our history, part of our life, part of England itself.'[25]

Paxman agrees with this, but also makes the necessary qualification, 'In developing a sense of national identity, the achievement of the Church of England was not so much what it proclaimed but what it made possible. There is a case for saying that the invention of the Church of England *was* the invention of England. However, this is not say that the English are a churchy people.'[26] For, just like the English family, which is important and yet does not provide the infrastructure, religion became privatized. This was particularly noticeable in relation to the tolerance of varieties of religion. 'In fact, I never met with an

English Catholic who did not value, as much as any Protestant, the free institutions of his country, or who divided morality into two sections, one consisting of public virtues, which might be safely neglected, and the other of private duties, which alone need be observed. ... I said only that I breathed freely in a country in which liberty and religion were united.'[27]

The paradox of extreme individualism and sectarian separation, combined with intense religious belief was obvious to Tocqueville as it is today. Religion, though supposedly separated from politics in a secular State, is everywhere. Yet it is also a private matter. Some thought it left religion almost empty. 'It was a curious result, in which the civility and religion of England for a thousand years ends in denying morals, and reducing the intellect to a saucepan.'[28]

Understanding all of this is more difficult in England because of the feature of the conservation of the outward forms. 'The English, abhorring change in all things, abhorring it most in matters of religion, cling to the last rag of form, and are dreadfully given to cant.'[29] And the cant, or hypocrisy, which amazed foreigners, makes it difficult to penetrate below the surface. I see this every day in Cambridge University, the bells, the processions, the chapels, the rituals, but what do people believe in their hearts?

Religion seeped into everything, as I now discover from my life as a schoolboy or through conversations with Japanese friends who are shocked at how religious even an agnostic like myself is. Christianity is there in English poetry, philosophy, art, music, architecture and every branch of life; yet it is different from the *ancien regime* religious pacts of the Continent or much of Islam or Confucianism. In Britain, was a useful first mover, as in the philosophy of Descartes, but not a place where the mind rests. The God of the English was often a relatively tolerant, curious and in the end puzzling deity.

♦

THE TYPE OF modernity of which I see early traces in England is one of moral ambiguity and relativism. Religion is constantly in conflict with pressures from social, political and especially economic forces. One way to examine this is to look at something which is a feature of all religions, namely the concept of radical or ever-present danger or Evil.[30] This takes us into many of the more complex areas of religious belief.

Detailed village records, diaries, letters, proverbs and other sources suggest that people in England from at least the fifteenth century do not seem to have been much concerned with the Devil and absolute Evil. A satisfying explanation of the absence of absolute Evil, the Devil and Hell is related to many wider features. It is clearly no coincidence, for example, that England was the only major European nation to have no Catholic Inquisition and no inquisitorial process under law. The terror of evil was not encouraged.

Another part of the solution for the curiously 'modern' attitudes from the later Middle Ages at least, is provided by two of those who wrote in England during the period under consideration, namely Shakespeare and Milton. One of the most striking features of both, making them seem 'modern' and relevant to us, is that they are concerned with a grey world where good and evil are interchangeable, where it is impossible to be certain, to have absolute moral standards, where nothing is entirely black or white. This is clearly the case in Shakespeare's treatment of his central characters – Hamlet, Brutus, Prospero, Macbeth. For them, the choices are difficult, there is no absolute standard, things are not what they seem.

Shakespeare suggests reasons why good and evil have become blurred. Money, he shows, could change one into the other. Here he is touching on a central paradox. In a capitalist society, evil becomes good, good evil. Karl Marx quoted Shakespeare approvingly because he had seen this central feature.

> What is here?
> Gold? yellow, glittering precious gold? ...
> Thus much of this will make black, white; foul, fair;
> Wrong, right; base, noble; old, young, coward, valiant.
> . . .
> This yellow slave
> Will knit and break religions; bless the accurs'd;
> Make the hoar leprosy ador'd; place thieves,
> And give them title, knee, and approbation,
> With senators on the bench...[31]

Thus, gold transforms everything, from black to white and back again; it brings together as equivalents things that are not really on the same plane and divides things that are naturally together. Man is no longer able to discriminate between what is good, what evil.

This confusion is echoed in Milton's *Paradise Lost*, which concerns the battle between good and evil. Yet the struggle is not between two opposed sides, but within the same principle. The poem is an attempt to state the paradox that good and evil are entirely separate, yet also the same. It grapples with the problem of how evil emerged at all, for it arose out of goodness. The problem is given one formulation in the myth of the garden of Eden, where evil was present even in a perfect Paradise. Once evil has emerged as distinct from goodness, having become separated, the problem for both is to prevent their mutual contamination and a tendency to become joined again.

The attempt to foil God's attempt to bring the fallen angels back into his mercy is the subject of many of Satan's famous lines.

> If then his providence
> Out of our evil seek to bring forth good,
> Our labour must be to prevent that end,
> And out of good still find means of evil

The world has to be redefined in order to achieve this.

So farewell hope, and with hope farewell fear,
Farewell remorse: all good to me is lost; Evil be thou my
Good[32]

Yet, just as evil has emerged out of the principle of good, so it is possible for good to emerge from evil. This is the constant threat to the fallen angels; that God may win them back and turn their evil into good, for the power of goodness is very great: 'abashed the devil stood, And felt how awful goodness is'.[33] Ultimately, good and evil are not separable. Heaven and Hell, the Devil and God are in essence different aspects of the same power.

Milton's poem could be seen as the eloquent expression of the tragic recognition that the simplicities of a childlike black and white vision were not sufficient. It is all a matter of how we look at things, a subjectivist world in which man cannot depend on any external, eternal, objective, moral laws. Milton needed to justify the ways of God to man; as a result, each man would act as a judge upon God, rather than the reverse. Morality was in the eye of the beholder. As Pope would put it, 'Pleasure, or wrong or rightly understood / Our greatest evil, or our greatest good'.[34]

Pascal had summarized this view in the seventeenth century. 'We hardly know of anything just or unjust which does not change its character with a change of climate. Three degrees of polar elevation overturn the whole system of jurisprudence. A meridian determines what is truth.... There is not a single law which is universal'.[35] Alexander Pope took the next step, representing the culmination of a trend towards ethical relativism which argued from growing evidence that every civilization had its own appropriate moral system.

All nature is but art, unknown to thee;
All chance, direction which thou canst not see;
All discord, harmony not understood;

All partial evil, universal good;
And, spite of pride, in erring reason's spite,
One truth is clear, Whatever is, is right.[36]

It is possible only to raise a few questions and hint at an answer to the problem of the origins of the disappearance of pure evil. Both the answer and the problem are encapsulated in St Paul's warning that 'The love of money is the root of all evil' (1 Timothy 6: 10). This dismissal of avarice is one of the central pillars of that Judaeo-Christian tradition upon which western civilization is based. Yet, it could equally well be argued that the love of money is an equally important pillar of this civilization.

Adam Smith most clearly exposed this foundation of modern society, a feature without which modern societies would immediately collapse. As he put it, 'The division of labour, from which so many advantages are derived, is not originally the effect of any human wisdom, which foresees and intends that general opulence to which it gives occasion. It is the necessary, though very slow and gradual, consequence of a certain propensity in human nature which has the propensity to truck, barter, and exchange one thing for another.'[37] This division of labour and all that flows from it is thus based on a propensity, that is, in the ethical terms laid down by the formal theology, evil. The foundations are laid on individual acquisitiveness, the love of money and pursuit of profit. Thus, good and evil are mixed in the roots of modern society.

Yet money, and all it symbolizes, is the root of all evil in a deeper sense than this. Viewed from outside the system, money can be seen to do something even more insidious. It subtly eliminates the very concept of evil. Or, rather it makes it impossible to discriminate between good and evil, throwing people into that confusion that cast the angels from Paradise and afflicted Shakespeare's central characters. 'Money', which is a shorthand way of saying capitalistic relations, market values, trade and exchange, ushers in a world of moral confusion.

This effect of money has been most obvious where a capitalistic, monetary economy has clashed with another, opposed, system. Thus it is anthropologists, who have worked in such areas of conflict, who have witnessed most dramatically the effect of the introduction of a monetized economy. They have noted how money disrupts the moral as well as the economic world. As Kenelm Burridge, for example, writes of the effect of money in Melanesia: money complicates the moral order, turning what was formerly black and white into greyness. Money, he argues, 'reveals the vice in cultivated virtues, allows no vice without some virtue, concedes an element of right in wrong-doing, finds the sin of pride in an upright fellow.... money invites a complex differentiation and multiplication of the parts and qualities of man.'[38] More broadly, it is money, markets and market capitalism that eliminate absolute moralities. Not only is every moral system throughout the world equally valid, as Pascal noted, but, within every system, whatever is, is right.

The consequences of money and the mentality associated with it are equally apparent to the major sociological thinkers. One of the most eloquent descriptions of the way in which money destroys moral polarities, qualitative difference is by George Simmel: 'By being the equivalent to all the manifold things in one and the same way, money becomes the most frightful leveller. For money expresses all qualitative differences of things in terms of "how much?" Money, with all its colourlessness and indifference, becomes the common denominator of all values; irreparably it hollows out the core of things, their individuality, their specific gravity in the constantly moving stream of money. All things lie on the same level and differ from one another only in the size of the area which they cover.'[39]

The consequences of this moral revolution were already apparent to people in the most developed capitalist economy, England, by the eighteenth century. What had happened was that capitalism had fully triumphed. It has now become clear that what was considered to be the root of all evil, namely the love of money, was also the root of all that was good, namely the bargaining, market principle of Adam Smith. This paradox was so horrifying in its implications that, when it was pointed out starkly, there was fierce condemnation. The man who made the unspeakable truth known was Bernard Mandeville, a Dutchman who had settled as a doctor in London, in his *Fable of the Bees*. The sub-title of the work summarized the theme: it was 'Private Vices, Public Benefits'. The work was first published in 1714, alongside a doggerel poem entitled 'The Grumbling Hive: or, Knaves Turn'd Honest', first published in 1705. The theme of the poem was that it was out of the private passions and vices of the citizens – their lusts, acquisitive spirits and aggressive competition – that public benefits flowed. As Mandeville rhymed,

> Thus every part was full of Vice,
> Yet the whole Mass a Paradice;
> Flatter'd in Peace, and fear'd in wars
> They were th'Esteem of Foreigners,
> And lavish of their Wealth and Lives,
> The Balance of all other Hives.
> Such were the Blessings of that State;
> Their Crimes conspired to make 'em Great;
> And Vertue, who from Politicks
> Had learn'd a Thousand cunning Tricks,
> Was, by their happy Influence,
> Made Friends with Vice: And ever since
> The Worst of all the Multitude
> Did something for the common Good.[40]

In other words, out of vice and evil passion came forth wealth and goodness. Evil lay at the heart of good in a capitalist society, just as evil had lain at the heart of good when the good angels had arisen to build a new world in the midst of Paradise. Mandeville's message was that, if one tried to be privately virtuous, the public world would collapse. Right at the end of the *Fable* Mandeville concluded that:

After this I flatter my self to have demonstrated that neither the Friendly Qualities and kind Affections that are
natural to Man, nor the real Virtues he is capable of ac-
quiring by Reason and Self-Denial are the foundation of
Society; but that what we call Evil in this World, Moral
as well as Natural, is the grand principle that makes us
Sociable Creatures, the solid Basis, the Life and Support
of all Trades and Employments without exception: That
there we must look for the true origin of all Arts and Sciences, and that the moment Evil ceases, the Society must
be spoil'd if not totally dissolv'd.[41]

This was Mandeville's central message, and it was incorporated in the great work that was written by the very moral
Adam Smith, and which would outline the basis of the capitalist
system: 'Without any intervention of law, therefore, the private
interests and passions of men naturally lead them to divide and
distribute the stock of every society, among all the different employments carried on in it, as nearly as possible in the proportion
which is most agreeable to the interest of the whole society.'[42]

Thus private vice, passions and interests have merged into
public good and ironically, the foundations of Paradise were laid
in Hell, and Hell in Paradise. The serpent of desire propped up
the tree of the knowledge of good and evil. Or, to put it another
way, the serpent was also the tree. By being that tree, he led to
the ultimate confusion, the inability to distinguish between good
and evil. When the fruit was tasted, it was found that, rather than
containing the new knowledge that enabled man to discriminate
good from evil, it contained the deadly knowledge that it was
now impossible to distinguish the two.

What is clear is that, at least at the popular level in England,
the ambivalences and contradictions were present back to the
start of the sixteenth century. It is possible to argue that ordinary
people in England had for centuries been accustomed to a world
not of absolutes, but of relative good and evil, where all could

be changed by money. It is appropriate and hardly fortuitous that Shakespeare should have provided the most exquisite expressions of that uncertainty in the midst of the period, or that in its full flowering in the eighteenth century Alexander Pope should have summarized the indecision and confusion so grandly:

> Placed on this isthmus of a middle state,
> A being darkly wise, and rudely great:
> . . .
> He Hangs between; in doubt to act, or rest;
> In doubt to deem himself a god, or beast;
> . . .
> Chaos of thought and passion, all confused;
> Still by himself abused, or disabused;
> Created half to rise, and half to fall;
> Great Lord of all things, yet a prey to all;
> Sole judge of truth, in endless error hurled:
> The glory, jest, and riddle of the world![43]

*

THIS SET OF never-resolved oppositions was beautifully reflected in the Anglican Church. It seems to have operated very much like English law – as a form of oil which lay between the different spheres of English life. It tolerated ambiguities and conflicts and adjudicated between them. Jeremy Paxman, who quotes several writers to this effect, recognizes this. '"The *via media* is the spirit of Anglicanism," wrote T.S.Eliot of the sixteenth century. "In its persistence in finding a mean between Papacy and Presbytery the English church under Elizabeth became something representative of the finest spirit of England of the time." Paxman continues, 'Dr Robert Runcie saw the vagueness for which it is castigated as a strength. "There are other churches in Christendom which take pride in their lack of ambiguity – in doctrine or leadership, or in monolithic interpretation of the Gospel. Anglicanism, by contrast, is a synthesis which necessarily unites thesis and antithesis."[44]

The political theorist D.W.Brogan also describes the creative inconsistency of the English church, its refusal, like the law, to be intolerantly based on certainties, its role as a religion which is not fundamentalist. He notes that many are irritated by the impossibility of defining the doctrine or practice of the Church of England and they 'are appalled by the toleration of incompatibles that is the genius of Anglicanism. To treat Christianity thus is very English...

> Before the Reformation, the central authority might impose order and doctrinal coherence. But once that control was removed, the absence of any English appreciation of the attractions of consistency, of the repellent character of anomalies, made it certain that whatever form organized religious life took in England it would not be coherent and consistent as it was in the Europe of Geneva or the Council of Trent ... The Church of England may only be the Church that the majority of English people stay away from. But they want it to be there to stay away from; it is their spiritual home whenever (which is not very often) they feel they want one. They would not be at home in a more functional institution, in a Church which knew its own mind and followed out to their logical conclusions the generally accepted premises of its doctrines. Such a Church would be, in one sense, a more respectable institution, but it would be very much less an English institution.'[45]

We might add that again it is like the English family – which may also be the only one where the majority of English people stay away from – but as the Church, they want it to be there to stay away from.

CHAPTER NOTES

1. Thomas, *Religion*

2. Thomas, *Natural*, 22

3. Saussure, *Foreign*, 317

4. Montesquieu, *Spirit*, I, 312

5. Rochefoucauld, *Frenchman*, 95

6. *Quotations*, 97

7. Saussure, *Foreign*, 191

8. Rochefoucauld, *Frenchman*, 92

9. Disraeli, in *Quotations* (Oxford), 129

10. Emerson, *English*, 175

11. Pevsner, *Englishness*, 66

12. Miller, *First*, 397

13. Pollock quoted in Campbell, *Yeoman*, 289

14. Rasmussen in Wilson, *Strange*, 258

15. Taine, *Notes*, 290

16. Huizinga, *Confessions*, 70

17. Huizinga, *Confessions*, 76

18. Fox, *Watching*, 356

19. Quoted in Fox, *Watching*, 354

20. Quoted in Paxman, *English*, 101

21. Freeman, *4th Essays*, 290, 287, 289, 240

22. Maitland, *History*, I, 21

23. Rochefoucauld, *Frenchman*, 85

24. Burckhardt, *Reflections*, 121

25. Bell, *English*, 7

26. Paxman, *English*, 100

27. Tocqueville *Memoir*, II, 398

28. Emerson, *English*, 188

29. Emerson, *English*, 174

30. This is based on Macfarlane, *Culture*, chapter 5

31. Timon of Athens, Act IV, scene 3 (quoted by Marx, *Grundrisse*, 163).

32. Milton, *Paradise Lost*, book I, line 157; and book IV, line 108

33. Milton, *Paradise Lost*, book IV, line 846

34. Pope, *Essay on Man*, epistle 2, line 91

35. Pascal, *Pensées*, II, 126ff,

36. Pope, *Essay on Man*, epistle 1, line 289

37. Smith, *Wealth*, I, 17

38. Burridge, *New*, 45

39. Simmel, *Sociology*, 414

40. Mandeville, *Fable*, 67-8

41. Mandeville, *Fable*, 67-8

42. Quoted in Hirschman, *Passions*, 110–1

43. Pope, *An Essay on Man*, epistle 2

44. Paxman, *English*, 100-1

45. Brogan, *English*, 104-5

CHAPTER 16

NATIONAL CHARACTER

ALL ATTEMPTS TO define 'national character' are doomed to failure. Whenever we try to describe any nation or country it soon becomes clear that it changes over time, varies over class and region, is inconsistent and people's character shifts with the situation.

If this is a general difficulty, then defining English character is an extreme case. As David Hume well observed, the only really strong things one can say about English national identity is that the English have no particular identity. 'We may often remark a wonderful mixture of manners and characters in the same nation, speaking the same language, and subject to the same government: and in this particular the English are the most remarkable of any people that perhaps ever were in the world.' The result is that 'the English, of any people in the universe, have the least of a national character; unless this very singularity may appear to pass for such.'[1] Elspeth Huxley was right: 'Take a dozen Englishmen and ask them – "What is England like?" – and you will get a dozen answers.... England is forty million different things to forty million different people; you cannot describe it in a page, or a chapter, or in a dozen volumes.'[2]

This diversity and contradictory nature is not due to physical factors. 'As to physical causes, I am inclined to doubt altogether of their operation in this particular; nor do I think that men owe anything of their temper or genius to the air, food, or climate'.[3] Hume believed it was the result of a mixed political system – monarchy, aristocracy and democracy combined – and a mixed religion. 'All sects of religion are to be found among them.' Consequently, 'the great liberty and independency, which every man enjoys, allows him to display the manners peculiar to him.'

If we pursue Hume's line of argument further, we can see that the contradictions of character arise from the separation of spheres or institutions. The central theme of this work is that we are dealing with the strangeness of modernity with its clashing values of hierarchy and equality, individualism and co-operation, tolerance and aggression. When one separates the spheres of life and there is no determining infrastructure, it becomes impossible for any one organizing principle – kinship for many societies, religion for others, communism for others – to make people alike. Chairman Mao for a time imposed uniformity – dress, life style, and gender status – as have other such regimes. Yet England was the extreme opposite to this – a mass of competing fragments, a thousand flowers blooming.

In such a confused situation all I can do is to follow a few outside observers and just note some tendencies and traits which, while not at all uniform, and varying over the past, nevertheless seem to capture something of the quintessence of these strange islanders.[4]

A True Born Englishman's a contradiction!
In speech, an irony! In fact, a fiction![5]

♦

ONE PRONOUNCED FEATURE of the upper middle-class English was noted by Tocqueville. Married to an English wife, spending some years in the country and seeing its reflection in America, Tocqueville noted English reserve and meditated on the reasons. 'Many people attribute these singular anti-social propensities, and the reserved and taciturn bearing of the English, to purely physical causes. I may admit that there is something of it in their race, but much more of it is attributable to their social condition, as is proved by the contrast of the Americans'.[6]

He particularly noted the reserve when two Englishmen met abroad:

> If two Englishmen chance to meet at the Antipodes, where they are surrounded by strangers whose language and manners are almost unknown to them, they will first stare at each other with much curiosity, and a kind of secret uneasiness; they will then turn away, or, if one accosts the other, they will take care only to converse with a constrained and absent air, upon very unimportant subjects'.[7]

He partly explained it by the fear that intimacy might leave a person open to demands from others. In other words, the obligations to help and support a fellow Englishman could not easily be rejected once an approach was made. Furthermore, I suspect, it was difficult to judge the social class and background of another Englishman so far from home.

Tocqueville was probably right that this could not be explained by climate, though Taine wondered about this: he believed that the fog and humidity partly leads to the independence of the English.[8] Others thought it might be an ancient trait brought by the Anglo-Saxons, part of an aggressive individualism. 'The Barbarians brought with them that staunch individualism, as the modern phrase is, and that passion for doing as one likes, for the assertion of personal liberty ...'[9] Some thought it was related to their religion. 'Methodism and Protestantism in general prevailing and religious sentiments conform so exactly to the melancholy and taciturn nature of the English.'[10]

◆

TO ILLUSTRATE A number of contradictory features, here is the picture painted by four observers. The first is the Frenchman Saussure. 'Englishmen are said to be very proud; certainly many are so, but in general they are more cold and reserved than really proud, and they are taciturn by nature, especially when compared to the French'. He then writes that 'Though twenty men will be sitting smoking and reading newspapers in a tavern, they talk so little that you will hear a fly buzz; their conversation is interrupted by long pauses, and an isolated, "How do you do?" will alone prove to you that they are aware you are there, and have nothing more to say to you'. As for the character of English women: 'I must now give you my experience of the character of English women. I find them gentle, frank, and artless, and they do not try to conceal their sentiments and passions'.[11]

Later the Scotsman Miller in his *First Impression* gave the following account. 'Lay-out of fields and houses. Englishman's home is his castle – separateness and individualism of the English.' 'Unlike the English, the Scotch form, as a people, not a heap of detached particles, but a mass of aggregated ones'. The non-neighbourliness and separateness of the English struck him: 'neighbour seems to know scarce anything of neighbour'. Likewise the individualism of the English when compared to the Scots, for example 'the Englishman stands out more separate and apart as an individual...Englishmen some what resemble in this respect particles of matter lying outside the sphere of the attraction influences, and included within that of the repulsion. The population exists as separate parts, like loose grains of sand in a heap, not in one solid mass'.[12]

D'Eichtal also noted this contrast. The Scots were not at all 'starchy, formal and fastidious like their neighbours, whose lack of free-and-easiness often makes them very tedious'.[13] Taine found the same. He noted that 'there are men of education, even learned men, who have travelled, know several languages and yet are embarrassed in company'. While 'this kind of awkwardness and shame, entirely physical, is normal to the Germanic peoples', he noted the special English features, 'Reserve, caution and understatement. Specially English features – complete self-mastery, constantly maintained sang-froid, perseverance in adversity, serious-mindedness, dignity of manners and bearing, the avoidance of all affection or swaggering…'[14]

Pevsner gives another example of understatement and a low-key approach.

> Thus the English portrait also keeps long silences, and when it speaks, speaks in a low voice… Or, to put it differently, the English portrait conceals more than it reveals, and what it reveals it reveals with studied understatement. These men and women illustrate what Jane Austen in *Emma* calls "the true English style" by "burying under a calmness that seems all but indifference, the real attachment".[15]

This was somehow English and not carried to America in the same way. It seems to be something to do with the English in their own class and club system. Emerson noted 'A Yorkshire mill-owner told me, he had ridden more than once all the way from London to Leeds, in the first-class carriage, with the same persons, and no word exchanged.' Or again 'In short, every one of these islanders is an island himself, safe, tranquil, incommunicable. In a company of strangers, you would think him deaf; his eyes never wander from his table and newspaper.' They were vigorous, but 'This vigor appears in the incuriosity, and stony neglect, each of every other. Each man walks, eats, drinks, shaves, dresses, gesticulates, and, in every manner, acts, and suffers without reference to the bystanders, in his own fashion, only careful not to interfere with them, or annoy them.' In sum, on this island, 'Cold, repressive manners prevail. No enthusiasm is permitted except at the opera. They avoid everything marked. They require a tone of voice that excites no attention in the room.'[16]

I have noticed some of these characteristics through my middle-class life. My grandfather and my uncles had a strong reserve, shyness almost, despite being highly accomplished and successful. It was something that strikes me in many English autobiographies. John Stuart Mill observed of his own father, 'I believe him to have had much more feeling than he habitually showed, and much greater capacities of feeling than were ever developed. He resembled most Englishmen in being ashamed of the signs of feeling, and by the absence of demonstration, starving the feelings themselves.' He added, '...in truth, the English character, and English social circumstances, make it so seldom possible to derive happiness from the exercise of the sympathies, that it is not wonderful if they count for little in an Englishman's scheme of life.'[17]

The reserve is shown even in the gestures – or lack of them – of the English, as an Italian visitor noted with puzzlement. 'Why is it that the English gesticulate so little, and have their arms almost always glued to their sides? For the same reason, I believe: the rooms are so small that it is impossible to wave one's arm without breaking something, or inconveniencing somebody.'[18] While southern Europeans and even the French gesticulate a lot, communicating as much with their hands and faces as with words, the English are normally rather passive, inscrutable, stiff upper–lipped.

The reserve, separation and modesty is clearly linked to the clash of loyalties – one has to step carefully in the minefield for one is pulled by economic, religious, kinship and political ties, yet never a slave to any one of them. Hence the delight of the English in those moments of relaxation, when things are suddenly certain, as in war, sport, hobbies, music, or in any endeavour which suddenly galvanizes the English so that they are doing things together and have something to share. I found this at school and throughout life – when participating in some 'game' one felt at ease with people. Otherwise, what could one talk about with passion?

Some of the ambivalences are again caught by Emerson. 'The manners and customs of society are artificial – made-up men with made-up manners; – and thus the whole is Birming-hamized, and we have a nation whose existence is a work of art; – a cold, barren, almost arctic isle, being made the most fruitful, luxurious, and imperial land in the whole earth.' He wrote that '…here exists the best stock in the world, broad-fronted, broad-bottomed, best for depth, range, and equability, men of aplomb and reserves, great range and many moods, strong instinct, yet apt for culture.' 'They are positive, methodical, cleanly, and for-mal, loving routine, and conventional ways; loving truth and re-ligion, to be sure, but inexorable on points of form.' They were individualistic and private people. 'The motive and end of their trade and empire is to guard the independence and privacy of their homes.' 'The English have given importance to individ-uals, a principal end and fruit of every society. Every man is allowed and encouraged to be what he is, and is guarded in the indulgence of his whim.' Yet there was another side, for 'These private reserved mute family-men can adopt a public end with all their heat, and this strength of affection makes the romance of their heroes.'[19]

The caution in straying outside one's competence and the division of labour I have so often witnessed in Cambridge is linked to the irony, understatement, modesty already alluded to.

Shyness, diffidence, arrogance and conceit make up a curious blend.

There are a number of other characteristics. One is the self-confidence and arrogance, the feeling that the English are the best people in the world and indeed that they are normal and everyone else is odd. Saussure commented. 'I do not think there is a people more prejudiced in its own favour than the British people, and they allow this to appear in their talk and manners. They look on foreigners in general with contempt, and think nothing is as well done elsewhere as in their own country, and certainly many things contribute to keep up this good opinion of themselves, their love for their nation, its wealth, plenty, and liberty, and the comforts that are enjoyed'.[20] Or as Tocqueville noted, England 'has less sympathy than any other modern nation; that she never notices what passes among foreigners, what they think, feel, suffer, or do, but with relation to the use which England can make of their actions, their sufferings, their feelings, or their thoughts; and that when she seems most to care for them she really cares only for herself'.[21]

The self-confidence may be galling but it also had positive effects. As Laing observed 'The self-respect, the sentiment of individual worth, the mutual confidence between man and man in the fair dealing and integrity of each other, which are both the effects and cause of a sound moral feeling in society, and of a high social character adapted to independent action ... form the basis of civil liberty and constitutional government.'[22] Emerson also noted that 'the English stand for liberty. The conservative, money-loving, lord-loving English are yet liberty-loving; and so freedom is safe: for they have more personal force than other people. The nation always resist the immoral action of their government.'[23] Montesquieu connected individualism and liberty: 'every individual is independent', 'this nation is passionately fond of liberty'.[24] 'Every Englishman is an island', observed the German poet- philosopher Novalis at the end of the eighteenth century.[25] So it is no surprise that Robinson Crusoe alone on his island was the national model. 'Marx already observed that Robinson was a favourite character with the economists, but he is present even more in the backs of the minds of philosophers, even if they did not so frequently invoke him by name.'[26]

It was this pugnacious, self-confident, independent character which many thought was the secret of English success in the nineteenth century. Tocqueville wrote 'seeing the Englishman, certain of the support of his laws, relying on himself and un-aware of any obstacle except the limit of his own powers, acting without constraint; seeing him inspired by the sense that he can do anything, look restlessly at what now is, always in search of the best, seeing him like that, I am in no hurry to inquire wheth-er nature has scooped out ports for him, and given him coal and iron. The reason for his commercial prosperity is not there at all: it is in himself.'[27] Emerson felt the same. 'You cannot account for their success by their Christianity, commerce, charter, common law, Parliament, or letters, but by the contumacious sharp-tongued energy of English *naturel*, with a poise impossi-ble to disturb, which makes all these its instruments.'[28]

This independence was combined with a love of eccentricity. 'They were grateful to me for the eccentricity of my escapade. The English are always attracted by eccentricity.'[29] They were rather informal – which could lead into what might be thought of as bad manners. 'It would be impossible to be more easy-going in good society than one is in England. Formality counts for nothing and for the greater part of the time one pays no attention to it. Thus, judged by French standards, the English, and especially the women, seem lacking in polite behaviour… they hum under their breath, they whistle, they sit down in a large arm-chair and put their feet on another, they sit on any ta-ble in the room and do a thousand other things which would be ridiculous in France, but are done quite naturally in England.'[30]

Thomas Burke notes a small example of the eccentricity in the naming of inns and pubs. 'Letting themselves go in their true current of emotion and sentiment, they found such names as the *Who'd Have Thought It? – Mrs Grundy's Arms – The Old Friends – Magnet & Dewdrop – Darby & Joan – Horn of Plenty – Baker & Basket – Sun in Splendour – Rent Day – Mortal Man – Merry Month of May – Bel & the Dragon – Labour in Vain – Tippling Philosopher – Good Intent – Castle of Comfort – Cat & Mutton – World Turned Upside Down.*'[31]

♦

THE CONTRADICTIONS COULD lead to a complete disjuncture between words and actions which seemed hypocritical. 'There is one point in which the English seem to me to differ from ourselves, and, indeed, from all other nations, so widely, that they form almost a distinct species of men. There is often scarcely any connexion between what they say and what they do'.[32] It could lead to a provincialism which had its good and its bad side. 'Instinctively the Englishman is no missionary, no conqueror. He prefers the country to the town, and home to foreign parts. He is rather glad and relieved if only natives will remain natives and strangers, and at a comfortable distance from himself.'[33]

It also seemed to be tied to a certain perpetual childishness, gaucheness, refusal to grow up. 'But if you get to know them closer, they are very kind and gentle; they never speak much because they never speak about themselves. They enjoy themselves like children, but with the most solemn, leathery expression; they have lots of ingrained etiquette, but at the same time they are as free-and-easy as young whelps. They are as hard as flint, incapable of adapting themselves, conservative, loyal, rather shallow and always uncommunicative; they cannot get out of their skin, but it is a solid, and in every respect, excellent skin.'[34]

The fact that a good deal of the most widely read children's literature in the world over the last two centuries, from *Alice in Wonderland* and *Winnie the Pooh* to the *Lord of the Rings* and Harry Potter novels have been written by English authors is intriguing. 'This unwillingness to grow old is an essential feature of the English folk lore of the twentieth century. When the learned scientists of the future endeavour to trace the origin of the Peter Pan myth, as no doubt they will, they will be obliged to recognise that it is peculiar to this island. Every continental Tom Thumb is a kind of dwarf, a quaint being which retains the body of a child, while possessing the intelligence of a man, but Peter is neither a monster nor a precocious imp, he is merely the Eternal Babe which every Englishman carries in his breast.'[35] It may even be linked to the love of games; 'Sport allows children to become Men and Men to Remain Children longer.'

♦

AS I POINTED out at the start, every one of these characteristics has its obverse. The reserve goes alongside another aspect noted by Saussure. 'I have also remarked that the passions of this nation are extremely strong and violent; they cannot bear failure, and customs and example are, I think, a great incitement to them'.[36] Provincialism and self-esteem also go with anxiety and restlessness. As Karl Werner noted, if we are looking for the quintessence of modern capitalism, we might choose one word '*Unruhn*, which means "in perpetual movement", but also anxiety, agitation – the English word 'unrest', but also 'restlessness'…'[37] They tend always to be busy – except when they appear immobile, gazing at a fishing float or a cricket ball.

At their best, they are as Cobbett described them. 'Never servile; always civil. This must necessarily be the character of *freemen living in a state of competence*. They have nobody to envy; nobody to complain of; they are in good humour with mankind.'[38] Some even find them steady, honourable, reasonable and good masters of mankind during their moment in the sun. 'His adventures are all external; they change him so little that he is not afraid of them. He carries his English weather in his heart wherever he goes, and it becomes a cool spot in the desert, and a steady and sane oracle amongst all the deliriums of mankind.'[39]

Others found them odd and inscrutable – particularly in their humour. 'You may well believe, my very dear mother, that these people have another kind of mentality, another kind of taste, a different way of thinking and feeling. The sort of wit which pleases them most is what they call *humour*, it does not consist in making witticisms but of seeing things from a new point of view and that depends more on the oddity of personality than on a prolific mind.'[40]

They were certainly a mixed bunch. 'My opinion on the whole of Englishmen is, that among them you find more sensible, thoughtful, trustworthy, and noble-hearted men than in any other nation; but, on the other hand, a great number of them are whimsical, capricious, surly, and changeable, being one day devoted to one thing and next day caring for it no longer.'[41] They were often prudish and guilty about sex. 'At the London Zoo a lady went up the Keeper of the hippopotami. "Tell me," she said, "is that hippopotamus a male or a female?" The keeper looked at her in a shocked manner: "That, ma'am," he replied, "is a question which should only interest another hippopotamus."[42] But they were also licentious and bawdy, as many cartoons by Rowlandson or the poems of Rochester show.

They could be earnest, but also tended to be happy to compromise. Speaking of the rise of the Whig party, Acton wrote that 'The very essence of the new Party was compromise. They saw that it is an error to ride a principle to death, to push things to an extreme, to have an eye for one thing only, to prefer abstractions to realities, to disregard practical conditions.'[43] Nothing was worth killing for and the deepest offences were not moral or political but to do with etiquette, as in the public school motto – 'manners makyth man'. 'Of all offences against English manners which a man can commit, the three following are the greatest: to put his knife to his mouth instead of his fork; to take up sugar or asparagus with his fingers; or above all to spit anywhere in a room...'[44]

They were narrow, but focused. 'What you say of the simple character of the English is true. Their perception is just, somewhat narrow, but clear: they see only what they look at; they do well only one thing at a time'.[45] Their hero was the White Rabbit with his large watch, hurrying to 'The Duchess, the Duchess'. 'The Englishman is not covetous of money, but he is supremely covetous of time. It is wonderful how exactly the English keep to their appointments. They take out their watch, regulate it by that of their friend, and are punctual at the place and hour.'[46] A strange mixture of deference and obsession with time.

♦

AFTER THIS CONTRADICTORY set of observations let me just jot down a few thoughts of how this odd set of characteristics, still recognisable today, but in its hey-day in the sixteenth to twentieth century, and in the middle class, fits with the argument of modernity and its separations.

The English, as we have seen, seem to have been a turbulent mix of contradictory characteristics. When he visited Manchester, Tocqueville found that 'Here humanity attains its most complete development and its most brutish; here civilisation works its miracles, and civilised man is turned back almost into a savage'.[47] Emerson wrote that 'The English composite character betrays a mixed origin. Everything English is a fusion of distant and antagonistic elements. The language is mixed; the names of men are of different nations, three languages, three or four nations; – the currents of thought are counter...'[48] He continues, quoting Bacon:

> "Rome was a state not subject to paradoxes"; but England subsists by antagonisms and contradictions. The founda-

tions of its greatness are the rolling waves; and, from first to last, it is a museum of anomalies.[49]

The outcome in English character was the result of conflict and compromise. The Englishman, wrote George Orwell, 'is a symbol of the strange mixture of reality and illusion, democracy and privilege, humbug and decency, the subtle network of compromises, by which the nation keeps itself in its familiar shape'.[50]

Many writers have pointed to the contradictions built into the very essence of a modern world. Bruno Latour suggest in *We Have Never Been Modern* that by artificially segmenting the unity of reality which modernity has to do, it does not banish tensions, but rather creates more hybrids as he calls them. In Mary Douglas' terms, we just push the dirt, the blurred boundaries, under the carpets or into corners. It is still there.[51]

Or again Tocqueville highlights the monstrous confusions and inconsistencies of the legal and bureaucratic system of Britain. It is a terrible muddle, a hall of mirrors, terribly 'unprincipled' – yet Tocqueville in the end prefers it to the clear absolutism of France. Veliz points to the same muddle in aesthetics. Drawing on Ruskin's *Stones of Venice,* he points to the clutter, the inconsistency, the absence of purity in the Gothic world, the muddle of English cities and streets, the sweet disordered English rose, the winding English road, as others have put it.[52]

A.P. Herbert points out the same in relation to the inconsistencies and confusions and crossed principles of English law. Are snails wild or tame, is a flooded footpath a road or a river, is a woman within the judgement of the reasonable man? F.W. Maitland also points out the inconsistencies in English law, the various compromises and counter-pressures.[53]

The reason for these outcroppings of inconsistency is obvious. When there is a determining infrastructure it brings everything into line. If kinship underpins everything, as it does in tribal societies, or religion in Hinduism and Islam, or politics in Communism and Fascism, or the market in extreme forms of neo-liberal American thought, then everything can be read off from it. There is consistency because there is a common base, or lowest common denominator. The cost, of course, is that it leads to the loss of liberty, oppression, the imprisonment of the soul and the mind. The world of *Brave New World* or *1984* are at least internally consistent.

On the other hand, the essence of the modern world is that there is no defining infrastructure. Things fall apart, the centre cannot hold. Mere anarchy is not loosed upon the world, but certainly chaos and confusion is often there. Basically the four spheres of our life are constantly in productive tension – politics, religion, economy and society. So there is an everlasting struggle, with no sphere triumphant.

In such a situation adults have to live in a world of endless compromise, of endless situations where the best is the enemy of the good, in an Einsteinian world of relativity where all principles can be bent by some other force. It is a Dirac or Schrödinger quantum world where a cat can be both alive and dead at the same time. It is a world perfectly caught by the Oxford mathematician Dodgson (Lewis Carroll) when he took a child, full of absolutes, into the magical world down the rabbit hole and through the looking glass.

What people have to do, therefore, is to create escapes, pools of consistency, a sense or meaning outside the contradictions in arenas of 'sanity'. These are sometimes the hybrids of which Latour writes. Sometimes it is captured in humour, irony, satire, ridiculous invention – the Goons, Monty Python, Gulliver's Travels, Oscar Wilde and Bernard Shaw, Shakespeare and so many others.

Or there are retreats into bounded areas – love, nature, games, children's stories and other parallel worlds with their own rules.

The Romantic and Pre-Raphaelite movements are classic examples of all this – Wordsworth, Keats and Coleridge are the great exponents, and later Tennyson and Matthew Arnold follow the same theme. These are not escapism – they are absolutely essential to rest the doubting and conflict-facing mind.

All these are important and generated by modernity and its tensions. Life after the invention of modernity is an endless oxymoron, 'both/and' as the Japanese would put it. It is there in all the great poets and novelists and playwrights in the British tradition over the last thousand years.

In the usual run of societies, an individual lives in an embedded world where all the currents – economic, kinship, religion, and politics – are flowing in one direction. So the flow is swift, certain and can be reasonably well described. There are 'patterns' to the cultures, as the anthropologist Ruth Benedict put it in the title of her book.[54]

Modernity is different. In order to help us to understand the contradictory forces, Tocqueville uses an image of a pool in a rushing stream where contrary flows meet and swirl. 'When one examines what is happening in the United States closely, one soon discovers two contrary tendencies; they are like two currents flowing in the same bed in opposite directions.' At other times he described more than two contrary flows. For instance he talked of '…the great American fight between the provinces and the central power, between the spirit of independence and democracy, and the spirit of hierarchy and subordination.'[55]

The restless, swiftly changing cascade is what struck him forcefully. 'Restlessness of character seems to me to be one of the distinctive traits of this people. The American is devoured by the longing to make his fortune; it is the unique passion of his life; he has no memory that attaches him to one place more than another, no inveterate habits, no spirit of routine; he is the daily witness of the swiftest changes of fortune.'[56] He comments that 'Often born under another sky, placed in the middle of an ever moving picture, driven himself by the irresistible torrent that carries all around him along, the American has no time to attach himself to anything, he is only accustomed to change and ends by looking on it as the natural state of man.'[57] Although Tocqueville saw this tendency in its extreme form in America, he constantly states that much of its inherent logic was taken from England. The result was a paradox which is one of the central features of modern capitalism, that desire always outstrips achievement.

◆

CERTAINLY I FOUND 'learning to be English' through the twelve or so years of boarding school and university, not an easy task. Like the language itself, it could only be picked up by example and painfully brought into the inner habitus. Few people could explain how you do it, how you 'Become a Brit', the title of George Mikas' book. An anthropological lesson might have helped, but no-one talked about it. You learnt the identity like cricket or dancing or riding a bicycle, by constant practice of the movements.

A few elementary rules were there, but otherwise it was a style, a posture, and an internalized and instinctive habitus. And like learning to ride a bicycle, falling off and hurting oneself was part of it until you suddenly did it.

Thoughtless and selfish, careful and caring – it is all there in my mother's account of my childhood character at the age of seven. I was deeply flawed, riven, conflicted, and yet was being trained to be self-confident and a leader of men.

How could it be otherwise? 'Ah what a dusty answer finds the soul when hot for certainty in this our life', is a line from Meredith which I loved at University. 'The best lack all conviction, the worst are fully of passionate intensity' (Yeats) – we were the best. We were cynical – 'democracy was the worst of all political system, except for the rest which were even worse' as our great war leader Churchill put it. We were hypocritical – believing in equality yet for decades playing a central part in the slave trade and forcing opium on the Chinese in the name of religion and liberty. We were devout, yet we did not really believe in anything. We were sceptical and realist, yet also very trusting of others. We had a low opinion of human nature, as intrinsically evil, violent, which needed curbing and always sceptical of the gap between words and actions and talk of the general good. And yet also idealist, grown up children, full of philanthropy. Indeed a strange set of beings who flattened the earth and gave birth to the modern world from this small island of Britain – for good and bad.

CHAPTER NOTES

1. Hume, *Essays*, 122

2. Huxley, *East*, 229

3. Hume, *Essays*, 118-9

4. An excellent account of English character is given in Langford, *English*.

5. Daniel Defoe, quoted in Paxman, *English*, 58.

6. Tocqueville, *Democracy* (abridged), 222.

7. Tocqueville, *Democracy* (abridged), 221

8. Taine, *Notes*, 61

9. Arnold, *Culture*, 102

10. D'Eichtal, *French*, 106

11. Saussure, *Foreign*, 177-8, 205

12. Miller, *Firsts*, 398, 399, 395

13. D'Eichtal, *French*, 76

14. Taine, *Notes*, 54, 145

15. Pevsner, *Englishness*, 79

16. Emerson, *English*, 100-1, 83, 83, 89

17. Mill, *Autobiography*, 43 128

18. Count Pecchio in Wilson, *Strange*, 177

19. Emerson, *English*, 78, 104, 84-5, 86, 232, 79

20. Saussure, *Foreign*, 177

21. Tocqueville, *Memoir*, II, 416

22. Laing, *Observations*, 268-9

23. Emerson, *English*, 110

24. Montesquieu, *Spirit*, I, 308, 309

25. Quoted in Singer, *Sword*, 44

26. Gellner, *Thought*, 104

27. Tocqueville, *Journeys*, 106

28. Emerson, *English*, 230

29. Benjamin Constant in Wilson, *Strange*, 127

30. Rochefoucauld, *Frenchman*, 34

31. Burke, *Inns*, 37

32. Tocqueville, *Memoir*, II, 352-3

33. Santayana in Wilson, *Strange*, 242

34. Capek in Wilson, *Strange*, 247

35. Cammaerts, English, 148

36. Saussure, *Foreign*, 198

37. In Hall and Mann, *European*, 173

38. Cobbett, *Cottage*, 122

39. Santayana in Wilson, *Strange*, 243

40. Bonstetten in Wilson, *Strange*, 106

41. Saussure, *Foreign*, 195

42. Maurois in Wilson, *Strange*, 261

43. Acton, *Modern*, 217

44. Prince Puckler-Muskau in Wilson, *Strange*, 175

45. Tocqueville, *Memoir*, II, 365

46. Count Pecchio in Wilson, *Strange*, 178

47. Tocqueville, *Journeys*, 96

48. Emerson, *English*, 42

49. Emerson, *English*, 75

50. Orwell, *Lion*, 46

51. Latour, *Never*; Douglas, *Purity*

52. Veliz, *Gothic*

53. Herbert, *Law*

54. Benedict, *Patterns of Culture;* yet when describing Japan she had to use a contradictory metaphor – *The Chrysanthemum and the Sword.*

55. Tocqueville, *Democracy*, I, 477, 483

56. Tocqueville, *Journey to America*, 182

57. Tocqueville, *Journey to America*, 183

CHAPTER 17

THE ENGLISH PATH

THERE ARE FOUR possible views about when 'The Great Divergence' which led to our modern world began. One is that it is a very ancient divergence. This would argue that in terms, not of productive output, but of religion, politics, society, ecology, economic organization and law and other factors, Europe and China/India had diverged more or less from the beginning of recorded history. Though many of the Neolithic technologies spread out across the whole of Eur-Asia, and the Axial revolution affected them all, there are strong grounds for thinking that there have been deep differences between the different parts of Eurasia for thousands of years.

The second time scale suggests that after the fall of the Roman Empire and the rise of medieval Europe, the paths of the two ends of Eurasia split again. Here there is a divergence in Europe away from the kind of centralized civilization that had gone before. This covers most of Western Europe up to about 1200.

The next divergence is the one which particularly interests me and I cover in my account. This is the divergence between England (and to a certain extent peripheral parts of Europe such as Holland and Portugal and Sweden) and continental western and eastern Europe. This is the divergence which started from the eleventh century and made England a very different place from most of Europe by 1500.

This difference increases and is the traditional period when people believe Britain incubated the industrial and agrarian revolutions, not doing something entirely new, but building on the earlier divergence to become wealthier and more urban. This covers the period 1500-1800 and by the end of it England is the first industrial nation.

After 1800 there is the growing gap between other parts of Europe – Germany, Belgium, France in particular, became 'modern'. By the end of the nineteenth century much of Western Europe (and also America and Japan) were very different from China and India.

Much of this is accepted. The contentious one is the third divergence, between about 1200 and 1500, which goes against much conventional wisdom of Marxist and other historiography. That assumed that the divergence within Europe, which set England apart, only occurred from the sixteenth century. I shall therefore end by setting forth an alternative narrative.

♦

MONTESQUIEU AND TOCQUEVILLE both traced what they considered to be the extraordinary historical trajectory of England back to the 'German woods'. Not surprisingly, particularly after the Nazi interlude, such a Germanist interpretation fell into deep disfavour. And if it has any overtones of manifest destiny or the racial superiority or purity of the Germanic or English peoples it is clearly both unacceptable and untrue. Nor is it a sufficient explanation in itself. Many people came out of the

'German woods' – in fact Germanic tribes conquered all of the countries in Western Europe in the two centuries after the fall of Rome. Yet different parts of Europe ended up in a very different situation a thousand years later.

Nevertheless, for a full and convincing story of how, against all traps and tendencies, the modern world was finally invented by way of the small island of Britain, we need to go back to the period around the collapse of the Roman Empire. The social and political structure of the Germanic peoples, the Anglo-Saxons, who colonized England had certain features which were to be important over the next thousand years.

Firstly, the Germans were a rural people, cattle herders and farmers who lived in small villages. Unlike the Romans, an urbanized civilization, the Germanic peoples' heart was in the shires. The pronounced preference even for the wealthy was to live in the countryside. This characteristic lasted.

Secondly, the Germanic peoples were a commercially minded people. They may have started as mainly subsistence farmers, but within a couple of centuries they had produced a sophisticated market system with a great deal of trading, the best silver coinage in Europe and busy ports. They were certainly proto-capitalists (and indeed the word 'capitalism' has its root in the word for 'livestock').

Thirdly, they did not live in communities with a defined legal status, but in straggling villages, which soon contained a church, a manor house, and some common land. It was a unit of government but without the sense of legal or emotional closeness of blood and identity which constitutes communities in many parts of the world. The only legally recognized 'community' was the borough.

Fourthly, they had a particular kinship system. The Romans had traced descent through males. The Anglo-Saxons traced their kin through both males and females. Roman Law gave the male head of households great power over children and over women. The Germans had no such patriarchal power built into their law and gave independence and equality to both women and children. The Romans gave joint legal rights in property to parents and children, while the Germans gave no intrinsic rights of inheritance to their children.

Soon, under the influence of the Church, in England parents were allowed to make wills leaving some or all of their property to whom they wished. Children tended to leave home at a very young age to work or be educated in another family. Except perhaps amongst the aristocracy, where marriage was important to practical concerns, marriages were made by the children on the basis of love. After marriage, the new couple would live in a separate household from their parents

The Romans had a set of hierarchical legal statuses – nobles, commoners, and slaves. The Germans had no such legal statuses. They had slaves for several centuries, but even this status was fading by the ninth or tenth century and was not incorporated into Common Law. So all social orders were permeable, for instance wealth could buy the status of an aristocrat.

The Romans devised a sophisticated written legal system based on a set of principles worked out in great detail. The Germans had powerful touring judges who sat with local people (juries) to administer a precedent-based, oral, and flexible system of common and customary law.

The language laid down by the Anglo-Saxons remained largely unchanged in its deep structure of the grammar and syntax for the next thousand years, though constantly being modified and added to. Unlike Latin and the Romance languages of the continent, it scarcely recognized status differences and the gender markings it contained were soon lost.

The Romans had a centralized, top-down, political system which, certainly by the later Roman Empire, was expressed in a form of a centralized dictatorship. The Germans in their conquests had operated a loosely federated or 'feudal' system. Here there were contractual ties between superior and inferior, with the inferior swearing allegiance and support, in return for protection and land. Power was dispersed and delegated downwards.

Through the seventh to ninth centuries this political system became incorporated into larger kingdoms so that by the eighth century Alfred united the whole of England under one rule, a Crown that was contractual but powerful. Thus by the tenth century, with the admixture of Viking influence, there was an independent, wealthy, integrated nation with a specific legal, political and social system.

The political system that had developed before the country was converted to Christianity, so that when mainly Celtic missionaries brought the new faith, the Church grew up parallel to, but not fully integrated with, the Crown. There were thus already countervailing forces, a powerful Crown, a powerful Church, growing merchant and farming communities, powerful aristocrats. No single force was dominant.

England was not exceptional. There was a similar pattern over much of north-western Europe. For example, the Normans, second-generation Vikings, were hardly distinguishable from the people they conquered in England. Much of southern Scotland was also similar, as was much of northern France, Germany and Scandinavia. If we had travelled over Europe at the end of the eleventh century we might have been surprised at its uniformity. From the twelfth century, however, a great divergence began to occur between England and much of continental Europe. In England, the characteristics described above persisted and were even re-enforced.

WE MIGHT HAVE expected the persistence of these patterns over all of Europe as the contract-based feudal system developed. And indeed it did continue to a certain extent for a century or so. The rapid integration and growth of Europe from the eleventh to twelfth centuries saw the developments of those separations and oppositions and productive tensions which Guizot maps so well in his *Civilization in Europe*.[1]

This was the golden period described in Richard Southern's *The Making of the Middle Ages*. It was the time of the founding of the first universities, the flourishing of the Benedictines and Cistercians, the building of the first cathedrals, the revival of ancient learning by way of Arab scholarship, the rapid development of cities and trade, the rapid growth of population, the introduction of new technologies such as the windmill and the mechanical clock. It looked as if all of Europe was moving towards what we have defined as 'modernity'.

Then, between the thirteenth and eighteenth centuries, almost all of continental Europe, moved in another direction. This is a huge topic, so I shall only sketch in a few of the landmarks. One was the rise of a pact between the State and the Church, demonstrated above all in the Crusades and in the savage repression of the Albigensians and the forming of the Inquisition. Church and State were now unified in most of Europe, working together against external (Moorish, Arab) foes, or internal enemies (heretics, Jews and, later, witches). By the eighteenth century there was a strong, control of deviation of all kinds. This did not happen in England.

Secondly there was a growing separation and institutionalization of legal differences between status groups or estates. There was instituted blood nobility, a separate educated bourgeois, a special clerical class and a vast peasantry. The peasants owned their land in a system not found in Britain, yet this meant that they had no desire to move off their holdings and when they needed more would sharecrop for larger owners.

Much of what happened can be examined through the progress of the 'Reception' of late Justinian Roman law. This emphasized legal differences – class, gender, familial, royal. Kings were absolute; nobility were a separate caste; men were intrinsically superior to women; fathers were absolute rulers of their children; cities were separated off from the countryside, the court from the country.

What happened over the centuries was a freezing, a growing rigidity. It is tempting to blame the terrible Black Death for this and no doubt it exacerbated a trend, but it could have worked both ways. In Britain it raised the price of labour and wiped out serfdom. In most of the Continent it tied the peasantry even more firmly to the land and in eastern Europe it foreshadowed the second re-enserfment of the population. So Europe turned into a vast, peasant-based, civilization with a huge gap between literate and illiterate, town and country, the rulers and the ruled.

It seems obvious that a structural reason for this was the continental problem of landed boundaries. Basically a ruler could exert centralizing power by threatening to throw those who disobeyed to marauding outsiders. To fight off the adjacent enemies a country had to keep a large standing army. This in turn required extortionate taxes and a large centralized bureaucracy. It was the exact antithesis of Adam Smith's three *desiderata*: there was little peace, easy taxes or due administration of justice. The populace, often restless, often starving, were kept in control by force, by summary punishment, an armed militia, spies and informers.

Over the centuries this led to a situation which even by the fifteenth and sixteenth centuries meant that a person travelling through Europe no longer felt that it was uniform, as it had been three hundred years earlier. All along the sea margin of Europe, where attacks were easier to fend off, namely Scandinavia, Holland, Portugal and Italy, there was greater freedom and continuity. Yet over the great plains of central Europe the slide towards absolutism and the immiseration of four fifths of the population was well advanced.

Despite the attempts of Henry VIII to introduce a strong tie between Crown and Church, England escaped most of this. By the fourteenth century it held much of France, then it sank back to a small power on the edge, only starting to grow into an offensive overseas expansion toward the end of the sixteenth century.

As we have seen in earlier accounts of fifteenth and sixteenth century travellers from Europe, or of those going from England to Europe, people expressed their surprise at the wide gulf which now seemed to separate off this island. So by the middle of the sixteenth century there were already two worlds: that of England (and southern Scotland and parts of Wales), and to a certain extent Holland, Scandinavia and pockets in Italy and Portugal on one side, and much of the rest of the Continent on the other.

The world which existed in England was already a 'modern' one. That is to say the four spheres were institutionalized and separate. There was an autonomous, instituted economy, as Adam Smith realized, with a functioning market, a great deal of trading, a developed manufacturing base, widespread use of money, an elaborate division of labour. There was an uniform, autonomous and widely respected legal system. There was a separate political system, with a Crown under the Law, parliaments, devolution of power to the localities, an efficient and relatively fair taxation system.

There were flourishing and free universities in Oxford and Cambridge (and four in Scotland). There was widespread and growing affluence with rapidly improving transport, housing, clothing, new foods and new drinks. There was no legal distinction between classes, but rather a constant scramble for money and status. The countryside was widely pervaded by 'urban' values in relation to time, money and status, and was filled with an educated and wealthy gentry and small farmer and artisan 'middling sort'.

This is the world which Chaucer and then Shakespeare depicted in the fourteenth and sixteenth centuries. It is the world where Francis Bacon in the early seventeenth century believed that man could take control of nature through understanding its hidden laws. It is the world where England, now effectively Britain from the seventeenth century, was no longer seeking to hold an empire in France, but rather to explore and profit from overseas trade in the Americas and the Orient.

In the eighteenth century people on this island launched the first industrial civilization. This was to transform human history more than any single event since the development of settled agriculture. In relation to agriculture it developed the most efficient system in the world. Britain was well towards controlling a quarter of the planet by the end of the eighteenth century.

These two hundred and fifty years have many special features: the development of institutionalized science, the rapid growth of various technologies in shipbuilding, glass, ceramics, weaving. It was a world where early replacement or supplementation of human energy through wind, water, animals and coal grew rapidly, where communication costs were reduced by canals, roads and soon railways, where wealth flowed into the nation, particularly with sugar, tobacco and the profits of the slave trade.

BY THE START of the eighteenth century England no longer just surprised visitors, it astonished them. They had found a new world, with little resemblance to the *ancien regime* countries from which they had come. It seemed an extraordinarily 'modern' place. It seemed to have a peculiar key to success which it was passing on to its colonies and conquests.

The development of the many inter-connected aspects of 'modernity' was like the proverbial difficulty of a camel passing through the eye of a needle. It was not an easy accomplishment. Using Rostow's metaphor of the take-off of an aeroplane, it requires a long runway, a long time period of increasing speed and a powerful thrust from a powerful engine.[2] As we can see after the event, England was large enough, rich enough, free enough and practical enough to escape from the agrarian traps which the classical economists had outlined and had believed to be inescapable. England did something which had hitherto never even been imagined. Even a century later, in the middle of the nineteenth century, many intelligent people such as John Stuart Mill still believed it to be impossible.

The exceptional nature of what happened is clear. There were no signs of the 'escape' happening anywhere else in Europe or in other parts of the world. Indeed the reverse was happening. The only possible candidate was Holland. Yet it was too small, too vulnerable by land, too dependent on commerce rather than manufacture and, crucially, it lacked coal. It was a high-level commercial Empire, similar to, though larger than Venice or the other early successes in Italy.

All the different parts of the combination lock were in place when Adam Smith was writing his great treatise on the *Wealth of Nations* published in 1776. Among other things he explained why humans had reached the limits of growth, though he also explained some of the conditions which would allow us to squeeze a little extra wealth out of a finite world.

What was finally needed to open the door was, ironically, happening down the corridor from Adam Smith in Glasgow University where James Watt was working on the double condenser steam engine, which would more effectively unlock the power of thousands of years of sunlight stored in coal.

So great was the lead of Britain at this point that even though the technical solution was now known, and the vast coal and iron of the Ruhr could be exploited, it was still another two generations before any other European country began to industrialize, or three generations before the first followers outside Europe, Japan and north America, began their industrial revolutions. The story of the outwards spread of the modern world from England is a complex and interesting one. Since it is a whole new chapter, I shall not deal with it here, but just refer to the excellent account in C.A.Bayly's *The Birth of the Modern World, 1780-1914* which synthesizes much of the recent research on the topic.

♦

PERHAPS I CAN end by returning again to the question of the invention of the modern world. To a large extent the components of our world have come from all over the globe. It is worth quoting a small part of Ralph Linton's account of how our material culture is drawn from everywhere. He imagines the beginning of an American citizen's day.

> Our solid American citizen awakens in a bed built on a pattern which originated in the Near East but which was modified in Northern Europe before it was transmitted to America. He throws back covers made from cotton, domesticated in India, or linen, domesticated in the Near East, or wool from sheep, also domesticated in the Near East, or silk, the use of which was discovered in China. All of these materials have been spun and woven by processes invented in the Near East. He slips into his moccasins, invented by the Indians of Eastern woodlands, and goes to the bathroom, whose fixtures are a mixture of European and American inventions, both of recent date. He takes off his pajamas, a garment invented in India, and washes with soap invented by the ancient Gauls. He then shaves, a masochistic rite which seems to have been derived from either Sumer or ancient Egypt.

Linton continues in this way for another four similar paragraphs and ends,

> While smoking he reads the news of the day, imprinted in characters invented by the ancient Semites upon a material invented in China by a process invented in Germany. As he absorbs the accounts of foreign troubles he will, if he is a good conservative citizen, thank a Hebrew deity in an Indo-European language that he is 100 per cent American.[3]

Yet, while all this is true, it is also true that much of the wealth of world inventions was funnelled for a while through one small island, and then spread around the world by its Empire, and in particular by way of North America. It is wrong for an Englishman to boast, so we can leave it to a Chilean academic to claim that 'We were all born in a world made in England and the world in which our great-grandchildren will mellow into venerable old age will be as English as the Hellenistic world was Greek, or better, Athenian.'[4]

Among the important 'exports' from England which have been considered are the industrial revolution, the agricultural revolution, the model of democratic politics, many principles of English law, many aspects of modern science and a number of important technologies including railways. Also important is the language, which Paxman considers to be 'the greatest legacy' of the English. 'It is the medium of technology, science, travel and international politics. Three quarters of the world's mail is in English, four fifths of all data stored on computers is in English and the language is used by two thirds of the world's scientists… an estimated one quarter of the entire world population can speak the language to some degree.'[5]

Others might argue that it is English games and sports, previously listed, which have been its greatest export, others that it was the English educational system or its literature. Yet there are many other things one might think of. Some of them are rather surprising. 'The English created modern tourism with the Grand Tour and Thomas Cook's first package tour. They developed the first modern luxury hotel (the Savoy with electric lights, six lifts and seventy bedrooms). Charles Babbage produced the world's first computer in the 1820s. A Scot, John Logie Baird, was one of the inventors of television, in an attic in Hastings... Sandwiches, Christmas cards, Boy Scouts, postage stamps, modern insurance and detective novels are all products "Made in England".' Or we might dream with Macaulay that it was 'the imperishable Empire of our arts, our morals, our literature and our laws', which would be the English legacy.'[6]

Perhaps the greatest legacy is not in any specific thing, but in the relations between parts of our lives. I believe that modernity and its freedoms and benefits emerge from the never-ending tension caused by separating and balancing parts of our lives. England was the first country which successfully held the demands of the State, the Church, the Family and the Economy in some kind of balance where none came to dominate. This leads to personal responsibility and freedom. It also leads to endless contradictions and confusions. So perhaps the great contribution of England is to show that muddle, confusion, contradiction and paradox should be welcomed.

When Huizinga tried to understand the character of his adopted country he felt that 'To generalise about "the" British, I soon realised, was nothing but foolishness. There were at least two or three vastly different Englands, if not many more, and their obvious dissimilarities were not only a matter of class...' So he approvingly quoted another long-time student of the English in the twentieth century, Paul Cohen-Portheim: 'the endless contradictions that confront one at every step and to grasp how it is that this country is at once the most aristocratic and the most democratic in the world ... how medieval chivalry and the commercial spirit confront one another in it; how the English philistine is counterbalanced by the imaginative Englishman and the shopkeeper by the conqueror; how the romanticism of a Byron and the fanatical genius of a Turner or a Blake could spring from such a prosaic and matter-of-fact environment'.[7]

The English were lucky yet they were no better than the rest of us (speaking from Scotland, my other ancestry), let alone from the wider world. They were often oppressive and though they provided a bridge into our modern world they did this on the back of the Scots, Welsh, Irish and slaves and workers around the world. Yet if England had not existed, if it had not separated out economy, society, politics and religion, it is difficult to see that I would be writing this on a sophisticated computer, sitting in a quiet garden in the Cambridge fens, while a busy world hums and the latest ricochet of the effects of English imperialism and democracy unfolds in one of its former colonies, Egypt. England and Britain may be the past, but they are also the future. And the new world Empires, of China, India and elsewhere will take up the white man's burden more effectively if they understand something of the path which, against all likelihood, led us to where we now are.

CHAPTER NOTES

1. Guizot, *History*

2. Rostow, *Theory of Economic Growth*

3. Linton, *Study of Man*, 326-7

4. Claudio Veliz, quoted in Paxman, *English*, 63. See Veliz, *Fox*, throughout for this argument, especially chapters 5 and 7.

5. Paxman, *English*, 235

6. Quoted in Huizinga, *Confessions*, 202

7. Huizinga, *Confessions*, 80

BIBLIOGRAPHY

Note: As noted in the text. All books published in London, unless otherwise indicated.

♦

Acton, Modern: John Acton (Lord Acton), *Lectures on Modern History* (1907)

Ady, Candle: Thomas Ady: *Candle in the Dark* (1656)

Allen, 'Yangtze': Robert C. Allen, 'Agricultural Productivity and rural Incomes in England and the Yangtze Delta, c. 1620-c.1820', working paper on Robert C. Allen's website at Nuffield College, Oxford (2006)

Allen, 'Wages': Robert C. Allen and others, 'Wages, Prices, and Living Standards in china, 1738-1925', Oxford University, Department of Economics Working Paper No.316 (2007)

Allen, British: Robert C. Allen, *The British Industrial Revolution in Global Perspective* (Cambridge, 2009)

Arnold, Culture: Matthew Arnold, *Culture and Anarchy* (Cambridge, 1981)

Bacon, Essays: Francis Bacon, *The Essayes or Counsels Civill & Morall* (Everyman Library edn.)

Baker, History: J. H. Baker, *An Introduction to English Legal History* (2nd edn., 1979)

Barker, Character: Ernest Barker (ed.), *The Character of England* (Oxford,1947)

Barrington-Moore, Origins: Barrington Moore, *Social Origins of Dictatorship and Democracy, Lord & Peasant in the Making of the Modern World* (1969)

Becon, Works: Thomas Becon, *The Catechism with other pieces written by him in the reign of King Edward the Sixth* (Cambridge 1844), ed John Ayre

Bell, English: G.K.A. Bell (Bishop of Chichester), *The English Church* (1942)

Benson, College: A.C. Benson, *From a College Window* (2006)

Bennett, Anglosphere: James, C. Bennett, *The Anglosphere Challenge* (2004)

Bernal, Science: J.D. Bernal, *Science in History* (1957)

Betjeman, English: John Betjeman, *English Cities and Small Towns* (1943)

Blaut, Colonizer's: J.M. Blaut, *The Colonizer's Model of the World* (New York, 1993)

Bloch, Feudal: Marc Bloch, *Feudal Society* (2nd ed., 1962), tr. L.A. Manyon, 2 vols.

Boesche, Tocqueville: Roger Boesche, T*he Strange Liberalism of Alexis de Tocqueville* (New York, 1987)

Boswell, London: *Boswell's London Journal 1762-1763* (Heinemann, 1951), ed. F.E.Pottle

Braudel, Capitalism: Fernand Braudel, *Capitalism and Material Life 1400-1800* (1967)

Brenner and Isett, 'England': Robert Brenner and Christopher Isett, 'England's Divergence from China's Yangzi Delta', *Journal of Asian Studies,* vol. 61, No. 2 (May, 2002)

Brogan, English: D.W. Brogan, *The English People, Impressions & Observations* (1944)

Bryant, 'Divergence': Joseph M. Bryant, 'The West and the Rest Revisited', *Canadian Journal of Sociology,* vol. 31, no.4 (Autumn, 2006)

Burckhardt, Reflections: Jakob Burchardt, *Reflections on History* (1950)

Burke, Popular: Peter Burke, *Popular Culture in Early Modern Europe* (1978)

Burke, Inns: Thomas Burke, *English Inns* (1946)

Burridge, New: Kenelm Burridge, *New Heaven, New Earth, a study of millenarian activities* (1971)

Burt, Letters; *Burt's Letters from the North of Scotland.* Intro. R. Jamieson. (Edinburgh 1876), 2 vols.

Caldwell, Fertility: John C. Caldwell, *Theory of Fertility Decline* (1982)

Campbell, Yeoman: Mildred Campbell, *The English Yeoman Under Elizabeth and the Early Stuarts* (Yale, 1942)

Cammaerts, English: Emile Cammaerts, *Discoveries in England* (1930)

Cecil, English: David Cecil, *The English Poets* (1947)

Chamberlayne, Present: John Chamberlayne, *Magna Britannia Notitia: or The Present State of Great Britain* (33rd edn. of the South part, called England; and the twelfth of the North part, called Scotland. 1737)

Clark, Subsistence: M.R. Colin Clark and M.R. Haswell, *The Economics of Subsistence Agriculture* (3rd edn., 1967)

Cohen, Scientific: Floris E. Cohen, *The Scientific Revolution, a historical inquiry* (Chicago, 1994)

Coke, Reports: Edward Coke, *Reports* (c1777), edited George Wilson

Comenius, Orbis: Johannes Comenius, *Orbis Sensualium Pictus*. (1672; facsimile reprint, Sydney, 1967)

Common Weal: *A Discourse of the Common Weal of this Realm of England* (1581; Cambridge, 1954), ed. Elizabeth Lamond

Defoe, Journal: Daniel Defoe, *A Journal of the Plague Year* (Everyman edn., 1963)

Diamond, Guns: Jared Diamond, *Guns, Germs and Steel* (1997)

Dorson, Peasant: Richard M. Dorson (ed.), *Peasant Customs and Savage Myths, selections from the British folklorists* (1968)

Douglas, Purity: Mary Douglas, *Purity and Danger, an analysis of concepts of pollution and taboo* (1966)

Drescher, Tocqueville: Seymour Drescher, *Tocqueville and England* (Harvard, 1964)

Duchesne, Uniqueness: Ricardo Duchesne, *The Uniqueness of Western Civilization* (Leiden, 2011)

Elvin, Pattern: Mark Elvin, *The Pattern of the Chinese Past* (1973)

Emerson, English: Ralph Waldo Emerson, *English Traits* (Boston, 1884)

Fischer, Albion's: David Hackett Fisher, *Albion's Seed* (Oxford, 1989)

Fortescue, Governance: John Fortescue, *The Governance of England* (Oxford, 1885), ed. Charles Plummer

Fox, Watching: Kate Fox, *Watching the English; The Hidden Rules of English Behaviour* (2005)

Fox, Emergence: Edward W. Fox, *The Emergence of the Modern World* (1972)

Frank, ReOrient: Andre Gunder Frank, *ReOrient, Global Economy in the Asian Age* (California, 1998)

Freeman, Growth: E.A.Freeman, *Growth of the English Constitution* (1998)

Freeman, First Essays: E.A. Freeman, *Historical Essays*, 1st Series (1886)

Freeman, 4th Essays: E.A. Freeman, *Historical Essays*, 4th Series (1892)

Fukuyama, Trust: Francis Fukuyama, *Trust* (1995)

Fukuzawa, Autobiography: Yukichi Fukuzawa, *The Autobiography of Yukichi Fukuzawa* (New York, 1972), tr. Eiichi Kiyooka

Geertz, Agricultural: Clifford Geertz, *Agricultural Involution* (California, 1968)

Gellner, Nations: Ernest Gellner, *Nations and Nationalism* (Oxford, 1983)

Gellner, Plough: Ernest Gellner, *Plough, Sword and Book* (1988)

Gellner, Legitimation: Ernest Gellner, *Legitimation of Belief* (Cambridge, 1979)

Gellner, Nations: Ernest Gellner, *Nations and Nationalism* (Oxford, 1983)

Gellner, Thought: Ernest Gellner, *Thought and Change* (1969)

George, London: M.D.George, *London Life in the Eighteenth Century* (1965)

Gibbon, Decline: Edward Gibbon, *Decline and Fall of the Roman Empire* (Chandos Classics edn., no date)

Gibbon, Autobiography: Edward Gibbon, *The Autobiography* (Oxford, 1959), ed. Lord Sheffield

Goldstone, Why Europe: Jack Goldstone, *Why Europe?* (2008)

Goode, World: W.J.Goode, *World Revolution and Family Patterns* (New York, 1968)

Goody, East: Jack Goody, *The East in the West* (Cambridge, 1996)

Goody, Eurasian: Jack Goody, *The Eurasian Miracle* (Cambridge, 2010)

Guizot, History: François Guizot, *The History of Civilization in Europe* (1846; Penguin edn., 1997)

Hall and Mann, European: John Hall, Michael Mann and Jean Baechler (eds.), *Europe and the Rise of Capitalism* (Oxford, 1988)

Harbison, Spaces: Robert Harbison, *Eccentric Spaces* (1977)

Harrison, Description: William Harrison, *The Description of England* (1577,1587; Cornell, 1968), ed. Georges Edelen

Hazard, European: Paul Hazard, *The European Mind* (1680-1715) (1953)

Hearn, East: Lafcadio Hearn, *Out of the East* (1927)

Herbert, Uncommon: A.P.Herbert, *Uncommon Law* (1937)

Hirschman, Passions: Albert O. Hirschman, *The Passions and the Interests* (Princeton, 1968)

Hobson, Evolution: John A. Hobson, *The Evolution of Modern Capitalism* (revised ed., 1926)

Hodgson, Venture: Marshall Hodgson, *The Venture of Capitalism* (Chicago, 1977)

Horton, 'Open': Robin Horton, 'African Traditional Thought and Western Science' in Robin Horton and Ruth Finnegan (eds.), *Modes of Thought* (1973)

Huang, 'Great': Philip Huang, 'Development or Involution in Eighteenth-Century

Britain and China?', *Journal of Asian Studies*, vol.61, no. 2 (May, 2002)

Huff, Science: Toby E. Huff, *The Rise of Early Modern Science, Islam, China, and the West* (Cambridge, 1993)

Huizinga, Confessions: J.H. Huizinga, *Confessions of a European in England* (1958)

Hume, Essays: David Hume, *Essays, Literary, Moral and Political* (1873)

Huxley, East: Elspeth Huxley, *East Africa* (1941)

Italian Relation: *A Relation, or rather a true account of the Islands of England... About the year 1500*, trans. C.A. Sneyd (Camden Society, 1848)

Jacob, Scientific: Margaret C. Jacob, *Scientific Culture and the Making of the Industrial West* (Oxford, 1997)

Jacques, China: Martin Jacques, *When China Rules the World* (2009)

Jaspers, Goal: Karl Jaspers, *The Origin and Goal of History* (1953)

Jones, European: E.L.Jones, *The European Miracle* (Cambridge, 1983)

Kames, Sketches: Lord Kames, *Sketches of the History of Man* (Basil, 1796)

Kroeber, Anthropology: A.L.Kroeber, *Anthropology* (New York, 1948)

Kussmaul, Farm: Anne Kussmaul, *Servants in Husbandry* (Cambridge, 1981)

Laing, Observations: Samuel Laing, *Observations on the Social and Political State of the European People in 1848 and 1849* (1850)

Landes, Prometheus: David Landes, *The Unbound Prometheus* (Cambridge, 1975)

Landes, Wealth: David Landes, *The Wealth and Poverty of Nations* (1998)

Langford, English: Paul Langford, *Englishness Identified* (Oxford, 2000)

Laslett, Illicit: Peter Laslett, *Family Life and Illicit Love in Earlier Generations* (Cambridge, 1977)

Latour, Never: Bruno Latour, *We Have Never Been Modern* (Harvard, 1993)

Li and van Zanden, 'Before': Bozhong Li and Jan Luiten van Zanden, 'Before the Great Divergence? Comparing the Yangzi Delta and the Netherlands at the beginning of the nineteenth century', unpublished paper (available from libzh@tsinghua.edu.cn)

Lloyd, Folk: A.L. Lloyd, *Folk Song in England* (1969)

Macfarlane, Justice: Alan Macfarlane, *The Justice and the Mare's Ale* (Oxford, 1981)

Macfarlane, Cambridge: Alan Macfarlane, *The Culture of Capitalism* (Oxford, 1987)

Macfarlane, Josselin: Alan Macfarlane, *The Family Life of Ralph Josselin* (Cambridge, 1970)

Macfarlane, Savage: Alan Macfarlane, *The Savage Wars of Peace* (1997)

Macfarlane, Individualism: Alan Macfarlane, *The Origins of English Individualism* (Oxford, 1978)

Macfarlane, Marriage: Alan Macfarlane, *Marriage and Love in England, 1300-1840* (1986)

Macfarlane, Letters: Alan Macfarlane, *Letters to Lily; On How the World Works (2005)*

Macfarlane, Making: Alan Macfarlane, *The Making of the Modern World* (2002)

McLynn, Crime: Frank McLynn, *Crime and Punishment in Eighteenth-Century England* (1989)

Maillaud, English: Pierre Maillaud, *The English Way* (Oxford, 1945)

Malthus, Population: Thomas Malthus, *An Essay on Population* (2nd edn., Everyman Library, no date), 2 vols

Maitland, History: F.W. Maitland, *History of English Law before the Time of Edward I*, with Sir F.Pollock (originally published in 1895, 2nd edn., Cambridge, 1923) preface by S.F.C.Milsom to the reprint of 2nd edn., Cambridge, 1968

Maitland, Political: F. W. Maitland, *Political Theories of the Middle Ages*, by Otto Gierke, translated and introduction by Maitland (Cambridge, 1900)

Maitland, Equity: F. W. Maitland, *Equity also The Forms of Action at Common Law; Two Courses of Lectures* (Cambridge, 1909)

Maitland, Collected: *The Collected Papers of Frederic William Maitland*, ed. H.A.L.Fisher (Cambridge, 1911), 3 volumes

Maitland, Constitutional: F. W. Maitland, *The Constitutional History of England* (Cambridge, 1919)

Maitland, 'Why': F.W. Maitland, 'Why the history of English law has never been written', in Maitland, *Collected Papers*, vol. 1

Maine, Communities: Henry Maine, *Village Communities in the East and West* (3rd edn., 1879)

Mandeville, Fable: Bernard Mandeville, *The Fable of the Bees* (Penguin edn., 1970), ed. Phillip Harth

Marx, Grundrisse: Karl Marx, *Grundrisse, Foundations of the Critique of Political Economy* (Penguin ed., 1974), trans Martin Nicolaus

Matthews, English: Kenneth Matthews, 'English Philosophers' in Impressions of English Literature (1944), ed. W.J.Turner

Mill, Autobiography: John Stuart Mill, *Autobiography* (Oxford, 1952)

Millar, Historical: John Millar, *An Historical View of the English Government...* (1812), 4 vols.

Miller, First: Hugh Miller, *First Impressions of England and its People* (3rd edn., 1853

Mokyr, Lever: Joel Mokyr, *The Lever of Riches* (Oxford, 1992)

Mokyr, Industrial: Joel Mokyr (ed.), *The British Industrial Revolution* (Westview, 1992)

Mokyr, Enlightened: Joel Mokyr, *The Enlightened Economy* (Yale, 2009)

Montaigne, Essays: *The Essays of Montaigne* (Oxford, 1935), trans E.J. Trechmann, 2 vols

Montesquieu, Spirit: Baron de Montesquieu, *The Spirit of the Laws* (1748; New York, 1975), tr. Thomas Nugent, 2 vols in 1

Morley, Seventeenth: Henry Morley (ed.), *Character Writings of the Seventeenth Century* (1891)

Morris, Why West: Ian Morris, *Why the West Rules – for Now* (2010)

Morris, West: Brian Morris, *Western Conceptions of the Individual* (New York, 1991)

Moryson, Itinerary: Fynes Moryson, *An Itinerary, containing his Ten Yeeres Travell* ...(Glasgow, 1907-8)

Mumford, Technics: Lewis Mumford, *Technics and Civilization* (1947)

North and Thomas, Rise: Douglass C. North and Robert P. Thomas, *The Rise of the Western World* (Cambridge, 1973)

Oschinsky, Walter: Dorothea Oschinsky (ed.), *Walter of Henley & Other Treatises on Estate Management and Accounting* (Oxford, 1971)

Orwell, Lion: George Orwell, *The Lion and the Unicorn* (1941; 1982)

Orwell, Pamphleteers: George Orwell and Reginald Reynolds (eds.), *British Pamphleteers* (1948)

Pascal, Penseés: Blaise Pascal, *Penseés* (Paris, 1844), ed. P. Faugère

Paxman, English: Jeremy Paxman, *The English* (Penguin, 1999)

Peacock, English: W. Peacock (ed.), *English Prose* (Oxford, 1921), vol. 1

Pearson, Elizabethans: Lu Emily Pearson, *Elizabethans at Home* (Stanford, 1967)

Pevsner, Englishness: Nikolaus Pevsner, *The Englishness of English Art* (1956)

Pomeranz, Divergence: Kenneth Pomeranz, *The Great Divergence* (Princeton, 2000)

Popper, Open: Karl Popper, *The Open Society and its Enemies* (1966)

Porter, Eighteenth: Roy Porter, *English Society in the Eighteenth Century* (revised edn., 1990)

Portheim, England: Paul Cohen-Portheim, *England, The Unknown Isle* (1930), trans. Alan Harris

Property of Things: Bartholomaeus Anglicus, *On the Properties of Things* (Oxford, 1975), trans. John Trevisa, 2 vols

Quotations: *The Penguin Dictionary of Quotations* (1960), eds. J.M. and M.J. Cohen

Quotations (Oxford): *The Oxford Dictionary of Quotations* (Oxford, 1950)

Roberts, Triumph: J.M. Roberts, *The Triumph of the West* (1985)

Rochefoucauld, Frenchman: François de la Rochefoucauld, *A Frenchman in England*, 1784 (Cambridge, 1933), trans and introduced by Jean Marchand and S.C. Roberts

Rogers, Work: Thorold Rogers, *Six Centuries of Work and Wages* (12th edn., 1917)

Rogers, , Industrial: Thorold Rogers, *The Industrial and Commercial History of England* (London 1892)

Rosenberg, Family: Charles Rosenberg (ed.), *The Family in History* (Pennsylvania, 1975)

Rostow, Stages: W.W.Rostow, *The Stages of Economic Growth* (Cambridge, 1962)

Rye, England: W.B.Rye (ed.), *England as seen by Foreigners in the Days of Elizabeth and James the First* (New York, 1865; 1967)

Salzman, English: L.F. Salzman, *English Life in the Middle Ages* (Oxford, 1926)

Saussure, Foreign: César de Saussure, *A Foreign View of England in the Reigns of George I and George II* (1902), trans Madame van Muyden

Shapin, Social: Steven Shapin, *A Social History of Truth* (Chicago, 1994)

Simmel, Sociology: Georg Simmel, *The Sociology of Georg Simmel* (Illinois, 1950), trans and ed., Kurt H. Wolff

Smith, De Republica: Sir Thomas Smith, *De Republica Anglorum* (1583; Cambridge, 1982), ed. Mary Dewar

Smith, Moral: Adam Smith, *The Theory of Moral Sentiments* (1759), George Bell, 1907

Smith, Wealth: Adam Smith, *An Inquiry into the Nature and Causes of the Wealth of Nations* (1775; Chicago, 1976), 2 vols in 1

Smith, Philosophical: Adam Smith, *Essays on Philosophical Subjects*, (Indianapolis, 1982)

Smith, Jurisprudence: Adam Smith, *Lectures on Jurisprudence* (Indianapolis, 1982)

Smith, Corporations: M.G. Smith, *Corporations and Society* (1974)

Sorokin, Sociological: Pitrim Sorokin, *Contemporary Sociological Theories* (1928)

Stewart, Works: Dugald Stewart, *Collected Works* (1856; reprint 1971), ed. Sir William Hamilton, 11 vols

Stubbs, Constitutional: William Stubbs, *Constitutional History of England* (Oxford, 1874-8)

Sugarman, 'Law': David Sugarman, 'In the Spirit of Weber: Law, Modernity and "The Peculiarities of the English"', *Legal History Program Working Papers*, Institute for Legal Studies, Wisconsin, Working Papers Series 2 (September, 1987)

Sumner, Folkways: William Graham Sumner, *Folkways* (1934)

Taine, Notes: Hippolyte Taine, *Notes on England* (1957), trans. Edward Hyams

Thomas, Religion: Keith Thomas, *Religion and the Decline of Magic* (1973)

Thomas, Natural: Keith Thomas, *Man and the Natural World* (1983)

Thompson, 'Peculiarities': E.P.Thompson, 'The Peculiarities of the English', *Socialist Register*, ed. Ralph Millband and John Saville (1965)

Tidrick, Empire: Kathryn Tidrick, *Empire and the English Character; The Illusion of Authority* (1990)

Tocqueville, Journeys to America: Alexis de Tocqueville, *Journey to America*, (1959) tr. George Lawrence 1959

Tocqueville, Recollections: *The Recollections of Alexis de Tocqueville* (1893; 1948), ed. J.P.Mayer, tr. Alexander Teixeira de Mattos

Tocqueville, Journey: Alexis de Tocqueville, *Journeys to England and Ireland* (New York, 1968), ed. J.P.Mayer, tr. George Lawrence and K.P.Mayer

Tocqueville, Memoir: *Memoir, Letters, and Remains of Alexis de Tocqueville* (Cambridge 1961), 2 vols

Tocqueville, Democracy: Alexis de Tocqueville, *Democracy in America* (1835, 1840; 1968), 2 vols. tr. George Lawrence

Tocqueville, Democracy (abridged): Alexis de Tocqueville, *Democracy in America* (1835, 1840; 1956), 2 vols. Abridged into one by Richard D. Heffner

Tocqueville, Ancien: Alexis de Tocqueville, *L'Ancien Regime* (1856; Oxford, 1956), tr. M.W.Patterson

Toynbee, History: Arnold Toynbee, *A Study of History* (new edn., abridged, Oxford, 1972)

Veliz, Gothic: Claudio Veliz, *The New World of the Gothic Fox* (California, 1994)

Voltaire, Letters: Voltaire, *Letters Concerning the English Nation* (1925)

Vries, Economic: Jan de Vries, *The Economy of Europe in an Age of Crisis 1600-1750* (1978)

Vries, Peking: Peer Vries, *Via Peking back to Manchester* (2003)

Walzer, Revolution: Michael Walzer, *The Revolution of the Saints* (1966)

White, Technology: Lynn White, *Medieval Technology and Social Change* (Oxford, 1980)

Wigmore, Panorama: W.H. Wigmore, *Panorama of the World's Legal Systems* (1928), 3 vols

Wilson, Strange: Francesca M. Wilson (ed.), *Strange Island; Britain through Foreign Eyes 1395-1940* (1955)

Wong, China: R. Bin Wong, *China Transformed* (1998)

Wormald, 'Feud': Jenny Wormald, 'Bloodfeud, Kindred and Government in Early Modern Scotland', *Past and Present*, 87 (May 1980).

Wright, Decent: Lawrence Wright, *Clean and Decent* (1966)

Wrigley, Energy: E.A. Wrigley, *Energy and the Industrial Revolution* (Cambridge, 2010)

Wrigley, 'Modernization':, E.A. Wrigley, 'The Process of Modernization and the Industrial Revolution in England', *Jnl. of Interdisciplinary History*, vol. III (1972)

ABOUT THE AUTHOR:

Prof. Alan Macfarlane, FBA, FRHistS, taught at the Department of Social Anthropology Cambridge University for more than 30 years and is now Emeritus Professor of Anthropological Science and a Life Fellow of King's College, Cambridge. He is the author or editor of 20 books and numerous articles on the anthropology and history of England, Nepal, Japan and China.

CPSIA information can be obtained at www.ICGtesting.com
Printed in the USA
LVOW12s2153040614

388619LV00040B/1197/P